THE LIMITED PARTNERSHIP

THE LIMITED PARTNERSHIP

Europe, the United States,
and the Burdens of Alliance

Josef Joffe

BALLINGER PUBLISHING COMPANY
Cambridge, Massachusetts
A Subsidiary of Harper & Row, Publishers, Inc.

International Standard Book Number: 0-88730-216-5

Library of Congress Catalog Card Number: 87-17837

Printed in the United States of America

Library of Congress Cataloging-in-Publication Data

Joffe, Josef.
   The limited partnership—Europe, the United States, and the burdens of alliance / by Josef Joffe.

        p.   cm.
     Bibliography: p.
     Includes index.
     1. North Atlantic Treaty Organization.   2. United States—Foreign relations—Europe.   3. Europe—Foreign relations—United States.   I. Title.
JX1393.N67J64   1987   341.7′2—dc19   87-17837

     ISBN 0-88730-216-5

For Christine

Contents

Acknowledgments

This book grew out of a research project supported by the Woodrow Wilson International Center for Scholars in Washington, D.C., where the author was a 1982/1983 fellow, and the Carnegie Endowment for International Peace in Washington, where he served as a senior associate until 1984. It is a pleasure to acknowledge a special debt of gratitude to Samuel Wells and James Billington of the Wilson Center and to Thomas Hughes, president of the Carnegie Endowment.

Each of these two institutions represents an ideal environment for scholarly research that is also bound up with the practical concerns of the political world at large. In each place the author was constantly confronted with sharp-eyed critics and better informed experts whose number is too large to allow for individual mention but whose contributions are gratefully remembered. Needless to say, neither institution bears any responsibility for the conclusions and assertions in this book. Portions of the text were previously published in *Foreign Affairs, Foreign Policy, The National Interest*, the *Washington Quarterly*, and *International Security*.

My special thanks go to Jane Lowenthal, the librarian of the Carnegie Endowment, for her tireless (and savvy) help in tracking down research materials and lost footnotes. The compliments normally reserved for typists, without whose patience and loyalty many a book would have gone unwritten, must go to my computer. Working in tandem with Xywrite III, he/it was a constant source of humming encouragement, thrown off course only by the author's collisions with the flawless logic of the machine. My real — and greatest — debt, however, is owed to three humans: to Christine, Jessica, and Janina Joffe, for granting me the freedom to write this book.

Two Continents Adrift

The history of the Atlantic Alliance is the history of its crises. To insist on that point is to stress another, less obvious one: the astounding longevity of this coalition. In the annals of the modern state system, the tie that binds the United States and Western Europe in a common defense stands out as the longest lasting alliance of free nations. No member has ever defected; none has ever threatened to defect. Indeed, with the accession of Spain in the thirty-fifth year of NATO's existence, the Alliance expanded at a time when other such leagues had long since disappeared.[1]

Crises Past and Present

There has been no end to quarrel—and no end to alliance. Nor did the tie prove strong only because the challenges have been weak. From Suez to Berlin, from Vietnam to Afghanistan, from the "Year of Europe" (1973) to the "Year of Euromissiles" (1983), confrontation was driven by interests properly billed as "vital" ones; and in each case, passions have soared because the stakes have been anything but paltry. When fight they did, the Allies have clashed over issues that define the very stuff of international politics—the security fears and the amour propre of nations: their power, pride, and position.

    The Suez Crisis of 1956 will remain forever etched in the collective unconscious of Britain and France. When the United States forced its two oldest allies out of Egypt, it did more than merely abandon them; in the process Washington was dismissing with barely concealed contempt their centuries-old history and vocation as great powers. Only two years earlier, it had been France's turn to humiliate the United States— when the French Parliament wrecked a five-year-old American campaign to have West Germany rearmed under the auspices of the European Defense Community. When, in 1961, the Kennedy administration greeted the Berlin Wall with a silent sigh of relief, it was demolishing the mainstays of the Federal Republic's foreign policy and, with it, the foundations of Chancellor Adenauer's tenure. To accept the partition of the German capital as cast in concrete was to accept the partition of the country itself, and that was the end of Adenauer's rule. He was forced out of office two years later. Though far apart in time and space, Suez and Berlin drove home the same message: superpowers protect the security of their lesser allies, but do not underwrite their ambitions.

In the years to come, the United States would be on the receiving end. When de Gaulle, in the 1960s, unleashed the fury of his rhetoric on the "twin-hegemony" of the superpowers, he meant above all the United States, not the heirs of the tsars; when he conjured up a "Europe from the Atlantic to the Urals," he did not mean to include America. In Vietnam the United States would suffer France's earlier fate in Indochina and Algeria. At first Washington could still count on its allies' symbolic support. But as the Vietnam War dragged on, Western Europe's discomfort turned into outright hostility—fueled by the noisy street demonstrations that presaged the antinuclear (and in part anti-American) revolt of the 1980s.

In the Yom Kippur War of 1973, the United States stood virtually alone at the side of Israel. Denied landing rights throughout continental Europe, the United States absorbed the brunt of Arab enmity while its allies hastened to forge their separate links with the oil producers of the Middle East. This was a fitting conclusion to the "Year of Europe" inaugerated in early 1973 by Henry Kissinger with his essentially correct—and therefore all the more insulting—pronouncement of America's interests as "global" and Europe's as merely "regional." Nor did the United States fare much better during the dual crisis triggered by the capture of the American embassy in Tehran and the Soviet invasion of Afghanistan at the threshold of the 1980s. While the Europeans delivered sympathy and measured diplomatic support, their hearts were really elsewhere. Precisely because of their dependence on the United States, they reacted as weaker allies always do: by keeping a safe distance from conflicts they do not accept as their own. During the 1986 American bombing raid on Libya—an action dedicated to combating international terrorism against the entire West—European discretion would gestate into almost Alliance-wide censure, with only Britain providing indirect military support.

The Nature of the Conflict

The history of the Alliance is the history of its crises because conflict is built into the very structure of this compact. There is, first of all, the corrosive effect of nuclear weapons. On the one hand, America's guarantee to its allies is essentially expressed in the language of the atom. On the other hand, nuclear weapons are literally the ultima ratio, posing an existential threat to guarantors, foes, and clients alike. Will the United States ever unsheathe that sword in the moment of truth? Or does the guarantee rest on a "cosmic bluff"? Hence, the West Europeans will always fear abandonment; hence, they will suspect *any* change in American strategy as a change in the nature of the commitment—for the worse, of course. And hence, they have *always* fought American doctrinal reforms, whether such reforms emphasized or diminished the role of nuclear weapons in Western strategy.

In the 1960s the Europeans drew no comfort from the American abandonment of "massive retaliation" in favor of "flexible response." Pushing conventional defense to the foreground, the new strategy was to lengthen the ladder of escalation and to postpone the nuclear moment of truth as long as possible. The Europeans resisted this strategy for years. For to mute the threat of instant retaliation was to weaken deterrence itself by lowering the immediate risks for the aggressor. Simultaneously, the new doctrine sharpened the specter of conventional devastation on a battlefield that was merely a "theater" for the United States, but home for the Europeans.

Nor did the Europeans like the renewed stress on nuclear weapons which, in the early 1980s, would center on such shibboleths as "warfighting" and "selective nuclear options." Where would such options be exercised first if not on the Continent? For its inhabitants, a "limited" nuclear war, even if fought with restraint and discrimination, would still be indistinguishable from general war and unlimited destruction.

The reason for these contradictory responses is easy to fathom. Henry Kissinger exposed the heart of the matter when he spoke of the "secret dream of every European": to "avoid a nuclear war but, secondly, if there had to be a nuclear war, to have it conducted over their heads by the strategic forces of the United States and the Soviet Union."[2] He might have added that Americans also have their "secret dream": if there *has* to be a nuclear war, let it be fought and contained far from American shores.

Such dreams are the stuff from which the Alliance's endless strategic quarrels are made. Though their fates are tied together by many bonds, *sacro eqoismo* naturally impels each side to shift the risk of nuclear war to the territory of the other. Whether the stress is on the conventional or on the nuclear, Europeans are always haunted by the unspoken quest for limitation that has informed every American strategic reform since "massive retaliation." To them, there is no assurance in a defense which might spare the superpowers, but turn the Continent into a neatly demarcated arena of East–West war. And this is precisely the reason the Europeans have greeted the latest act of the endless drama, the Strategic Defense Initiative, with less than applause. True, a United States shielded against Soviet missiles might discharge its nuclear obligations to Europe more readily than it would in a setting of assured mutual destruction. But deep in their psyches, the Europeans have no faith in a cocooned America—especially an America faced with a similarly sheltered Soviet Union. If each is deterred by the other's defenses, where will they fight if not in those areas where great offensive power has *not* been devalued by great defensive capabilities?

There is also no solace in too much or too little arms control. Allies huddling under the nuclear umbrella of a distant superpower naturally fear the din of confrontation, but they are just as quick to suspect betrayal when their patron is too eager for accommodation. Too much arms control, as in the early Carter years, spells "Big Twoism" at the expense of small-power security interests. SALT II, for instance, set out to stabilize the nuclear balance "at the top." The negotiating process did nothing to solve the problems of the regional imbalance in Europe; indeed, it helped to dramatize them—which is precisely the root of the Euromissile crisis of the 1980s. The specter of a "condominium" reemerged with clocklike predictability in the mid-eighties when the United States and the Soviet Union reached agreement in principle on the elimination of all medium-range nuclear weapons in Europe—as, for example, during the Reykjavík "nonsummit" of 1986.

Yet worse than too much is too little arms control, as during the first term of the Reagan administration. Rhetorical warfare and rearmament by the superpowers, though merely the ritualistic substitutes for real conflict, reveal tensions that disturb the tranquility of the nations in between. Moreover, the absence or denigration of arms control dramatizes the role of military might in international affairs, devaluing precisely those civilian assets—diplomacy and trade—on which smaller powers must rely for wielding their influence. Finally, the duels of the great constrict the freedom of the small, forcing the latter to choose sides instead of allowing them to balance interests and obligations. In short, nations that cannot provide for their own security do not like to be reminded of their existential dependence on others. And the costs of that dependence soar when there is either too much harmony or too much enmity between their patron and their main adversary.

A second source of endemic conflict is the inequality between the United States and Western Europe in power and resources. The United States is indeed a global power with global interests, and the European nations are regional powers whose immediate interests are only intermittently staked on faraway conflicts. In the global strategic arena there are only two contestants, the United States and the Soviet Union, and they are doomed to permanent rivalry. In the end there are no peripheries and no points of indifference.[3] The United States must worry about *any* event, no matter how distant, that might endanger the global balance. If not counteracted, small Soviet (or surrogate) victories in Africa, Afghanistan, or Central America might add up to a large victory—or at least embolden the only adversary who counts. Europeans, on the other hand, naturally worry about regional tranquility. As long as the European balance holds, they have little incentive to rush into conflicts that are, at best, only remotely their own. Indeed, they have every reason to avoid them because a confrontation at the periphery, say over Afghanistan, might earn them nothing but Soviet counterpressure at the core—which is, and remains, Europe.

Where responsibilities diverge, interests are bound to clash. The Europeans naturally resent American involvement in extra-European ventures because these either deflect attention and resources from the common defense of Europe (as during the Vietnam War) or entangle them in conflicts they would rather stay out of (as in Afghanistan or Libya). There is resentment even where allies pursue a common policy, as they did in Lebanon, but do not command the same means. While France and Italy shared the U.S. goal of a Lebanon reconstituted and a Syria contained, they could only act in tandem with American power. Given their limited means, these two countries had to follow the American lead in dispatching as well as in withdrawing troops from Lebanon—which did not make for harmonious relations with the United States. When interests exceed resources, dependence on stronger partners is dramatized. And when the strong obey their own interests rather than the pleas of their junior partners—as did the United States when it suddenly abandoned Lebanon in early 1984—lesser allies are left with little more than a fait accompli and food for thought about the follies of collaboration.

A third source of conflict flows from the inequality of vulnerability. Nations that look to others for their security have two choices. The first is to draw derivative strength from great intimacy. Dependents will thus try to persuade the alliance leader that their regional interests transcend local importance, that their quarrel with the common rival or his regional satrap is in fact part and parcel of the global contest. This was West Germany's strategy in the fifties and sixties; it continues to be the strategy of Israel or South Korea. And it is bound to breed resentment because great powers will just as instinctively seek to avoid so close an identification with the special claims of their allies.

The second choice is the exact opposite of the first. Instead of increasing intimacy with patrons, allies will seek to decrease dependence through separate arrangements with their adversary—also known as "Ostpolitik" or, *détente, entente et coopération*. Since junior partners can never fully rely on the pledges of their principals, they must reduce their exposure by giving their opponent as little reason as possible to threaten them. They must, in other words, propitiate the enemy. Uncertain insurance requires a measure of reinsurance, and since a world of only two superpowers leaves no alternative allies, reinsurance can only be had from the other superpower. Hence, the divisibility of conflict is built into the very structure of the contemporary alliance system. Indeed, the more the United States tried to harness its allies to the cause of neo-containment in the 1980s, the more the Europeans felt compelled to distance themselves from the call to arms, to reassure the Soviet Union, and to save as many pieces of their separate, regional détente as possible.

For those who are vulnerable and condemned to share a continent with the Soviet Union, a measure of accommodation bears no shame. It is in fact the rational response of the weak, who must seek to contain threats by conciliation because they cannot do so by confrontation. And there is a bonus effect to boot: a wider margin for diplomatic maneuver. To the alliance leader, however, such behavior invariably smacks of disloyalty. Demanding support his allies are loath to give, he feels hampered and betrayed. Hence arose the predictable collisions which shook the Alliance in the wake of the Afghanistan invasion and sundry Soviet sallies elsewhere around the world.

Yet even in tranquil times, a relationship of unequal vulnerability foreordains conflict. Bound by strategic ties, Western Europe and the United

States also happen to inhabit the same economic space. Vast disparities in economic power—the hallmark of the immediate postwar period—disappeared long ago. When it comes to economic size, the United States and Western Europe are truly equals, and in the realm of trade it is the European Community (EC) that dwarfs the United States. Yet economic parity has not made for equality of economic power and dependence, let alone for political serenity. Thus, the Allies' economic quarrels merely replicate the perverse dynamic of their politico-military relationship; although any American policy might soon be followed by its opposite, each and every policy change will invariably engender the same European reaction, namely, resentment and recrimination.

During the 1970s the Europeans bemoaned low interest rates and a freewheeling U.S. monetary policy because the world became flooded with cheap dollars and American goods gained an unfair export advantage. By 1981, the indictment was reversed. Now it was a harsh American deflationary regimen that imperiled world recovery and towering interest rates in the United States that supposedly negated European attempts to escape from an accelerating recession. Yet by 1985 (when the dollar-deutschemark parity had doubled from DM 1.71 in 1980 to DM 3.47), the American currency was no longer too cheap but too dear. Accused of hogging exports in the late seventies the United States was now blamed for absorbing too many imports and inflicting a $200 billion budget deficit on the rest of the world. By 1987, when the dollar had again gone through a precipitous drop (to around DM 1.80), resentment had turned full circle, and the stage was set for a replay of the endless drama of economic might and economic dependence.

The pattern is perverse, but the reasons are not hard to fathom. Equality of economic size is not identical with equality of vulnerability. While Western Europe boasts a collective gross national product larger than that of the United States, its collective economy is hardly "e pluribus unum." The United States represents a single market harnessed to a single currency and a single political will; the European Community represents twelve largely self-contained economic entities bereft of both. Dominance comes easy when the competition, even if nominally superior in the aggregate, is dispersed and disunited. Dominance is enhanced when one side commands a global currency that chains everybody else's to the almighty dollar, whether it is tied to gold as in the early postwar decades, or freely floating as in the years after the 1971 "Nixon Shock."

When the dollar was embedded in a system of fixed exchange rates, the American government could evade fiscal restraints by printing more dollars and exchanging paper claims for goods and services abroad. When the dollar was cut loose, Washington could still circumvent fiscal discipline by luring funds from abroad with the promise of high rates of return. (By 1983 foreigners financed one-half of the federal deficit.) Nothing could better dramatize the singular dominance of America's global currency than Washington's laissez-faire strategy in the mid-eighties. Whether the dollar was seen as too high (1985) or as too low (1987), it was not America's monetary authorities that were forced to intervene but their partners in Japan and Western Europe. In the world economy as elsewhere, power is when consequences are suffered by others.

Where vulnerability is unequal, effects are rarely distinguishable from threats. If the United States inflates, it exports inflation; if the United States deflates, it exports unemployment and banking crises—and in each case by dint of its sheer economic weight. In the world economy the United States occupies a position akin to an elephant in a lifeboat. His intentions may well be benign, but the craft will gyrate wildly if this massive mammal shifts his position by only an inch or two. For lighter passengers, any movement at all threatens nasty consequences, no matter which way the beast is tilting. Though they might well outweigh the United States collectively, they suffer the problem of the many against the one. In theory the Europeans could discipline the United States, but to act in common they would first have to submit to the discipline of a common will. Such unanimity is not given to nations that prefer the limited loss of autonomy to the total loss of sovereignty.

What Has Changed?

Conflict is thus built into the very structure of the Alliance, and if the compact has endured in the face of so many strains, it must be that it rests on a foundation of common purpose (or dependence) stronger than the pulls and pushes of inherent discontent. There is comfort in crises that do not kill—like those fevers which betray not decrepitude but underlying health and superior resistance. The French have a familiar saying for continuity amidst chaos: *plus ça change . . . .* On the other hand, there is the counsel of caution ascribed to Napoleon's mother: *pourvu que ça dure,* "provided that it will last."

What, if anything, is different about the 1980s? Prima facie, at least, there is a twofold change that transcends the familiar crises of the past, betraying not the familiar tremor of clashing interests but the rumble of shifting foundations. Though in each collision, there is a sense of déjà vu that evokes the solace of, "This, too, will pass," there is a still deeper level at which premises rather than policies are at stake, where the real struggle is not about the course but the very purpose of the Alliance.

There is, first, the political level; while it is true that NATO has never been able to forge a common response to "out-of-area" challenges, there is after all a difference between, say, the Suez and the Afghanistan crises. In spite of the high stakes involved, Suez was at heart a family quarrel between the United States and its two oldest Western allies. Though that crisis had grave long-term consequences (accelerating France's quest for nuclear independence and Britain's decline from empire), it did not detract from the Alliance's primary purpose as a coalition against the Soviet Union. The rupture over Afghanistan, however, did more than merely reassert the classic distinction between core and periphery, between interests subsumed under the terms of the Alliance and those that fall outside NATO's ken.

The root of the quarrel was an irreconcilable split in perceptions of NATO's raison d'être, namely, Soviet power. While the United States portrayed the Soviet invasion as incontrovertible proof of Soviet expansionism and hence as *casus foederis*, the West Europeans chose to define that foray as sui generis—as driven not by aggressive but by defensive intent. In itself, the quarrel over Soviet motivations may have been dramatic but not truly novel. What was distinctive, new, and enduring was the transformed relationship between Western Europe and the Soviet Union that underlay the Euro-American battle over the meaning of Afghanistan and most East–West issues to follow. The crucial difference was the new position of Europe in the global conflict between the two superpowers; in contrast to the forties, fifties, and sixties, Europe was now not just stable but ultrastable—a sheltered island of peace amidst violence and turmoil beyond the Continent's shores.

Thus, with ancient conflicts (over Berlin and Germany) safely enveloped in the formal agreements of the 1970s, the West Europeans had come to look at the Soviet Union no longer as a looming threat but as an indispensable partner in détente. Indeed, with military stability seemingly frozen in perpetuity, political evolution and the reassociation of Europe's two halves moved to center stage; and there the Soviet Union, being in control of the prize, holds more trumps than the United States. For Western Europe, these enduring changes—analyzed in Chapter One —have added up to a permanent détente imperative. To be sure, the imperative is balanced by military dependence on the United States. Yet it is precisely this dependence that motivates détente as reinsurance and, consequently, Western Europe's abiding unwillingness to confront the Soviet Union except for the gravest of provocations.

In sum, Afghanistan was not just a reenactment of past out-of-area clashes between the United States and its major West European allies. This crisis dramatized the limits of alliance not only outside Europe but on the Continent itself. Afghanistan posed a new and as yet unresolved question: can an alliance endure whose key members take such widely divergent views of the nature of the threat and of the necessities of cooperation with the coalition's reason for being, the Soviet Union?

That question receives added urgency from changes that are also bound to persist in the second area, the domestic level. The antinuclear demonstrations that drove hundreds of thousands in the early 1980s to protest against neutron bombs, *Pershing II*, and cruise missiles have long since subsided. (The ineradicable nuclear troubles of the Atlantic partnership and the new societal response to them in the eighties are addressed in Chapters Two and Three.) Yet something else has remained embedded in the polities of major West European countries. In Britain and in the Federal Republic, to take but the two most obvious cases, the democratic left (Labour and SPD, the West German Social Democratic Party) has turned squarely against nuclear weapons—and also, if more obliquely, against their provider, the United States. While Labour and the SPD do not attack the rationale of alliance, they do want to do away with the Alliance's ultima ratio—yet without being truly prepared to add to NATO's conventional might. The implications of that position cannot be overdrawn. If potential governing parties in two key countries are willing to face the Soviet Union without those weapons that NATO has treated as an indispensable counterweight to Soviet power since 1949, then they must also be willing to propitiate the Soviet Union to the point where its open exercise of power is no longer necessary.

On the moral-psychological plane, this position has come to be known as "equidistance between the superpowers." In practice, however, the term is misleading because most social democratic parties of northwest Europe as well those forces to the left of them—like the Greens—are in fact closer to the Soviet Union on key issues than to the United States. The opposition to the deployment of intermediate-range nuclear forces (INF), to the Strategic Defense Initiative (SDI), and to the first use of nuclear weapons, marks off one area of commonality: the quest for zones free of nuclear and chemical weapons marks off another. Conversely, there is nary a case where the democratic left of Scandinavia, West Germany, the Benelux countries, and Britain actually agrees with the United States—be it Nicaragua, military intervention against the purveyors of international terror, or the American arms control posture.

To be sure, each of these parties, even West Germany's Greens, would loudly reject the label of "anti-Americanism." Nor would they praise the Soviet Union as a model of societal and political development. Yet in stark contrast to the fifties and sixties, Western Europe's democratic left —with the exception perhaps of the French and Italian Socialists—has abandoned anti-Sovietism as the classic mark of distinction which used to separate communist from social democratic parties throughout much of the postwar period. And most of the latter would probably agree that the real threat to Europe's well-being does not flow from Gorbachev's Russia but from Reagan's America—that it is the United States which impedes arms control, peace, and understanding. While none of these parties has improved its electoral chances in the process (see Chapter Three), they do represent large segments of their populations. And that points to a fundamental reorientation in West European society which is surely the great price of NATO's secular success: a deeply rooted sense of security has pushed the benefits of alliance into the background while casting its burdens into the glaring light of dependence. Questioned only from the fringes in decades past, an intimate alliance with America—one that transcends a mere one-sided guarantee pact—now demarcates the critical cleavage between the leftist and center-right parties in Europe's Northern Tier.

The Federal Republic offers the most telling case of transformation, which is why that country assumes a special place in this book. Nowhere else are the sluggish forces of continuity more evident than in West Germany; nowhere else, however, are questions about the future raised more insistently than in the land between the Rhine and the Elbe. And that is hardly an accident. The Federal Republic is the core of the ancien système. It is the symbol and the product of Europe's partition, at once the bulwark and the victim of the Continent's bipolar order. On the other hand, no European nation has profited more from that system than West Germany. Prostrate in 1945, it had become the European pillar of the Atlantic coalition by 1955. Situated athwart the frontlines of the Cold War, it is also the main benefactor of European security *made in the USA*.

Yet as the demand for security dwindled in the wake of the grand settlement of the early 1970s, so did a major reason for the assiduous cultivation of the Federal Republic's Atlantic links.[4] Indeed, since that watershed, West Germany has acquired a new role in the Atlantic system: still its easternmost brace, the half-nation has consciously begun to act as a bridge between East and West. This role had been suppressed in the past by a grating security imperative, but was nevertheless permanently dictated by geography and by *raison de nation* vis-à-vis the other half of Germany, which fulfills an analogous linchpin role in the Soviet sphere. Continuity has asserted itself in many guises; for example, in West Germany's abiding attachment to the Alliance, and in electoral verdicts (such as in 1983 and 1987) that repudiated those—the Social Democrats and the Greens—who would loosen the tie that binds. Yet there is also the rising voice of discontent, and that, too, is most stridently heard in the Federal Republic. Why must the Germans continue to pay the highest price for bipolarity? Why cannot the Germans be like everybody else?

Nor is discontent only a European problem. Though electorally far less significant, a similar revolt against the long-standing assumptions of the Alliance has been brewing in the United States. It is in many ways a mirror image of the West European phenomenon. In Europe the challenge comes from the democratic left; in the United States it is voiced by the neo-conservative right—and it is spreading into the center where internationalist Republicans (like former National Security Adviser Henry Kissinger) and internationalist Democrats (like Senator Sam Nunn) have begun to question the price of America's pledge to Europe.

If resentment in Europe centers on American demands for fealty, U.S. critics condemn its dwindling supply. If Americans charge abandonment, their allies denounce arrogance. If the European left dreams of a United States content to play the undemanding protector in the last resort (as a kind of over-the-horizon presence), their transatlantic counterparts dream of a Europe that could defend itself and thus deliver all the benefits of the current system without the excruciating costs of entanglement. And on the extremes in both camps, there are those who would do away with the Atlantic system altogether. Is not the United States an "occupying power," doing unto the West Europeans what the Soviets are doing to their hapless East European vassals? That question is echoed on the opposite shores of the Atlantic by those who see Europe as a drain on American power that could be better invested elsewhere.

Critics on both sides are, ironically, joined by the same assumption: that the price of entanglement has come to exceed its profits. Each side sees itself as the victim of the other, above all, in the realm of security. Extreme European voices depict the Atlantic system as a conspiracy against the peoples of Europe, a conspiracy that has turned the Continent into a nuclear "shooting gallery of the superpowers" while simultaneously imposing an oppressive regime of conquer-and-divide on an ancient civilization. American critics see their country similarly entrapped—by a

Western Europe unwilling to shoulder the burden of its own defense while demanding that the United States continue to play nuclear hostage to Europe's well-being. This is surely the impulse that underlies the search for strategic alternatives in the name of "conventional deterrence," analyzed in Chapter Four. Proposals for "no-first-use," "mobile defense," or "conventional retaliation," though spanning different ideological quarters, are all designed to postpone the dreaded moment of truth when the United States might have to trigger the nuclear apocalypse on behalf of its European allies.

What is the common denominator of discontent? One key difference between the contemporary challenge and those of the past is the historic success of the Atlantic coalition. Alliances are at risk when they either fail or succeed in their primary purpose: to best or to contain the common enemy. Most of the Alliance's past crises have revolved around the classical question of any alliance: Can NATO protect its members in the face of threats that were said to bring about its own undoing—the rise of Soviet power, the repetitive Soviet assault against Western positions in Europe (like Berlin), and the waning credibility of the American nuclear guarantee? The contemporary crisis stems from the opposite of fear—from a deeply entrenched feeling of security that reflects the realities of the Continent's ultrastability. That feeling dramatizes burdens and denigrates benefits. It highlights a stable superstructure of peace while obscuring the foundations laid in a distant past. Could not the structure stand on its own? Indeed, could not Europe and America try their hands at a new architecture—one that would satisfy the yearnings of guarantors and beneficiaries better than the ancien système?

That is the underlying question Americans and Europeans have begun to pose ever more insistently since the beginning of this decade. The conclusion of this book (Chapter Five) tries to limn an answer to that question in the light of history and the factors that continue to shape the international relations of the Euro-American system. Europeans might want to dispense with their unloved protector, but how will they protect themselves in the face of rivalries and fears—the source of murderous conflict in the past—that were subsumed in the Pax Americana constructed in the wake of World War II? Americans might dream of letting their onerous allies fend for themselves, but what if the bet on devolution goes wrong? Though Americans and Europeans yearn for different roles than the ones the postwar system has assigned to them, evolution has not changed the most fundamental given of that system. Caught in an inexorable conflict with the Soviet Union, the United States cannot yield Western Europe without yielding the greatest prize of them all to the one and only rival that matters.

These are the historical givens which dictate dependence and the burdens of alliance—with no end in sight. Yet nations act not only in terms of realities, they also resent them. And history offers neither examples nor reasons why sovereign nations would suffer such dependence without end.

Notes

1. This point deserves to be emphasized: NATO is the *only* multilateral alliance that has survived the Cold War. In 1986 the de facto rupture of ANZUS (Australia, New Zealand, the United States) completed the disintegration of the extra-European multilateral alliance system forged by the United States in the 1950s. The first to falter was CENTO (the Central Treaty Organization joining Britain, Iraq, Turkey, Pakistan, and Iran, with the United States as de facto member), followed by the unheralded demise of SEATO in the wake of the Vietnam War. (The Southest Asia Treaty Organization encompassed the ANZUS nations as well as France, Britain, the Philippines, Thailand, and Pakistan.)
2. Henry A. Kissinger, "The Future of NATO," Opening Remarks at conference organized by the Center for Strategic and International Affairs, Brussels, September 1–3, 1979, in Henry A. Kissinger, *For the Record: Selected Statements 1977–1980* (Boston: Little, Brown, 1981), p. 241.
3. Cf. the seminal analysis by Kenneth N. Waltz, "The Stability of the Bipolar World," *Daedalus* (Summer 1964).
4. That settlement comprises the Quadripartite Berlin Agreement; it quarantined an ancient source of trouble, the so-called Eastern Treaties with Moscow, Warsaw, and Prague, by which the Federal Republic had enveloped the conflict over borders in pledges of acceptance and renunciation-of-force agreements; and the "Basic Treaty" with the German Democratic Republic, by which Bonn established formal relations with East Berlin.

CHAPTER 1

Détente versus Alliance

At the threshold of the 1980s, the Atlantic Alliance was caught in a vexing paradox. The main conflict in Europe was no longer between East and West but between the United States and its own allies. To put the matter so baldly is hardly an exaggeration. While the Soviets counted their blessings, the West Europeans and the United States indulged in a confrontation that ran deeper and lasted longer than any of their disputes in decades past. Although the crisis had visibly abated by the mid-eighties, it laid bare fissures that resisted complete fusion. The conflict went to the very core of the relationship and, as a result, the paradox offered a paradigm that transcends the lessons of yesteryear.

Crises Old and New

In sharp contrast to earlier quarrels, when the issues arose one by one, the crisis of the 1980s spared no area of the relationship—whether it was nuclear strategy, arms control, détente, trade, or money; the Soviet Union, Iran, or Poland. Yet the fight over specifics merely obscured the fact that fundamentals were at stake: irreducible differences in interest, outlook, and ambition; the liberties of the weak and the prerogatives of the strong; the limits of allegiance and the claims of alliance. For the first time, conflict burst through the confines of governmental discord, reaching deeply into European societies shaken by fear of nuclear war and stirred by counterelites who attacked the wherewithals of deterrence—meaning the policies of the United States. Finally, there were moments when the very raison d'être of the Atlantic compact seemed to hang in the balance—when Europeans talked as if the United States posed a greater threat to their well-being than the Soviet Union, and when

Americans came to question the value of partners who behaved more like adversaries than allies.

The unprecedented depth of the crisis, and its paradigmatic nature, derived from yet another paradox: it should not have happened. It began in the final days of the 1970s, when the Soviet Union invaded Afghanistan. To be sure, Soviet armies had marched across borders before, but then only against their own allies. The Soviets had also used force outside their own bloc before—in Ethiopia and Angola—but then only indirectly and with the help of various surrogates. In any event, Moscow had been protected by the brutal rules of bipolarity—unwritten, but accepted by default ever since the bloody suppressions of East Germany in 1953 and Hungary in 1956. Afghanistan, however, signaled a direct and unmasked blow to the status quo. It was the first time since World War II that the Soviet Union had attacked a neutral country, and that country happened to be perilously close to the main sources of Western energy supplies.

In theory, such a foray should have provoked the entire West. Executed within a few days, the Soviet move displayed not only an unfamiliar readiness for risk-taking but also some impressive capacities for rapid power projection. In theory, the invasion of Afghanistan should have revised some firmly held assumptions about Soviet behavior, and it should have elicited a uniform Western reaction. In practice, it did not. Instead, it accelerated the continental drift between Europe and the United States. Far from infusing the West with a renewed sense of unity, the thrust into Afghanistan would leave a legacy of distrust and resentment which, in retrospect, was to make the many quarrels of the past look like a series of minor family squabbles.

To illustrate the historical difference, it is instructive to compare Afghanistan with the Suez and Cuba crises. In the fall of 1956 the United States humiliated its two oldest allies, France and Britain. The Eisenhower administration joined hands with Moscow to mobilize the United Nations in condemnation of Paris and London. And to add injury to the insult, the United States resorted to sheer economic blackmail. In the wake of the Suez Canal expedition, there was a massive run on the British pound. To stabilize the currency, Britain required an immediate $1 billion loan; American help was offered on the condition that London announce an immediate cease-fire.[1] Yet the alliance held because Eisenhower was merely applying brutal political and economic pressure; by contrast, the Soviet leader Nikita Khrushchev had threatened London and Paris with nuclear rockets at the same time that he was crushing the Hungarian revolution.

Nothing could dramatize the difference between the sixties and the eighties more vividly than Western Europe's response to the Cuban missile crisis. In 1962 relations between Bonn, Paris, and Washington were anything but harmonious. General de Gaulle's challenge to American hegemony had already blossomed into a full-scale offensive. And in the aftermath of the Berlin Wall (1961), Chancellor Adenauer's ancient fear of superpower collusion at the expense of German interests had hardened into sheer paranoia. Yet when the missile crisis broke, the two European leaders did fall into line behind President Kennedy. So did Prime Minister Harold Macmillan, who had been chancellor of the exchequer when Britain begged the United States for financial succor to stave off the attack on the pound in 1956.

In Paris, de Gaulle told Kennedy's emissary, Dean Acheson, "If there is war, I will be with you."[2] When the French president was informed about the naval quarantine of Cuba, he replied, "It is exactly what I would have done." Asked whether he wanted to see the aerial reconnaissance photographs, he declined, because "a great government such as yours does not act without evidence."[3] In spite of past humiliations and acute resentments, the three major European leaders closed ranks with Kennedy because there was something more crucial at stake than their own quarrels with Washington: the global balance between East and West.

Afghanistan, however, brought forth very different reactions. Within days of the invasion, the French foreign minister, François-Poncet, proclaimed that it would be a "grave error to westernize the Afghanistan affair" since it was primarily a conflict between the Soviets and the Islamic world rather than an East–West confrontation.[4] His president, Valéry Giscard d'Estaing, viewed the conflict even more indifferently, depicting Afghanistan as a kind of internal police action, "Moscow [having] acted in its own sphere of influence."[5] And to Jimmy Carter's claim that the invasion was "the greatest threat to peace since the Second World War,"[6] Chancellor Helmut Schmidt replied tersely, "I cannot forget that Warsaw Pact troops are only 30 miles from my own home in Hamburg."[7]

Jimmy Carter, who had experienced an epiphany in the meantime ("this action of the Soviets has made a more dramatic change in my own opinion of what the Soviet's ultimate goals are than anything they've done in the previous time I've been in office"),[8] reaped only disappointment, while Kennedy had easily gained European solidarity eighteen years earlier. In his diary, Carter wrote:

A long meeting with the Chancellor. He was primarily on the defensive because I persisted in asking what more the Federal Republic would do to help us with Afghanistan, and what actually they had done that provides pressure on the Soviet Union. The answer to both those questions apparently is "Nothing," except that Schmidt recommitted himself firmly and personally . . . that he and Giscard d'Estaing would join us in the Olympic boycott. (March 10, 1980)[9]

Whereas Charles de Gaulle had refused to negotiate with "l'Empire totalitaire" as long as the Soviets focused their pressure on Berlin and Cuba, his successor, Valéry Giscard d'Estaing, rushed off to Warsaw in May 1980 to pay his respects to Leonid Brezhnev—a move that signaled an early end of the Soviet Union's diplomatic quarantine by the West. A few weeks later the German chancellor traveled to Moscow where he appealed to Brezhnev to contribute to the "defusion of the dangerous crisis." Simultaneously, however, Schmidt proclaimed his government's "will to peace," stressing that "the policy of détente and cooperation with our Eastern neighbors" was one of the "pillars" of West German diplomacy.[10]

If in previous crises the purposes of alliance had served to swiftly contain internal dissent, this time it seemed no longer clear who the enemy was. It appeared immaterial that one superpower had dealt a nasty blow to the status quo by invading a neutral country whereas the other, even if haphazardly, was trying to restore the balance. In European eyes, both superpowers were no longer quite rational, both were trying to rob Europe of the precious fruits of détente, and both—as Helmut Schmidt was wont to reiterate ad infinitum—lacked a sorely needed "war avoidance strategy"—one which would heed the so-called lessons of 1914.

The chancellor's cautious resort to historical metaphor betrayed an ambivalence that, in turn, reflected the mounting dilemmas of European politics: how to save détente on the Continent without playing into Soviet hands elsewhere; how to please the American protector without affronting the Russians; how to show firmness abroad without risking repudiation at home. Those who were not in power, however, could afford to shrug off the dilemmas and indulge in resentment pure and simple. The former French interior minister, Michel Poniatowski, announced that France wanted no part of a "supersuicide of the superpowers."[11] Former German Chancellor Willy Brandt, the architect of Ostpolitik, denounced the "venomous stammering" of the superpowers, condemned "sterile agitation" in the wake of Carter's call to arms, and appealed to Germans and Europeans alike to stand ready "to save what can be saved" of détente.[12] In December 1980, when the Polish crisis escalated amidst apparent indications of a Soviet invasion, he castigated those in Washington who "indulge in an orgy of impotence." Nor was Poland a problem for the Alliance. "Poland has a great deal more to do with Poland than with the relationship between East and West."[13]

As in George Orwell's *Animal Farm*, the distinctions between friends and foes vanished. Worse, in a classic textbook example of psychic displacement, fear and frustration were not turned against the aggressor but against the protector. The most striking case in point was a letter that German novelist Günter Grass (*The Tin Drum*) and three of his writer friends addressed to Chancellor Schmidt: "Since Vietnam at the latest, the American government has forfeited any right to moral appeals. . . . The limits of Alliance loyalty are reached when peace is jeopardized wantonly or negligently." There was no crisis, the authors of the letter stated, for "nobody was attacking us, nobody is threatening us." Hence, they concluded, declarations of firmness were strictly "childish." Instead, "we Germans ought to use every possible means, every possible compromise to save the peace."[14]

Nor was the general populace so far behind the indignant avant-garde. A confidential poll sponsored by the West German government in the spring of 1980 revealed that:

- half of the West German population supported "more independence" vis-à-vis the United States (29 percent did not);
- 60 percent opposed the "stationing of more and new atomic weapons" on West German soil (in favor were 24 percent); and
- 45 percent viewed "military neutrality of the Federal Republic and the German Democratic Republic" as a useful way of safeguarding the peace (34 percent were opposed).[15]

During the Korean War the European allies had dispatched military contingents to the Asian battlefront; during the Vietnam War most of them had offered at least political support. Afghanistan was closer to home than either of these two theaters. Yet at the beginning of the 1980s, Europe's message to the United States was that détente and conflict were —and should be—divisible, that it would not allow the United States to pull it into conflicts that were not its own, leading Jimmy Carter to note in wistful cadences,

Nations ask us for leadership. But at the same time, they demand their own independence of action. They ask us for aid. But they reject any interference. They ask for understanding. But they often decline to understand us in return. They ask for protection, but are wary of obligations of alliance.[16]

What Détente Has Wrought

The blurring of the security issue ("Who threatens whom?") confirms the suspicion that Afghanistan marked a qualitatively different crisis in European–American relations. How can this transformation of psychology and politics be explained?

On the most obvious level, the answer is that of Under Secretary of State Lawrence Eagleburger, who told a Vienna audience, "Détente for you, for Berliners, for Germans, has made a difference, but for us it has been a failure."[17] In the first place, the Europeans—and the Germans in particular—have profited far more heavily from the decade of détente (1970–1980) than has the United States. The Europeans remember the recurrent confrontations of the past, from the Berlin Blockade (1948–1949) to the Berlin Crisis (1958–1962), and compare them with the unprecedented era of stability in the seventies. It was a decade that saw the quasi-settlement of World War II (also known as the "New Ostpolitik"); the Four-Power Agreement on Berlin which at least cauterized a perennial trouble spot; the drawing together of the two Germanys; the flourishing of trade; and a good deal of person-to-person interaction across what used to be known as the Iron Curtain. While crises and confrontations multiplied elsewhere, Europe remained a solitary island of peace.

The American experience during this decade was more sobering. Reacting to the hapless, costly, and society-rending intervention in Southeast Asia, the United States had cut back on its worldwide commitments and had begun to de-emphasize the weight of military power in its foreign policy. At the beginning of the 1970s, the exhaustion of the Truman consensus had forced the Nixon administration to play the game of balance-and-containment with an increasingly empty hand. When Jimmy Carter came to the presidency, he was determined to dispense with balance and containment by dint of sheer proclamation. "We are now free," he announced in 1977, "of that inordinate fear of communism which once led us to embrace any dictator who joined us in that fear," and he promised a policy based on "constant decency in its values and optimism in our historical vision."[18] Yet while they were defining a more modest role for their country, Americans saw Soviet armaments grow apace, followed by geopolitical forays stretching from Angola to Afghanistan. And in spite of SALT I and sundry other agreements concluded with the Soviets in the heyday of détente, the military balance deteriorated for the United States both strategically and conventionally, globally as well as locally.

For the United States détente did not "work"; for the Europeans it did, precisely because the Soviet Union had shifted the focus of the competition from Europe to the strategic arms arena and to the Third World. Because the East–West conflict unfolded no longer in and over Europe, as it had in the forties and fifties, the Europeans tried to disengage from the confiict. They reacted to Afghanistan, for instance, with obsessive attempts to snatch as many pieces of détente as possible from the jaws of the rattled giants. Nor was arms control discredited in Europe just because it had yielded nothing tangible after so many years of barren negotiations, like those on Mutual and Balanced Force Reductions (MBFR) begun in Vienna in 1973. What mattered more in Europe was the conviction that arms control had not been a palpable failure either. And that conviction was informed by a peculiar assumption: that the process (negotiation) was more important than the end (reduction); indeed, that the process *was* the end, namely, the continuous reaffirmation of détente. Hence, there was no backlash in Europe born out of frustration. While many Americans came to associate the SALT period with the onset of unbridled Soviet opportunism, Europeans congratulated themselves that, on the Continent at least, the steady growth of Soviet military power had not translated into political pressure or armed adventurism. Throughout the 1970s the Soviets had remained on their best behavior in Europe. Détente was not "oversold" in Europe, as critics claim it was in the United States, simply because it had in fact delivered on its key promise: stability.

Second, and precisely because détente worked, the Europeans have acquired new vulnerabilities—like contiguity with the Soviet bloc—that the United States does not share. The West German case is, as usual, the most telling case of transformation. Before the New Ostpolitik, the Federal Republic was America's most faithful junior partner in Europe because of its peculiar conflict with the East, which centered on Bonn's refusal to consecrate partition and the territorial redistribution following from World War II. Conducted from a position of weakness, conflict with the East necessarily translated into a unique degree of dependence on the

West. To compensate for its weakness in the face of Soviet pressure, the Federal Republic had to gain derivative strength; to garner that strength, it paid in the currency of loyalty and deference to American (and French) policy. The New Ostpolitik radically revised that balance sheet. By conceding to the Soviets what the realities demanded, Bonn not only shed a good number of the old fetters but also acquired new stakes. With the new freedom in the West came new obligations in the East. Once the Federal Republic had committed itself to a cooperative relationship with East Germany, Eastern Europe, and the Soviet Union, vulnerabilities were not so much unshouldered as shifted eastward.

When the Afghanistan crisis broke, about 300,000 German ethnics had been allowed to emigrate from Eastern Europe and the Soviet Union. But an estimated three million still remained—as unwitting hostages to good relations between Bonn and its eastern neighbors. In effect, *all* the achievements of Ostpolitik—especially the fitful process of reassociation between the two Germanys which has to substitute for the impossible goal of reunification—are hostages to détente in Europe. West German trade with the Soviet Union had grown more than tenfold during the decade of détente, from 544 million rubles in 1970 to 5.78 billion in 1980. (During the same decade, French trade with the Soviet Union rose by a factor of 7, Italian trade by a factor of 6.5, and Belgian trade by a factor of 8.)[19] Though the aggregate figures are comparatively small (West German trade with Switzerland exceeds its Soviet trade), sectoral dependencies are not. A good portion of West European exports to the Soviet Union flow from declining industries (such as steel and machinery in West Germany) or highly protected sectors (such as agriculture in France). These areas are particularly dear to the hearts of West European governments, all of whom resisted categorically when Jimmy Carter sounded the call for boycotts and embargoes in the wake of the Afghanistan invasion. By contrast, American trade with the Soviet Union has always been small, its growth lagging far behind the expansion of European eastward trade during the détente decade. The same holds true for every other area of cooperation. Since the United States shares few ties of interdependence with the Soviet bloc, it had very little to lose from the outbreak of "Cold War II."

Third, the uneven distribution of détente's costs and benefits had left a heavy imprint on the domestic bases of foreign policy in Europe and the United States. In Europe the sustained decline of East–West hostility, the steady progress of trade and travel, and the perception of ultra-stability between the blocs, had realigned domestic priorities away from defense and toward public welfare and private prosperity. Having taken root abroad, détente had also wrought a secular change in the nature of the domestic consensus. The West Europeans had indeed lost their "inordinate fear of communism" because the threat itself—internal as well as external—had lost its sting.

In Italy the Communist Party (CPI) had progressively severed its ties to Moscow, straining hard to gain domestic respectability on the road to a "historic compromise" with the ruling Christian Democrats (which included the acceptance of NATO). Though much closer to their pro-Soviet origins than the CPI, the French Communists had embraced their country's national deterrent while whitewashing their Stalinist image in search of an electoral alliance with François Mitterrand's Socialists. In West Germany, the most fiercely anti-Communist member of NATO until the mid-sixties, the transformation went even further than in Italy and France, and for more complicated reasons.

In Italy and France the Communist parties had shifted toward what Italians call the "majority zone," for domestic reasons—in order to acquire a chance of gaining a long-denied share of governmental power. In West Germany, on the other hand, the accommodating impulse came from outside the country, and it acted to change not only parties but the entire polity. The Federal Republic's "Communist Party"—the main challenge to the legitimacy of the existing order—was its counterstate across the Elbe River, the German Democratic Republic (GDR), its real Communist party having been outlawed in 1956. If in France and Italy the Communists moved to accommodate the majority consensus, the majority consensus in West Germany moved to accommodate East Germany and, by extension, the entire Soviet bloc. Once the Federal Republic had shifted from an exclusive preoccupation with Westpolitik toward Ostpolitik and détente, yesterday's public enemy—the East Germans and their allies—had to be legitimized as today's and tomorrow's partner in cooperation. The diplomatic opening to the East demanded societal change at home, and thus the systematic dismantling of the anti-Communist consensus of the Adenauer era.

Germany's "historic compromise" was thus achieved when the Italian version was but a gleam in the eye of CPI leader Enrico Berlinguer—in the early 1970s, when the treaty network with the East opened the gate to cooperative coexistence with the members of the Warsaw Pact. Diplomacy dictated a nonconfrontational ideology, and once détente was in place, its fruits continued to nourish the new consensus to the point of virtual irreversibility. If the Left and the Right in West Germany had once been sharply polarized in matters of Ostpolitik, by 1980 they were united in a tacit grand coalition that resisted American fealty demands in the name of good neighborly relations and détente-minded realism. (Having fought Willy Brandt's Ostpolitik with a vengeance, Helmut Kohl's Conservatives would continue that policy with nary a modification after the ouster of the Social Democrats in 1982.)

By 1980 the fear of confrontation and the claims of tranquility loomed far larger in Europe than the problems of the military balance, Soviet opportunism, or instability in the Third World. In the United States, however, public opinion had moved in the opposite direction during the decade of détente. The Vietnam-induced revulsion against entangling obligations and the use of military force had yielded to the "new patriotism" which flowered into the Reagan consensus of the 1980 presidential election. The popularity of defense spending was on the upswing, and *détente* turned into a word that signified credulity and lack of resolve. No wonder then that the confrontation between Europe and the United States would transcend the specifics. The divergent responses to Afghanistan suggested that fundamental perceptions and beliefs on the opposite shores of the Atlantic were drastically out of phase. And the clash was not just over tactics but over weltanschauung, to wit:

Arms control. If Americans came to question arms control both as a process (stabilizing East–West relations) and as an end (slowing the arms race), the Europeans continued to view the enterprise as a crucial ingredient of détente and as an imperative goal in its own right. In Europe arms control continued to command not only broad-based but even growing support; in the United States the restoration of military strength loomed larger than its reduction through negotiation. The clash of public moods was emblematically illustrated by the opposite approaches taken by the United States and Europe to theater-force modernization and to SALT.

In Europe the 1979 NATO decision to deploy 572 intermediate-range missile systems could only be bought with an ironclad commitment to arms control talks with the Soviets—as a substitute or alibi for the installation of cruise and Pershing II missiles four years later. In the United States, by contrast, President Carter felt compelled to pay for a SALT II agreement with a massive rearmament program (like the MX missile and a host of conventional add-ons). Put differently, arms control was the price of rearmament in Europe; across the ocean, rearmament was the price of arms control—and even that was not enough to buy the ratification of SALT II in the Senate.

Détente. In the early seventies, Europeans and Americans had embarked on the road of détente with a tidy theory in hand. Together, they
would cast a net of interdependence around the Soviets, enmeshing them
in trade and technology transfers, credit lines, and arms control agreements. Having acquired a stake in cooperative relations with the West,
the Soviet Union would behave according to Western standards—like
any other reasonable power which values peace and prosperity more
highly than the costly pleasures of aggrandizement. The Soviets, so the
theory ran, would not risk the horn of capitalist plenty for geopolitical
adventures in the Third World.

By the same theory, Soviet contraventions should have been met by
the denial of cooperation and the cutting of links. Yet in practice, Western policy did not follow the logic of linkage but rather the détente differential between the United States and Europe. Having little to lose from
the breakdown of superpower détente, the United States reacted to the
rumblings of Cold War II with sanctions and rearmament. Counting their
many blessings, most Europeans stressed not only the validity of the
original concept but also the need for more rather than less détente in
times of tension. If Americans were struck by the deterioration of the
global military balance, Europeans worried about the threat to regional
tranquility. Hence, they invoked the "1914" analogy and the danger of
miscalculation created by an ill-considered call to arms. Americans, on
the other hand, pointed to "Munich" and the danger of Soviet miscalculation stemming from its perception of Western weakness. Conscious of
the burden of global containment, the United States called for resistance
on a global scale. Scrambling to shore up the dikes around the Continent, the Europeans responded, "Why risk détente here just because it
has broken down elsewhere? Shouldn't we pocket our regional gains instead of gambling them away in extra-European disputes which call for
different chips anyway?"

The Soviet Union. For Americans, Afghanistan posed a threefold
threat. A move so close to the Persian Gulf was fraught with grave implications for global stability and Western energy supplies; it suggested that
Soviet objectives tended to expand with Soviet military means; and it
dramatized an inherent Soviet opportunism which could only be checked
by countervailing power. The Europeans took a more benign view, stressing the defensive motives of the Soviet Union. They saw the thrust into
Afghanistan as a limited response to a set of circumstances that were sui
generis; they emphasized the unique vulnerability of a multinational empire to fundamental challenges from beyond its borders, and invoked

the age-old Russian trauma of encirclement and invasion as guideline for a Western strategy that ought to reassure rather than provoke the Soviets.

With equal insistence, Americans and Europeans claimed superior wisdom in their opposing analyses. The din of mutual recrimination merely helped to obscure the obvious: that an irreducible difference of interests lay at the root of all their disputes. It was these interests that colored their perceptions, not their perceptions that brought on the clash of American and European interests.

The Transformation of the European System

Moods change, and change they did on both sides of the Atlantic as the United States and its European allies disengaged from their conflict after several years of seemingly endless contention. About halfway through the 1980s, another cycle of resentment and restoration had come to an end, and in part because of sheer exhaustion. Yet the interests that fed the conflict have not really changed, and neither has the stage on which it was enacted. The causes of the conflict have outlived its manifestations, and it is these causes—rooted in the interests of the Alliance members and the setting in which they must act—that endow the crisis of the eighties with its lasting relevance.

The noisy clashes over Iran, Afghanistan, and Poland, over Eastern trade and Western missiles, were but the denouement. The drama of what might be called *decoupling* began in the era of détente, which the United States and Western Europe entered in tandem in 1970 but exited in bitter confrontation. In the course of that decade, détente rewrote the scripts of the major actors while rearranging the stage that is Europe. Slow in the making and reaching beyond the particulars of day-to-day events, the transformation is fated to endure. Hence, we must look to the decade of détente for the forces that have changed some of the principal givens of the European–American relationship.

To begin, the very process of détente was destined to drive the Allies apart because it would offer rewards to the West Europeans that the United States could not possibly share. Détente had a built-in "success differential" that reflected not so much superior European skill or effort but the irreducible difference between the ways in which global and regional powers face their common adversary. In the superpower arena, where détente and Cold War are but variations on the enduring theme of rivalry, the United States had to manage a global conflict that continues to defy resolution. In the European setting, on the other hand, the conflict was more limited and thus less resistant to partial resolution. In short, there was a deal to be had for the Europeans, but not for the United States.

When détente began in the early seventies, the United States and its European allies had set out in similar directions. Yet the original harmony belied fundamental differences in goals and roles. As a global power, the United States could only pretend that a "stable structure of peace" could be fashioned, as one of the more famous shibboleths of the Nixon administration had it. That objective was bound to remain a will-o'-the-wisp, an inspiring myth crafted to reassure a domestic audience weary of Vietnam and eager to lighten the burden of universal containment. Détente as a "stable structure" could not deliver on its lofty promise because such a settlement must perforce evade the grasp of two superpowers doomed to permanent rivalry. Sheltered by a surfeit of deterrent strength, they cannot destroy each other. Equipped with overwhelming destructive power, they cannot trust each other. Between two nations that alone pose a mortal threat to each other's existence, there can be no permanent victory and no permanent peace, neither condominium nor withdrawal—only permanent competition.

Hence the precarious nature of all superpower détente. At times nervous confrontation has yielded to wary cooperation; at other times the relaxation of tensions has given way to partial collaboration. Yet none of these positions on the spectrum of possibilities has been stable. Solemn arms control agreements were merely the prelude to the rapid expansion of the strategic arsenals. Pledges to desist from "unilateral advantage" were only honored until the next crisis—as in 1973 when the celebrated U.S.-Soviet Agreement on the Prevention of Nuclear War was followed a few months later by the harbingers of nuclear confrontation during the Yom Kippur War. Superpower détente, in short, has been in the nature of a respite; it has never jelled into a stable agreement on fundamentals. Nor will it ever do so.

Détente between Western Europe and the Soviet Union proceeded from a more solid foundation. There was, first of all, an obvious trade-off that could form the core of a formal agreement, and it centered on the quid pro quo of access and acceptance. The Soviet Union wanted legitimacy for its postwar territorial gains in Europe and for the partition of Germany. The West Europeans, with the Federal Republic in the vanguard, wanted access—diplomatic, social, and economic—to the other half of the Continent being jealously guarded by Moscow. And the treaty network fashioned in the early 1970s followed precisely along these lines. In the so-called Eastern Treaties, Bonn bound itself to respect the post-war borders as inviolable, while all but recognizing its hostile brother, the German Democratic Republic. In the Helsinki Agreement of 1975, concluding the 35-nation Conference on Security and Cooperation in Europe, the West as a whole added its multilateral cachet to these pledges. In return, Moscow opened some doors in the wall of separation between Eastern and Western Europe. Embassies were exchanged between Bonn and the capitals of Eastern Europe; trade began to flourish; carefully controlled travel and emigration started to open up what was once known as the Iron Curtain. In short, Ostpolitik and regional détente added up to a quasi-settlement of World War II, lending the process a permanence that will always elude the United States in its dealings with the Soviet Union.

In the second place, Europe profited from a structural windfall of America's making. Henry Kissinger would make the point succinctly when he deplored the "divisibility of détente," which gave "Europe . . . a monopoly on détente and America a monopoly on defense."[20] That the Europeans would pursue such a "market-dividing" strategy was virtually foreordained by the nature of the American–European relationship vis-à-vis the Soviet Union. Precisely because the United States has to produce security on its own, and because there is no outside insurance against misplaced credulity, global détente will always run up against the stringent limits imposed by the existential threat the two superpowers hold over each other. The Europeans, however, were—and continue to be—sheltered by American might; their core security is guaranteed by a powerful patron across the sea. In the shadow of that guarantee, the security risks of regional détente were bound to pale. To resent the crafty "division of labor" by which "one side does the defense and other side does the negotiating"[21] was to resent the very postwar security system that the United States had built. The interests of a global power are global by definition, and great powers have always been compelled to pay a disproportionate share for the maintenance of the security system they built. Conversely, Charles de Gaulle was right when he proclaimed *"tout le monde est, a été ou sera Gaulliste"* ("everybody is, was, or will be Gaullist"). All small powers are intrinsically "Gaullist": they will seek to profit more from the security structures provided by the great powers than they will invest in those structures. Given this fundamental asymmetry between the strong and the weak, smaller allies will always be tempted to opt out of global conflicts and to enjoy the fruits of their sheltered existence, the counterpart of their dependence. It is a choice the strong do not have, and therefore the United States and the Europeans were predestined to decouple in the face of a crisis that engulfed Southwest Asia while sparing the Continent.

As an option, "selective détente" grows out of the very nature of the European–American relationship. As long as the Alliance endures, the United States will always "hold the ring," leaving the Europeans free to pursue their regional ambitions without fear of existential consequences. Selective détente, always a latent possibility, became a reality when the Soviet Union executed a historic reversal in its European policy. That shift points to the third reason why détente transformed the European stage. In the past, Soviet policy had been to intimidate Western Europe and to isolate West Germany while holding in reserve the never quite suppressed secondary option of Big Twoism, meaning collaborative arrangements with the United States at the expense of European interests. (That option flourished briefly under the aegis of the Nonproliferation Treaty sponsored jointly by the Soviet Union and the United States in the late 1960s.) The strategy of intimidation and isolation essentially achieved the opposite of what it intended. Soviet leaders from Stalin to Khrushchev, during crises from the Berlin Blockade in the forties to the Berlin Wall in the sixties, had regularly resorted to risk-laden gambits to gain predominance over Europe—yet aggressiveness had regularly failed them. Instead of separating the Europeans from their transatlantic guardian, Soviet pressure had increased their dependence on the United States, homogenizing interests and policies and driving the Federal Republic into an intimate (and deferential) partnership with Washington.

In the 1970s the Soviet Union offered a very different relationship to Western Europe, and the rewards were enormous. By shifting the global East–West competition from Europe, its ancient locus, to the Third World, the Soviet Union lifted the threat and thus the discipline from the European members of the Alliance. By offering them diplomatic access to Eastern Europe, the Soviet Union gained peaceful access to Western Europe's prolific resource base—credits, subsidies, technology transfers—which was after all one of the great stakes of the Cold War contest. And by extending cooperative coexistence to the Europeans while denying similar self-restraint to the United States in other areas, the Soviets achieved a separate truce in the world's foremost strategic arena.

Thus, Khrushchev's successor, Leonid Brezhnev, could proclaim in 1977, "The changes for the better [as a result of détente] are most conspicuous in Europe."[22] Merely by dint of its existence, that truce encouraged its own perpetuation. What was extended by the East could always be withdrawn, and nobody was more acutely aware of that silent threat than the West Germans, who had carried the brunt of Soviet pressure from the Prague Coup in 1948 to the Prague Invasion in 1968. After Jimmy Carter's post-Afghanistan epiphany, Helmut Schmidt and his foreign minister, Hans-Dietrich Genscher, never ceased touting the détente-minded *berechenbarkeit* (predictability) of West German foreign policy; they were signaling to the Soviet Union that Bonn knew well where its own intrinsic pressure points lay. And when the German chancellor blessed the fruits of détente ("We are living in more secure circumstances than the first 25 years after the war")[23] he unwittingly underscored the essence of Moscow's newly acquired influence over Western Europe. Power in its purest and most productive form makes threats unnecessary. Having been hostage to Soviet power in the past, the Europeans had now become hostage to Soviet good will.

A fourth factor of transformation derives from the purposes of détente. The short-term objective—the relaxation of tensions buttressed by contractual agreements—was shared by Americans and Europeans alike. Yet both sides attached quite different expectations to the outcome of the process, and those hopes would ultimately drive them into a clash over the basics, not the tactics. Aware that détente could not really dispatch the underlying cause of the permanent rivalry, the Nixon and Ford administrations were essentially pursuing a policy of containment-cum-balance by another name (détente), except that it had to be played out from a position of Vietnam-induced domestic weakness. In effect détente spelled "hegemony on the cheap," with regional allies being asked to assume some of the countervailing tasks that were traditionally executed through the direct application of American power. American détente policy in the seventies was conservative and geared to the status quo; it owed more to Bismarck than to George F. Kennan.

For the classic statement of containment was anything but status quo–bound. In 1947, George Kennan postulated that "the United States has it in its power to increase enormously the strains under which Soviet policy must operate, to force upon the Kremlin a far greater moderation and circumspection than it has had to observe . . . and in this way to promote tendencies which must eventually find their outlet in either the break-up or the mellowing of Soviet power."[24] Containment, then, was not intended to merely stop Soviet power but to *transform its nature*. Containment would either bring about the demise of the Soviet empire or prompt its internal reform along lines that promised a more pacific policy abroad.

The internal, domestic transformation of the Soviet system clearly was not the ambition of the Nixon/Kissinger détente. Their target had been the external behavior of the Leninist heirs to the tsars. A judicious blend of pressures (in that catalog the People's Republic of China loomed largest) and incentives would socialize the Soviet Union into the world system according to American rules of the game. Reassured by nuclear parity and lured by the cornucopia of capitalist riches, Moscow would come to act as a responsible citizen in the society of nations, eschewing the temptations of aggrandizement at the expense of Western positions. If containment à la Kennan, following traditional liberal dogma, sought stability through regime transformation (only "bad" states make "bad" policy), Nixon and Kissinger took their cues from the past masters of conservative diplomacy, like Palmerston and Bismarck. No matter how bad a state might be, it could still be taught to prefer the profits of stability and balance to the wages of opportunism and disorder.

These purposes were at best only partially congruent with those of the Europeans. As far as the means of détente were concerned, the Europeans shared only half of the American assumptions. Forced to conduct their policy from a position of military dependence on a United States that had done little to halt or match the Soviet military build-up in the 1970s, the Europeans quite naturally fastened on the incentive side of détente diplomacy while ignoring, even denigrating, the no less vital pressure side. They enthusiastically embraced the "carrots" and dispatched the "sticks" in a cloud of circular logic. They accepted the necessity for forging East–West links strong enough to give the Soviets pause before contemplating new expansionist ventures. Yet Europe refused to cut those ties when Moscow declined to live up to Western standards in Afghanistan and Poland, because to do so would have loosened the West's hold over the Soviet Union in future confrontations. For the Europeans détente had become irreversible, except for the most cataclysmic of provocations. After Afghanistan, sanctions remained for the most part symbolic, and even these were mainly honored in the breach. Among the allies in Western Europe, only the Federal Republic, Norway, and Turkey joined in the boycott of the 1980 Olympic Games in Moscow.

Yet to blame commercial avarice or military weakness for such behavior is to overlook the deeper causes. Western Europe's refusal to be dragged into what it regarded as America's quarrel with the Soviet Union was a matter of ends rather than means. For the United States and Western Europe were profoundly at odds when it came to the ultimate purpose of détente. If the United States sought to stabilize the status quo around the world, the West Europeans hoped to change it in their East European hinterland. And it is at this fork in the Western détente road where the weightiest causes of Alliance conflict were—and continue to be—buried.

West European détente policy was a heady brew of Kennan's ambitious ends and Kissinger's modest means. It was containment by carrot. It sought to change *patterns of rule* within the Eastern bloc (the "sources of conduct," to borrow from Kennan) rather than *patterns of foreign policy,* and to do so not by relentless pressure (as "Mr. X" had recommended) but by endless pliancy. For the Europeans détente has always been more than just the relaxation of tensions and the stabilization of the military milieu. Détente in Europe was to offer a framework which might allow the Soviets to loosen their stranglehold on the eastern half of the Continent. This was certainly the key thrust of German Ostpolitik. If reunification of the two Germanys was precluded by the realities of territorial possession, then the increasing permeability of borders and the cautious liberalization of regimes would mute the consequences of partition and ultimately even render irrelevant the quest for a unitary German state.

Unlike American détente, German (and European) Ostpolitik was irrevocably tied to domestic reform in the Soviet empire, which, in turn, demanded a reliably nonconfrontational posture. Proceeding on the assumption that the Soviet Union ruled by fear because of fear, Ostpolitik equated diplomacy in part with therapy. It called for feeding the Soviets a steady diet of reassurance, supplemented by a stream of material benefits which would outweigh the risks of partial devolution. With regard to Eastern Europe, West Germany (and, to some extent, Giscard d'Estaing's France) became the Soviet Union's silent partner in stability. Hence the minimal German tolerance—long before Afghanistan and Poland—for anything that might either destabilize Communist regimes or legitimize the reimposition of East bloc uniformity by force. In 1977 the West Germans were rattled by Jimmy Carter's human rights campaign (as a gratuitous insult to the Soviet Union); in 1978 they vacillated over the neutron bomb (because it might provoke Moscow); in 1979 the ruling Social Democrats barely consented to the Brussels Decision on intermediate-range nuclear forces (INF) because, as they correctly foresaw, such a decision would offer the Soviets a cause or pretext for tightening their grip over their East European vassals.

Contrary to American expectations, the Polish crisis (beginning in the summer of 1980 and escalating to the high point of martial law in December 1981) made little difference, even though it was closer to home than Afghanistan. Precisely because a Soviet invasion of Poland would reduce the essential rationale of Ostpolitik ad absurdum, the Germans waited apprehensively and secretly cursed the Americans for their renewed rush to confrontation. Given German premises, it was only logical that somebody like Willy Brandt (chancellor from 1969 to 1974) would seek to hold off the Americans and to reassure the nervous Russians by pooh-poohing the bipolar dimension of the crisis with comments like "Poland has a great deal more to do with Poland than with the relationship between East and West."[25]

Nor were the Germans alone as tacit collaborators in cohesion. David Watt, then the head of the Royal Institute for International Affairs in London, stated that "the real object of western policy is the creation and preservation of a situation in which there is maximum freedom [in Eastern Europe] compatible with the maintenance of the overall political status quo." And he added, "The Russians for their part want something that is, in practice, not so very different. . . . [There is], as it were, a furtive community of interests."[26]

The breathtaking gamble of Ostpolitik and European détente rested – and continues to rest – on a finely tuned trade-off between reassurance and subversion, between cooperation and co-optation. Reassuring the Soviets would allow them to relax the heavy grip of imperial control. Reassuring the regimes of the East would lower the risk of partial liberalization. Buttressed by economic side payments, these reassurances would help to breach barriers between states, societies, and individuals in Europe – healing the "great wound of World War II."[27]

In a prescient analysis published before the eruption in Poland, Pierre Hassner rightly questioned the assumptions of this approach. It was not clear, he wrote, "whether this increased self-confidence [on the part of Eastern regimes] is supposed to bring the elites to lower their guard and to promote an unwitting . . . structural change, thereby working against their own real interests, or whether the goal was a real stabilization which would allow them to keep their domination but dispense with the more pathological measures born out of insecurity."[28] If "lowering the guard" was the objective, what would prevent the regimes between East Berlin and Moscow from seeing through the game and pocketing the gains without paying in the currency of structural reform? If, on the other hand, the real goal was not benign subversion but a latter-day "Holy Alliance" that would insure regime authority minus the authoritarianism, the under-lying assumption was even more sanguine than in the first case. What if the Communist regimes were just constitutionally unable to accept con-ciliation from the West and extend it to their populaces without trigger-ing the next cycle of revolt and repression?

The imposition of martial law on Poland in the final days of 1981 dem-onstrated once more that the process has a built-in tendency to turn up-on itself. As in the two previous détentes—after Stalin's death in 1953 and the mini-thaw of the mid-sixties—the Polish self-invasion showed that neither the regimes nor the Soviets could respect the verdict of dé-tente once it threatened the Kremlin's political and pontifical empire in Eastern Europe. While the Soviet Union would seek to encourage the loosening of bipolarity in Western Europe, it was not prepared to coun-tenance such an outcome in its own glacis. And so, in 1981, the lofty assumptions of Ostpolitik and European détente collided head-on with General Jaruzelski's troops, which occupied their own country to fore-stall a replay of the Czechoslovakian invasion in 1968.

Yet no West European government has been prepared to accept the more brutal consequences of détente. Neither Afghanistan nor Poland could undo Western Europe's enduring commitment to regional détente. The French president, Valéry Giscard d'Estaing, put the abiding ratio-nale as well as any of his European counterparts:

This policy of détente has allowed for a change in the relations between the Euro-pean states. Thus, relations between France and certain European states—Poland, Romania, Hungary . . . East Germany—have been transformed, intensified and have certainly changed the existing situation in Europe. I tell you, for the benefit of those who talk so willingly about giving up détente, that this would plunge part of the populations of these European countries into despair, those who are our partners in the quest for détente.[29]

This rationale is shared by all European leaders, be they center-right or center-left, and it underlines a fifth change in the European setting. Transcending the mainstays of classic bipolarity, there is now a shadowy parallel system defined not only by all kinds of economic and political ties between the European members of the two blocs, but also by a West European *prise de conscience* that regards the East Europeans not as ene-mies but as hapless victims and even tacit allies. In the past the East Eu-ropean regimes were seen as creatures and cohorts of the Kremlin, in-distinguishable from the Soviet masters who had installed them as over-lords of their hapless populations. A Walter Ulbricht (who ruled East Germany until 1971) or a Janos Kadar (who was imposed on Hungary after the revolution of 1956) was seen to be no more deserving of friendly treatment than their Soviet patrons, regardless of the deprivations suffered by their captive subjects.

Yet today, neither Kadar nor Ulbricht's successor, Erich Honecker, is seen as a mere satrap of Moscow. Instead, the leaders of Hungary and East Germany (as well as Poland's General Jaruzelski) appear as prudent patriots who must strike a precarious balance between the realities of power and their countries' national aspirations.[30] Though chained to empire and beholden to an inimical ideology, the regimes of the East are silent partners in an all-European enterprise that must lighten the deadweight of bipolarity and pierce the barriers of partition. The East Europeans, hostages rather than hostile, must not be punished for Soviet transgressions. Instead, their margins of maneuver must be carefully enlarged through conciliation and cooperation.

From a global perspective, this tacit alliance between Western and Eastern Europe poses an insoluble dilemma: how to differentiate between the Soviet Union and the rest of the bloc. Differentiation collides mercilessly with a basic rule of Soviet bloc diplomacy in times of Soviet–American tensions: "Clients must not enjoy better relations with the West than the patron."[31] Therefore, the new benevolence must either be extended all the way to Moscow or suffer the full weight of Soviet wrath. From the timid beginnings of détente in the 1960s, various Western powers have tried to distinguish between Moscow and its subordinates, and in each case (Lyndon B. Johnson's "bridge-building" and Bonn's "policy of small steps" in the mid-sixties), these efforts foundered swiftly on the enduring shoals of imperial control. By long experience, the West Europeans have learned that the key to Eastern Europe ultimately remains in Soviet hands. Confronted with differentiation, Moscow has regularly responded with heavy-handed recentralization, either with overt force, as in the case of the Prague Spring, or obliquely, as in Poland in 1981.

Nor has the passage of time weakened the Kremlin's grip. Though the Soviet Union did tolerate a measure of separate inter-German détente during Cold War II—in part, because that relationship helped to separate the Federal Republic from the United States—it also demonstrated its continuing hold over the Westpolitik of its allies. The most significant test of that power came in 1984, when the Euromissile deployment had begun and the Soviet Union had ruptured its last remaining détente link to the United Sates—the arms control negotiations in Geneva. With the familiar exception of Romania, all members of the Warsaw Pact were forced to boycott the 1984 Olympic Games in Los Angeles.

Simultaneously, Bulgaria and East Germany were brought face to face with the niggardly limits of Soviet tolerance when their leaders were forced to cancel long-standing plans to travel to the Federal Republic.

As guardians at the gate, the Soviets are the ultimate beneficiaries of Western Europe's bloc-transcending collaboration with Eastern Europe, a collaboration from which there is now no turning back. Western Europe's scope for a policy of denial and countervailing pressure toward the Soviet Union is inexorably limited by its newfound sense of obligation toward the nations under Moscow's sway. Since the Soviets have perennially demonstrated that they can dictate the terms of interaction (and veto contacts altogether), even the most modest détente defies differentiation. Détente in Europe, unlike elsewhere, is either indivisible or impossible. It must either encompass the Soviet Union or collapse as a futile ambition.

As usual, the Federal Republic is the most instructive case in point. It is in Germany where the Soviet–American rivalry has divided the Continent, and it is in the Federal Republic where *raison de nation* dictates a *raison d'état* of permanent cooperative existence with a key member of the Soviet bloc, the German Democratic Republic. To protect the tortuous process of reassociation with East Germany for the sake of a common German nation, Bonn must protect its ties to Eastern Europe as well; and to shelter both, it cannot afford to alienate the Soviet Union. Indeed, no West European nation is prepared to sacrifice the silent partnership with Eastern Europe on the altar of the Soviet–American contest. Or, as Helmut Schmidt has put it, increasing global tensions "will indubitably compress the margin of maneuver of East European states and their governments."[32] Hence the lasting conflict of interests between the United States and its transatlantic partners. Being a global power, the United States must worry about the Soviet Union as a threat to worldwide stability and seek to restrain Moscow. As regional powers, the Allies must worry about the Soviet Union as a threat to Europe's evolution and try to reassure Moscow. The United States must preserve the status quo, the Europeans want to change it; such diverse aspirations do not add up to a prescription for harmony.

The sixth and perhaps most momentous change wrought by the decade of détente stems from a secular shift in the strategic balance that goes by the shorthand symbol of "parity." The U.S. loss of nuclear superiority, as both American and European strategists have never ceased to proclaim, has grievously, perhaps fatally, weakened "extended deterrence"—that is, the credibility of America's pledge to unsheathe its nuclear sword on behalf of its non-nuclear allies. In the existential crunch, so the argument goes, that pledge will be exposed as an empty bluff because the United States will not risk its own survival for the sake of other nations. And short of Armageddon, the new vulnerability bids the United States to accept risks on behalf of Europe more cautiously than ever before. Events have not borne out the pernicious effects throught to flow from strategic stalemate; in spite of their new surfeit of nuclear power, the Soviets have not been tempted to test in Europe the edifice of extended deterrence.

Still, beliefs are not always based on realities, and it is perhaps no accident that the onset of strategic equality, as codified in the SALT agreements of 1972, coincided with the great push toward Europeanwide détente at the beginning of the decade. Indeed, European détente follows quite smoothly, though not exclusively, from the premise of parity. Parity's presumed ill effects on the solidarity of America's nuclear guarantee have sharpened an ancient dilemma of all alliances. Since the weak can never rely completely on their patron's pledges, they have a *structural* incentive to improve the balance between insurance and risk, by propitiating the common adversary.[33] To compensate for their dependence on a great power that might stand aside during the moment of truth, smaller powers are perenially drawn toward policies that reduce their opponent's reasons for attacking them. To buttress the insurance afforded by their protector, weaker nations tend to take out reinsurance from their opponent in the form of side payments that spell conciliation and cooperation. In other words, if the supply of security declines, and if client states are unwilling or unable to make up the shortfall, they can reduce their demand for security through a policy of partial appeasement. (Total appeasement is not, of course, an option because that would be tantamount to defection and the end of alliance.)

Always latent, these incentives grow when the certainty of the patron's guarantee seems to dwindle, and they grow even more swiftly for allies placed geographically close to the locus of likely confrontation. Hence, it was to be expected that West Germany, more exposed and dependent than most, would take the lead in the pursuit of two seemingly contradictory but in fact entirely consistent policies. On the one hand, Helmut Schmidt (chancellor from 1974 to 1982) was the first to raise a public alarm over the sudden new menace posed by the soaring Eurostrategic potential of the Soviets; Backfire bombers and SS-20 missiles added a nasty regional edge to the perils of global parity. To pressure the United States into doing something about the SS-20—either by negotiating them away or by countering them with similar American systems—was to play the "supply-side" of Western European security. On the other hand, the West German chancellor was just as eager to reduce his country's demand for security—and all the more so in the face of Jimmy Carter's obtuseness about the separate Soviet missile threat arrayed against Western Europe. And so the West Germans were also the driving force behind regional détente—engineers of a studious effort at propitiation that would seek to dispatch any reasons the Soviets might have to exploit their expanding regional might.

The shaky nuclear balance might have remained only an abstraction —the object of endless debates, but safely confined to the routines of a small transatlantic strategic community. Yet what turned the quest for regional détente into sheer compulsion was Europe's perception of Jimmy Carter as a wayward and vacillating leader who would alternately ignore the threat and then fan it with a sudden switch toward militant containment. Defeat in Vietnam had weakened American power, and the nightmare of Watergate—the betrayal of public trust at the highest level of government—had weakened America's faith in itself. Yet instead of a restoration of that faith, Watergate was followed by the long decline under the presidency of Jimmy Carter, who would confuse the purposes of American power with wicked power politics and end up ignoring the demands of both.

In European eyes, the apparent collapse of American will was compounded by unmitigated confusion as the Allies contemplated the gyrations of American foreign policy between 1977 and 1980.[34] Over the course of three years, the Allies were confronted with a total about-face. In the beginning there was the abrupt turn toward "Wilsonianism": the almost blind neglect of power and conflict in favor of "world order" and "global issues." Scarcely three years later, however, there was the equally sudden shift toward "Trumanism" à la Carter: toward rearmament, rapid deployment forces, embargoes, boycotts—in short, a shift toward Cold War II. Worse, this mid-term reversal was but the background for rapid short-term oscillations that turned unpredictability into a steady routine (for instance, the notorious "neutron bomb")—where a policy was hardly announced before it was already disputed, reversed, or forgotten. At the same time the Europeans could not overlook what the United States seemed determined to ignore: a Soviet arms build-up across the entire spectrum of military power—but particularly in Europe—that had proceeded without pause for the better part of two decades and was virtually immune to the restraining effects of détente.

For the Europeans the confluence of Soviet ascendancy and American lassitude (whose onset, it must be said, had preceded Jimmy Carter by half a decade) added up to a need for political distancing. If their mighty protector could not act on behalf of its own vital interests, could it be expected to do so on behalf of the Allies' needs? Or, as Robert Tucker has put it, "the principal consequence [of all those developments] is that an imperfect protection cannot require more than an imperfect obedience."[35] Whatever parity had wrought was sharpened by an American stance that combined exhaustion with eccentricity; that pervasive uncertainty put a powerful impetus behind the various other reasons fueling Western Europe's quest for regional détente. Détente was to bear many fruits, but one was surely a reduction of Western Europe's dependence on the vagaries of American policy. Doomed to suffer the consequences of America's erratic twists and turns, the Europeans acquired a pressing motive to loosen the ties that bind. Conscious of their exposure to the lengthening shadow of Soviet power, the Europeans would perforce try to diminish Soviet incentives to capitalize on the newly favorable "correlation of forces."

Latent throughout the 1970s, decoupling via conciliation grew into a overriding imperative in the aftermath of Afghanistan, when the Europeans fought tooth and nail to insulate their regional détente against the rising tide of Cold War II. From the perspective of an alliance leader, Western Europe's behavior in the early eighties looks like a pernicious combination of cowardice and greed. Yet from a structural vantage point, these are the rational responses of the weak. Unable to take care of themselves, dependents must eschew the battles of the strong. Indeed, an ally's inclination to widen its distance from the alliance leader increases *pari passu* with the rise of hostility between this leader and the common adversary, and it does so for two reasons. First, the rising tension of superpower confrontation increases the smaller nation's dependence on the patron, thus reducing its freedom to maneuver in the interstices of the great power rivalry. Secondly, too close an identification with the alliance leader carries the risk of entrapment in a conflict that might prove more costly to the weak than to the strong, especially when the weak, by virtue of geographical position, can expect to become the first (and perhaps only) victim of limited nuclear war. Hence, dependent states tend to stand aside from the duels of the strong and, to reduce the threat to themselves further, will offer propitiatory side payments to the common adversary. As long as the smaller allies are not directly threatened, they will seek shelter in a divisible détente. This was precisely the structural imperative that determined West European policy in the aftermath of Afghanistan—and the root of the Alliance crisis of the 1980s.

Crisis and Continuity

In the early eighties, more and more American observers were prompted to predict the early demise of the Atlantic Alliance. "The most urgent crisis," wrote Irving Kristol in the pages of the *Wall Street Journal*, "is the impending collapse of NATO."[36] Nor were these gloomy assessments responding merely to the spats and spitting matches of the day. With so many frictions refusing to subside and betraying resentments that went to the very core of the Alliance, there was no comfort in the memory of crisis resolutions of the past. On either side of the Atlantic, a growing chorus of critics—predominantly on the right in the United States and on the left in Europe—argued that the burdens of alliance had finally come to outweigh its benefits. "What can America do," asked on American commentator, "to satisfy those who want equidistance from the two superpowers, who want defense (but not too much of it), who are more afraid of American sanctions than of events in Poland, more apprehensive about American than Soviet missiles, who want to be allies and mediators at the same time?"[37]

If American indictments reflected frustration with allies who turned their backs on America's global travails, European countercharges betrayed sheer fear. On the one hand, the United States was blamed for having done little to stem or match the 1970s build-up of Soviet power. On the other hand, American attempts in the 1980s to restore the balance were denounced as the first step toward confrontation, if not armed conflict. And in either case, as the same voices would claim (sometimes in the same breath), the victim would be Europe. If Americans suspected abandonment, Europeans feared entrapment in conflicts they refused to accept as their own. Nourished on a steady diet of security *made in the USA*, the Europeans recoiled in anger when the United States asked for payment in form of fealty demands that threatened not only the newfound tranquility of the Continent but also the stability of their body politics. For many Europeans—and not only for those who preached abdication in the name of peace and equidistance—the Alliance was suddenly posing an unbearable imbalance between rewards and costs.

This was also, of course, the American view; hence the familiar conflict routine of the early eighties when even the smallest dispute turned into an ominous symbol of either (European) disloyalty or (American) imperial hauteur. Driven by opposite interests, each side began to claim the right to change the terms of alliance in its own favor. Short of defeat or victory in war, this the deadliest moment in the life of any alliance.

As the United States asked more, the Europeans gave less; if Washington demanded obedience, the Allies insisted on freedom; and when the United States tried to impose discipline through punishment (as in the case of the export ban on American-licensed parts for the Euro-Siberian pipeline in 1982), the Europeans responded with sheer defiance. It was the longest battle of wills in the history of the Alliance, with the United States calling for boycotts, embargoes, and rearmament against the Soviet Union, and the Europeans withholding cooperation wherever possible and yielding it only whenever absolutely necessary. At the height of this grimmest of postwar contests, both sides had rapidly approached the point where alliances normally break up. Yet this alliance held — which is all the more puzzling considering that the underlying causes of the conflict have by no means disappeared.

Differences in vulnerability, power, outlook, and ambitions are fated to endure, and so are the new givens wrought by a decade of détente. Reluctant (and ill-equipped) to shoulder America's global burdens, the West Europeans will continue to resist entanglement in the quarrels of the superpowers — or in any quarrel of the United States, for that matter, as shown by the virtually universal European condemnation of the 1986 bombing raid on Libya. Unable to defend themselves without the United States yet wary of dependence, the Europeans will take care not to provoke their neighbor to the east. They are eager to lighten the deadweight of bipolarity and will steer clear of policies that offer the Soviet Union a cause or pretext to tighten its grip on Eastern Europe. Short of the resumption of Soviet pressures in Europe comparable to those of 1947-1962, regional détente and its trappings — trade, arms control, and cooperation — will remain a "permanently operating factor" in Europe.

If so, why did the Alliance return to more tranquil relations in the mid-1980s? One reason is a familiar phenomenon in the annals of international politics. Though the underlying conflict may defy resolution, passions dwindle when at least the immediate irritants disappear. Loyalty simply ceases to be an issue when demand for it no longer exists. The Teheran hostage affair — the source of so many frictions between the United States and its sympathetic but santion-wary allies — simply vanished from the agenda when the American embassy staff was released in January of 1981. Nor did the Allies ever resolve their conflict over Poland, where the very premises of action remained at odds. If the United States had openly sought to pressure Warsaw into liberalization and to deter the Soviets, the Europeans had tacitly tried to stabilize the regime and to dispatch Soviet incentives for intervention. Respite was finally provided by General Jaruzelski himself. Having undone Solidarity with an astounding economy of force, he presented the West with welcome relief from its Polish travails by announcing the "suspension" of martial law at the end of 1982, an act that removed at least the more visible means of suppression. Afghanistan, too, disappeared into the recesses of the Western collective unconscious because, after years of fighting, the Soviets could not inflict a decisive defeat on the rebels, let alone use their new possession as a springboard for further expansion.

Secondly, further alienation was halted by domestic forces on either side of the ocean. In the United States, it would turn out that the mood of national reassertion, which had flowered into the Reagan consensus of the 1980 election, was less than a clear mandate. While spending on arms remained popular, their actual use was not — except where military force was swift, cost-free, and victorious, as during the Grenada intervention in the fall of 1983. That the new mood fell short of a mandate was neatly exemplified in Central America and Lebanon. America's military involvement in the Lebanese free-for-all came to an abrupt end in 1984 after a one-man terrorist assault claimed the lives of 241 Marines. Nor did the revolutionary activism of the Sandinista junta offer an acceptable occasion for the overt use of American force. By the end of the first Reagan term, the administration would present to the world an astounding split between reputation and reality: strong on rhetoric but meek in action; muscle-bound but caution-prone; and committed to a policy of prudence that belied the president's earlier image as a trigger-happy innocent in search of global superiority.

That split was reflected in the ambivalence and evolution of public opinion. After surveying a wealth of data, two respected experts concluded just before Ronald Reagan's reelection in the fall of 1984:

In 1980 and 1981 the backlash against détente reached a high peak of intensity. The public mood was characterized by injured national pride, unqualified support for increasing the defense budget, and a general desire to see American power become more assertive. The public is now having second thoughts about the dangers of such an assertive posture at a time when the United States is no longer seen to maintain nuclear supremacy. The electorate is still wary, still mistrustful, and still convinced that the Soviets will seize every possible advantage they can; yet at the same time, Americans are determined to stop what they see as a drift toward nuclear confrontation. . . . The stage is being set for a new phase in our relationship with the Soviets.[38]

By huge margins (between 70 and 90 percent), Americans continued to believe that the Soviets had exploited détente for their own military build-up, are "constantly probing for weaknesses," and had lulled the United States "into a false sense of security." On the other hand, more than seven out of ten Americans also believed that the United States "has to accept some of the blame for the tensions . . . in recent years" and that it was "dangerous oversimplification" to see the Soviets as the "cause of all the world's troubles." Significantly, "Americans feel that the power imbalance that prevailed in 1980 has now been partly or wholly corrected and that more constructive negotiations are possible."[39]

If the political consensus would move from the right to the center in the United States, domestic change in Western Europe reflected an analogous shift from left to right. In Norway the Conservatives captured power in 1981; in 1982 left-of-center governments in Denmark and the Netherlands were replaced by right-of-center coalitions. Though the French Socialist party (in league with the Communists) had ousted Giscard d'Estaing in 1981, President Mitterrand would soon be acting like a composite of Ronald Reagan and Margaret Thatcher. After a short and hapless experiment in lavish deficit spending—which triggered inflation and capital flight—Mitterrand swung sharply right in 1982, toward a policy of fiscal and monetary restraint that owed more to Thatcher than to John Maynard Keynes. In foreign policy Mitterrand presented himself as a paragon of Alliance virtue. Unlike his predecessor—who had hoped to neutralize the Gaullists with a mildly anti-American policy of splendid aggravation and to propitiate the Communists with a mildly pro-Soviet policy of détente-minded conciliation—Mitterrand defied both domestic parties by excoriating Soviet arms-mongering and enthusiastically embracing the deployment of American Euromissiles. In June 1983 Margaret Thatcher's Conservatives inflicted a murderous defeat on Labour that mirrored Helmut Kohl's electoral triumph over the Social Democrats in March of that year. The center-right trend was broken only on the periphery where the electoral verdict brought left-wing governments into power (Greece in 1981 and Spain in 1982).

The decline of the social democratic Left throughout most of Western Europe cannot be attributed directly to foreign policy factors. Insofar as the issues themselves determine electoral behavior, the domestic economy regularly looms larger in peacetime than issues from the world outside. In the early 1980s, during the worst slump since the Great Depression, it was the issues of unemployment, inflation, and a creaking social security system that concentrated minds throughout the West. In part, social democratic parties were punished at the ballot box because they had presided over the onset of recession; they were ousted from power at the time when the politics of redistribution, which had fueled the

relentless expansion of the welfare state, collided with the harsh eco-
nomics of contraction.

Yet indirectly, foreign policy did play a role in realigning the structure of domestic power. Throughout the Northern Tier (most notably in
England and West Germany), the Left had assumed a vanguard role in
the battle against nuclear weapons. That campaign blurred the old distinctions between the democratic and communist Left and articulated not
only anti-American and neutralist sentiments but genuine fears. While
the left was evidently repudiated for domestic economy reasons, there
is another moral to the story. In England, Germany, and the Scandilux countries,[40] the attack against traditional defense policy foundered
because fears about détente and nuclear weapons were not powerful
enough to suppress the status quo instincts of the electorate. Instead,
the lackluster electoral performance of these issues underlined a neglected truth about the nature of Western domestic politics. While the shibboleths of pacifism and neutralism galvanized the few, they could not mobilize the many. (For a more detailed analysis, see Chapter Three.) This
outcome was hardly insignificant, however, given the unprecedented
clarity of choices facing the British and German electorates during the
national contests of 1983. The parties of the Left were as opposed to the
deployment of Euromissiles as their rivals on the Right were determined
to accept them in the absence of agreement with the Russians. To cast a
ballot in favor of Thatcher's Conservatives or Kohl's Christian Democrats was also a tacit sign of consent to the missiles, hence to the Alliance-
affirming policy these two leaders represented. Thus, a final moral cannot be excluded: that fears about nuclear weapons were outweighed by
doubts about parties who would proclaim loyalty to the Alliance while
rocking that cozy boat with noisy attacks on the weapons of extended deterrence and their American providers. Nor could it have escaped those
who voted against Labour and SPD in 1983 that these parties were, in
effect, more closely attuned to the goals of Soviet than Alliance policy.
Nor was that impression dispelled by the heavy-handed attempts of Soviet public diplomacy to skew the electoral verdict in favor of the Left,
particularly in the critical West German contest. (Had the Social Democrats won and then proceeded to make good on their program, the Euromissile deployment would have been postponed indefinitely. Yet on
March 6, 1983, they fared worse than in any election since 1961, and they
lost again on January 25, 1987.)

The shift in public mood and electoral allegiance, reflecting a sturdy
attachment to the transatlantic status quo, merely confirmed no less crucial trends in the realm of diplomacy, where the policies—each side's

attempt to impose its will on the other—had run out of steam. Which leads to the third, and more properly structural, reason for the easing of the Alliance tensions by the mid-eighties: the absence of trumps, triumphs, and options.

The essence of the 1980s crisis was the contest over the terms of alliance, with each side trying to force unacceptable choices on the other. As maximum, the United States hoped to recentralize the Alliance in the service of militant neo-containment while insisting, at the very least, on benevolent neutrality—hence on Europe's abstention from policies that would act as an "impediment to the restoration of America's power and position, whether in Europe or in the world beyond."[41] The problem was that the Allies wanted exactly the same thing. At a minimum, the West Europeans sought insulation; at a maximum, they wanted interference. They wanted to at least be left out of America's battles, and, ideally, to recentralize the United States under the banner of détente-minded East–West cooperation. In the end the maximal ambitions of both sides were frustrated. Europeans and Americans were forced to learn that allies cannot muster that kind of power within a coalition such as NATO. The traditional ultima ratio of nations-in-alliance has been the threat of abandonment (by leaders) or defection (by followers). Yet the brutal facts of the postwar international system preclude such a power-maximizing strategy. Bipolarity has emptied the ultimate threat of its reality. Can the United States credibly threaten an "agonizing reappraisal," as John Foster Dulles put it in 1954, when the French defied Washington on West German rearmament? It can denounce but never abandon its allies because, in doing so, the United States would be delivering a major strategic victory to the one and only adversary who counts. And on the other side, what choice do the West Europeans have in a world of only two superpowers, except to exchange one dependence for another?

Within a coalition such as NATO, members can normally generate enough power to block each other, hence to veto demands that would turn a separate will into the purpose of the whole. To block someone's designs is far easier than to move him in one's own direction because an intramural antagonist can always resist in the comfortable knowledge that he need not fear the ultimate penalty. And so, even an alliance leader will rarely succeed in imposing his will on the rest. Nowhere was this lesson exemplified more dramatically than in the Euro-American pipeline battle of 1982. In that year, the Reagan administration had tried to sever the massive link to the Soviet Union, the Yamal pipeline, which was to provide about 30 percent of Western Europe's natural gas supplies in the late 1980s. From the vantage point of a great power, the administration's sally made perfect strategic sense. If successful, it would deprive America's great adversary of billions of dollars in future hard currency income, a precious financial asset in the Soviet–American rivalry. In addition, the destruction of the Euro-Siberian gas link would deny the Soviet Union the political leverage over America's allies that such an energy dependence entails.

The West European governments (in London, Paris, Bonn, and Rome) regarded the tie not only as a boon to their ailing steel industries but also as the very symbol of Euro-Soviet détente, to be defended at all costs against Ronald Reagan's call to arms. And defend it they did with fierce tenacity. They shrugged off the first set of American sanctions (imposed on December 30, 1981), and they defied the second set (of June 18, 1982); that embargo would have significantly damaged the gas duct by stopping the transfer of vital turbine components (over which the United States retained a technological monopoly). In the end, however, it was the United States that "blinked," and on November 13, 1982, the Reagan administration lifted all restraints from American companies and their foreign subsidiaries engaged in the construction of the gas duct.

Earlier, Vice President George Bush had laid down the American rationale, the classic rationale of the dominant power: "We've heard a lot of protests from our European allies. I am sorry. The U.S. is the leader of the free world, and under this Administration we are beginning once again to act like it."[42] Why then did this exercise in leadership end in a rout? Le Monde's answer was to point out that the American war against the pipeline "had in fact done more damage to what [Reagan] wanted to strengthen—the cohesion of the Atlantic Alliance—than to the Soviet Union which he wanted to punish."[43] To cast the moral in more general terms: a superpower can force its will on lesser allies only by means that would also fundamentally weaken them, thus undermining the very raison d'être of alliance, which is to maximize collective strength. This built-in limit on the expenditure of American power explains precisely why the lesser allies can go to such great lengths when they defy their patron.

Yet those lesser nations had to relearn a similar lesson in the limits of power: their ability to defy was far stronger than their ability to impose their will on the United States. The Federal Republic of Germany was a perfect study in the politics of weakness amidst strength. Faced with America's turn toward confrontation, the West Germans were condemned to defend their stake in détente more vigorously than any other ally—which forced Bonn to the forefront of the intra-Alliance dispute. The Federal Republic was destined to play the leading roles in the drama—

both the protagonist and the victim. While everybody resented America's grating new fealty demands, the Federal Republic had to resist them more strenuously than anybody else because of its unique *raison d'état* and *raison de nation*. A revival of the Cold War, threatening to refreeze what détente had so painstakingly unthawed, would inevitably inflict the heaviest penalties on the Federal Republic. And West Germany would suffer twice—as a state and as a half-nation—because the fortunes of either will always be so thoroughly tied to a benign East-West climate in Europe. This is why the European-American crisis of the 1980s was essentially the German-American crisis writ large.

As a state—which must worry about its power and position in the world—the Federal Republic had more reasons than most to dread the advancing chill. Being the most exposed member of the Alliance (unlike France and England, it cannot seek prestige and protection in a national nuclear deterrent), West Germany has learned to associate East-West conflict in Europe with heightened dependence and impotence. All through the mid-1960s, the Federal Republic had remained tightly wedged between East and West: the strongest "civilian" power in Europe, but forced to defer to France and the United States for reasons of security; eager to apply its considerable resources, but unable to find a legitimate outlet in its natural hinterland to the east. Conversely, the era of détente had dramatically enlarged the margins of West German diplomacy. Less dependence spelled greater freedom, which, in turn, allowed for a role that was at last commensurate with West Germany's natural weight in the European order. Mercilessly hounded by the Soviets in times past, West Germany would quickly become Moscow's prime interlocutor; as such, Bonn acquired a position in Alliance councils that was a far cry from the enforced modesty of the fifties and sixties. For a state that was the product and prime victim of tight bipolarity, détente was not one option among many but the very condition for German self-assertion.

Raison de nation redoubles the urgency of the détente imperative. Détente in Europe has meant above all Ostpolitik—the policy of patient accommodation that refuses to challenge the political status quo in Eastern Europe precisely in order to transform it—pursued to the point when the falling barriers of partition might make reunification not so much possible as unnecessary. Indeed, Ostpolitik naturally sustains détente because such a subtly balanced strategy can only flourish in a permissive milieu: where bipolarity is loose rather than tight; where bloc discipline is low and regime confidence is high; where the risks of the East are outweighed by the rewards from the West; and where the Soviet Union need not brandish its power because its imperial sensitivities are respected by each and all. Ostpolitik, in short, has had to be Europeanized, to serve as a kind of categorical imperative for every state between the Atlantic and the Elbe—and never more so than in times of tensions between Europe's great flanking powers, the United States and the Soviet Union. According to Willy Brandt, the social democratic architect of German and European détente, "Today, we and other Europeans face the problem . . . of how to keep the deteriorating relations between Washington and Moscow from having a negative effect on Europe."[44] This message was essentially reiterated by Chancellor Helmut Kohl, a Christian Democrat, half a decade later: "Above all, we Germans, living in a divided country . . . where any international tension or deterioration of the political climate is felt with the sensitivity of a seismological station, have a pressing interest in successful [superpower] negotiations."[45]

Yet mere insulation was not enough to weather the advancing chill. Trying to harness its allies to the cause of neo-containment, the United States demanded loyalty, not neutrality. As a result, the West Germans were confronted with the deadliest bane of their foreign policy: a choice between their Western obligations and their Eastern mission. To act like a latter-day de Gaulle and deny loyalty to the United States was impossible for, unlike the general, Helmut Schmidt could not count on a strongly defended glacis to the east, a fact that had taken the existential sting out of de Gaulle's antics. West Germany *was* the glacis—all there is. Nor could Schmidt allow the United States to drag Bonn into its global quarrels with Moscow without sinning against every commandment of Ostpolitik and provoking Soviet retribution. None of the other European allies faced so painful a dilemma, and to avoid either horn, Schmidt was forced into a role that no German government, from Bismarck onward, had ever been able to sustain for any length of time.

To evade too close an identification with the United States without, at the same time, incurring the charge of disloyalty, Schmidt instinctively tried to straddle the conflict. In order to withstand the pull of either superpower, he tried to execute from a position of underlying weakness what Bismarck had only been able to play out (and even then without enduring success) from a position of underlying strength: the role of mediator and intermediary. He also had to save German Ostpolitik by defending European détente. To achieve both these goals, Schmidt tried his utmost to hold Moscow and Washington to the global bargain struck in the 1970s —to mute the conflict between the strong, which, if unchecked, would inevitably impose the most fearful choices on the weak. Putting himself forward as an "honest interpreter of Western policy," Schmidt proclaimed, "We have an important role to play in [preserving the dialogue between the superpowers], both toward our friends in the United States and toward the Soviet Union."[46]

In the aftermath of Afghanistan, the notion of being an "honest interpreter" (echoing Bismarck's famous offer in 1878 to play the "honest broker" between feuding Britain and Russia) became part of Schmidt's standard repertoire, yet Bonn was singularly ill-equipped to act as a bridge and a brace.[47] Though the clash between the great powers had been triggered on the "periphery" (Angola, Ethiopia, Afghanistan), the global contest inexorably returned once more to its ancient locus—Europe. And as in the bygone Cold War I days, the critical question was once more, who controls Germany, the country at the fulcrum of the East–West balance—too weak to hold its own and too strong to be left alone. It was in Europe that the Soviet Union was trying to inflict a major political defeat on the United States by executing a two-pronged decoupling strategy. First, by holding out the promise of selective détente to the West Europeans, Moscow hoped to gain their benevolent neutrality, if not active opposition, as a check on American designs to turn the Alliance into the forward bastion of militant neo-containment. Second, by defining Western Europe's refusal of American cruise and Pershing II missiles as the true test of détente-minded realism, the Soviets sought to thwart what the United States had come to see as the very symbol of American power restored. And it was in West Germany, the focus of all pressures, that the battle was going to be decided.

It was Helmut Schmidt's personal tragedy that he desperately clung to an equipoise when the times demanded choice, that he tried to play the mediator long after his country had turned into the foremost stake of the Soviet–American contest. His task had been forbidding from the very beginning; it became virtually impossible when France, the Federal Republic's closest ally in Europe, recognized that Gaullism would be reduced to mere posturing without Germany, that is, without an intact glacis to the East. The watershed was marked by the passage of power from Valéry Giscard d'Estaing to François Mitterrand in 1981—from a president (on the Right) who had been Schmidt's comrade in détente to a president (on the Left) who quickly subordinated socialist sentiments to the cold calculation of power realities in Europe. As Schmidt noted in retrospect, "Giscard had left the scene, and if you really want to try to explain the role I played internationally, you have to take into account this tandem."[48]

Immediately after taking office, Mitterrand proceeded to undo the continental entente that had allowed Schmidt to defy the more blatant American pressures. While the guardians of Gaullist orthodoxy bemoaned the new Atlanticism as sheer heresy against "the received diplomatic and military legacy,"[49] Mitterrand was in fact acting as the most faithful disciple of Charles de Gaulle. Stripped of its theatrics, Gaullism can only thrive given three vital insurance policies: a stable balance of power in Europe, a credible American nuclear guarantee, and a reliably integrated West Germany — a combination that endows France with a leverage consistently exceeding its natural weight.

Given the Soviet build-up in Europe across the full spectrum of military power — particularly the growing menace of Soviet Euromissiles that were devaluing France's modest national deterrent — and West Germany's apparent tilt toward pacifist nationalism, it was only logical that the new French president would hasten to link hands with the United States. Forgotten were the contemptuous epithets that Mitterrand had heaped on NATO in a book published just before his elevation to the presidency. In a chapter entitled, "The Phony Alliance," Mitterrand had waxed more venomous than even Charles de Gaulle in his most uncharitable moments: "I am no more attached to the Atlantic alliance than a Romanian or Pole is attached to the Warsaw Pact. . . . Nothing disposes me to postulate the necessity of the Atlantic alliance, and I would be satisfied with a situation which would render it defunct."[50]

Faced with the new *incertitudes allemandes*, Mitterrand's attachment to the Alliance soared. Precisely because NATO might indeed become "defunct," precisely because Gaullism minus a credible American deterrent and a sturdy German glacis would dwindle into empty-handed pretense, Mitterrand became the most stolid American ally in Europe. The Soviets, with their SS-20 missiles, "are destroying the equilibrium in Europe," proclaimed Mitterrand upon assuming office. "I will not accept this, and I admit that we must arm to restore the balance."[51] Casting a worried eye across the Rhine, Mitterrand's defense minister, Charles Hernu, warned, "The energies rising in the young people of our neighbors are now expressed through the distorting prism of pacifism; they are likely to give in to the temptations of a disastrous neutralism which would create a void."[52] Unlike Giscard d'Estaing, who had refused to take a stand on the Pershing II and cruise missiles, Mitterrand quickly embraced their deployment, reiterating ad infinitum that France's nuclear weapons were for France's protection only. And also unlike his predecessor, who had covered Helmut Schmidt's European flank against American pressures,

Mitterrand forsook socialist solidarity in favor of sacred *raison d'état*. While the Soviets were unleashing a ham-handed campaign in favor of West Germany's antimissile Social Democrats, Mitterrand traveled to Bonn just six weeks before the 1983 elections to make sure that Helmut Kohl's conservative coalition would carry the day. (Kohl had ousted Helmut Schmidt with a no-confidence vote the preceding autumn.) Speaking before the Bundestag, Mitterrand made it clear that he had no patience for his ideological confréres in Bonn: "Whosoever is staking his bet on 'decoupling' Europe from America, jeopardizes . . . the balance of power and thus the preservation of peace. . . . The elements of this indispensable balance must be maintained, and our peoples must remain assured that they will not succumb to the burden of . . . foreign domination."[53]

Two critical events marked the outer limits of Bonn's effort to Europeanize Ostpolitik and to turn the Federal Republic into a bridge and a brace between the feuding superpowers. One was Mitterrand's shift toward Reaganism *à la française*. Driven by the unsettling vision of their German neighbor adrift between East and West, the French thus robbed Bonn's diplomacy of its most vital continental support. Without the French prop, the center could not hold. To hold off the United States was one thing; to sustain a simultaneous conflict with Paris was a task that overtaxed the Federal Republic's resources and went squarely against an unwritten law of West German diplomacy: do not oppose both of your two most important allies at the same time.

The second watershed came with the imposition of martial law in Poland. If Mitterrand's calculated embrace of the United States drove home the conditional nature of French friendship (and hence the structural limits of the Federal Republic's autonomy in the West), the suppression of Solidarity by General Jaruzelski's troops dramatized the tenuous fortunes of German and European détente diplomacy. Its key premise is evolution through conciliation, a kind of "reverse Finlandization" that will promote a safe rate of change in Eastern Europe. Yet as the events in Poland showed, the dialectic of détente tends to operate in an opposite, and perverse, fashion. Instead of encouraging greater lenience on the part of the regimes and their Soviet guardians, the détente of the 1980s triggered a change that ended in revolt and renewed repression. That the real prize of détente remained elusive did not—and will not—change the driving premise of Western Europe's Ostpolitik, which is to treat the East Europeans as tacit allies rather than as adversaries. (By the end of 1984, three years after the Polish putsch, the succession of high-level visitors from Western Europe would signify the final collapse of Poland's diplomatic quarantine.) Yet there was a sobering effect nonetheless. As the prize receded, the price of détente was bound to seem higher, inspiring more caution in those who had risked dissolution in the West in order to encourage evolution in the East.

Though they were highly disparate events, the shift in French policy and the military coup in Poland reflected the same structural fact: the European system's enormous resistance to real change. Many years ago Stanley Hoffman described the postwar world as a "stalemate system," and he added, "Dreams are [its] victims."[54] The European system, based on the rivalry and countervailing powers of the United States and the Soviet Union, has brought unprecedented security to the Continent, but at the cost of freedoms denied and aspirations blocked. Order has been the counterpart of partition, and safety has been the brother of subordination—inflicted on the East but borne voluntarily in the West.

In the past forty years, various nations have tried to loosen the system's grip. Charles de Gaulle attempted to defy the "twin-hegemony" of the superpowers in the 1960s; Helmut Schmidt would later try to deflect the confrontation of the great by turning the Federal Republic into the guardian and helmsman of European détente. In the 1950s, the Hungarians revolted; in the 1960s, the Czechs tried to carve out a niche for themselves. And in the early eighties, a spontaneous mass movement in Poland tried to reclaim some of the freedoms lost to the regime imposed after World War II. Yet in each case, the dream collided with the realities of power and dependence in a "stalemate system" of unparalleled longevity in the annals of European history.

What is the nature of this system? The destruction of the European balance in two world wars left a twofold problem in its wake: how to constrain the potential of a resurgent Germany, the previous claimant to hegemony; and how to contain the might of the new contender, the Soviet Union. The solution had three parts: the permanent entanglement of Europe's flanking powers (via empire in the East and its voluntary analogue in the West); the partition of the Continent; and the integration of the divided Reich into the two opposing blocs. These elements define the balance; a fourth—the intrusion of nuclear weapons—has reinforced it to the point of virtual immutability. Whatever flexibility might have remained was suppressed by the awesome might of weapons that promise to obliterate the distinction between defeat and annihilation and, in Europe at least, have dethroned war as the ultimate arbiter of politics among nations.

Such a system does imply a lack of trumps, triumphs, and options. In the East the smaller members have learned from bitter experience that the Soviet Union will not hesitate to use force for the sake of empire. Indeed, the productivity of force—the exchange rate between violence and control—appears to have risen over the course of time. In Hungary in 1956, the Soviets had to fight a bloody war; in Czechoslovakia in 1968, only physical occupation was necessary to undo the Prague Spring; and in Poland in 1981, the Soviets had to resort to neither because the task of suppression was shouldered by the Polish army itself.

In the West, stability flows not from the imposition of force but from a combination of dependence and voluntary acceptance of obligations. While the West European states continue to chafe under a system that provides security at the cost of a large measure of abdication, they also continue to be unable or unwilling to generate a defensive potential commensurate with their economic and demographic strengths. (For a detailed analysis of this failure, see Chapter Five.) They resent, and continue to resent, the fact that they have entrusted their security, the ultimate responsibility of any nation-state, to a distant protector. Yet in the end, as the denouement of the Euromissile drama showed, the West Europeans preferred the extra burden of the missiles to the uncertain rewards of autonomy. In the mid-1980s the longest and fiercest revolt against their transatlantic guardian was muted by a renewed sobriety that arose for three reasons, all of which reflect the realities of the postwar "stalemate system."

First, the West European elites (and the majority of their populaces) emerged from the great crisis of the eighties with a sharpened sense of limits. The previous decade of détente had not delivered on its loftiest promises. Unable to shed its expansionist notion of security, the Soviet Union had not made the military concessions that the West Europeans had hoped to gain through political and economic cooperation. Instead of reducing its military threat against Western Europe, the Soviet Union increased it with a relentless drive for more and better arms, conventional as well as nuclear. And instead of granting a measure of devolution in Eastern Europe as a fair price for the loosening of bloc ties in the West, the Soviet Union rejected the verdict of détente when its own pontifical domain was imperiled by millions of Polish heretics flocking to Solidarity's reformationist cause.

Second, there were the limits of Western Europe's internal order, felt most painfully by its most potentially restless member, the Federal Re-

public. The turn of Mitterrand's France (abetted, after 1985, by his conservative prime minister, Jacques Chirac) toward the United States, Euromissiles, and rearmament was a not so subtle reminder that the French
were not prepared to underwrite the Federal Republic's national aspirations at the cost of an endangered military and political balance. Always
ready to invoke "Europe" when countering the demands of the superpowers, France has never allowed West Germany the freedom it claims
for itself. Indeed, France's freedom to act as the arbiter between the great
powers requires not only a sturdy military balance but also a Federal Republic firmly ensconced in the West. (Hence Mitterrand's, and then Chirac's, demonstrative attempts to revive the dormant military clauses in
the Franco-German Treaty of Friendship and Collaboration, as an additional anchor on the Federal Republic when it seemed to be straining
against its Western moorings.) By reminding Bonn of its Western obligations, Mitterrand merely enunciated a message that was soon echoed by
other governments when they glimpsed a future West Germany keeping
company with the West only at its own discretion. "We are all in agreement," proclaimed Italy's foreign minister, Giulio Andreotti, in the fall
of 1984, "that there should be good relations between the two Germanies.
. . . Yet there should be no exaggeration in this direction. Pan-Germanism
must be overcome. There are two German states, and two it should be."[55]

"In my view, it is a hoary illusion," said Helmut Kohl in the aftermath of the 1980s crisis, "to believe that the relationship between . . . the
GDR and the Federal Republic of Germany can really improve while the
global political climate remains at sub-zero temperatures." He also cited
an old folk saying from his home region: "A big stream carries the small
river with it."[56] That homily reveals a critical insight into the nature of
Europe's order: by itself, German power was imply too weak to transform that order; for change to occur, the systemic conditions had to be
right.

The third reason for the more subdued tone in Western Europe by the
mid-1980s was the fact that the United States had accepted certain limits.
The Reagan administration had surveyed the debris from years of conflict with its European allies, and did not overlook the Europeans' choice
of alliance over détente in the great Soviet–American test of strength
over the Euromissiles. Though prompted more by the changing mood of
the American public than by the necessities of alliance management, the
second Reagan administration began to temper neo-containment with
a good dose of neo-détente from 1985 onward. In March of 1985, arms
control negotiations with the Soviet Union (which the Soviets had rup-

tured after the arrival of the first Pershing II and cruise missiles in late 1983) resumed in Geneva. These talks were soon flanked by the pomp and pageantry of superpower summits—the encounters of President Reagan and Secretary-General Gorbachev in Geneva in 1985, and in Reykjavík in 1986.

Though none of these events spawned any substantive agreements, they did help to alleviate the conflict that had pitted the United States against Western Europe since the beginning of Cold War II in late 1979. They signified a measure of great power détente that had lain dormant since the invasion of Afghanistan. The return to summitry and arms control on the part of the superpowers bestowed the cachet of legitimacy on Western Europe's separate détente, which the Allies had been claiming as their inalienable prerogative and the United States had been condemning as a gratuitous act of disloyalty. With European détente so paralleled and enveloped, Alliance disaffection was doubly defused and and reassurance was doubly restored. The West Europeans had regained a legitimate margin of maneuver vis-à-vis the East, and the United States, once more engaged in the global détente business, had regained a measure of initiative—if not supervision—over the regional process.

During the intramural battle over the terms of their relationship, Europeans and Americans had come to blows but never even approached the end of alliance. Frustrated, each side had finally climbed down from its maximalist ambitions; sobered, Europeans and Americans both came to accept the limits imposed by the "stalemate system" on patrons and clients alike. Yet it was more than just exhaustion that reharnessed the antagonists to alliance. The contemporary international system is simply short on alternatives. And thus, a great power like the United States must tolerate the deviations of the smaller members because it cannot abandon them; to wield that club against allies is to wield it against oneself—against the very purpose that inspired the alliance in the first place.

Yet there is also solace in bipolarity. Leaders can tolerate unruly allies because their antics are ultimately constrained by their dependence. Both sides are free to deviate, but not free to defect. They are at liberty to roam because they run on a strong leash. There is little leverage while the long leash is uncoiling, but at the end of the line there is the sharp tug of mutual dependence. Alliance relations during the eighties ultimately conformed to this pattern. Rapidly drifting apart, the United States and Western Europe reversed course by mid-decade—when the Europeans began to reemphasize their alliance obligations, and the Reagan administration muted its penchant for confrontation with its rival superpower.

To recall NATO's history as the history of its crises is to recall a larger truth about the nature of the postwar order. Precisely because it is impervious to a real change as long as the world remains dominated à *deux*, the system's sturdy outer bounds can accommodate enormous strains and stresses within.

Notes

1. As recounted by Herman Finer, *Dulles Over Suez* (Chicago: Quadrangle Books, 1964), pp. 428–429.
2. As quoted in Arthur M. Schlesinger, Jr., *A Thousand Days* (Boston: Houghton Mifflin, 1965), p. 815.
3. As quoted in Robert F. Kennedy, *The Thirteen Days: A Memoir of the Cuban Missile Crisis* (New York: New American Library, 1969), p. 51.
4. As quoted in Ronald Koven, "U.S. Rebuffed by France," *Washington Post*, 7 Jan. 1980.
5. As quoted in *Le Figaro*, 10 Jan. 1980, p. 1.
6. State of the Union Address, January 10, 1980, *Public Papers of the Presidents of the United States: Jimmy Carter, 1980*, vol. 1 (Washington, 1981), p. 96.
7. James Reston, "A Talk with Schmidt," *New York Times*, 7 March 1980.
8. "Transcript of President's Interview on Soviet Reply," *New York Times*, 1 Jan. 1980.
9. Jimmy Carter, *Keeping Faith: Memoirs of a President* (New York: Bantam, 1982), p. 500. Even so, Schmidt promised too much, for the French *did* go to the Moscow Olympics in the summer of 1980.
10. Helmut Schmidt, "Tragen Sie zur Entschärfung bei" (Speech in the Kremlin, July 1, 1980), *Frankfurter Rundschau*, 2 July 1980, p. 2.
11. As quoted in William Pfaff, "Finlandization," *New Yorker*, 1 Sept. 1980, p. 31.
12. As quoted in "Mit den Amerikanern nicht in den Tod," *Der Spiegel*, 28 April 1980; Martin E. Süskind, "Die Zweifler üben sich in Solidarität," *Süddeutsche Zeitung*, 18 Jan. 1980.
13. In Harry Schleicher, "Nicht mit Worten tapfer sein" (Interview with Willy Brandt), *Frankfurter Rundschau*, 19 Dec. 1980, p. 5.
14. For the Grass et al. letter, see *Süddeutsche Zeitung*, 19 April 1980, p. 9.
15. As cited in "Mit den Americanern nicht in den Tod," p. 19.
16. Remarks Before the American Society of Newspaper Editors, April 10, 1980, *Public Papers — Carter, 1980*, vol. 1, p. 632.
17. As quoted in Leslie H. Gelb, "NATO Is Facing Paralysis of Will, Experts Contend," *New York Times*, 12 July 1981, p. A1.
18. Address at the Commencement Exercises, University of Notre Dame, May 22, 1977, *Public Papers — Carter, 1977*, vol. 1, pp. 956–957.
19. Calculated from Soviet trade statistics, as compiled by Angela Stent, "Economic Strategy," in E. Moreton and G. Segal, eds., *Soviet Strategy Toward Western Europe* (London: Allen & Unwin, 1984), p. 223 table 7.1.
20. As quoted in Ronald Koven, "Paris–Bonn Summit Seeks Joint Position on Carter's Policy," *Washington Post*, 4 Feb. 1980, p. A20.
21. See note 20 above.

22. Leonid Brezhnev, from a November 2, 1977 speech, reprinted in *Survival* (January/February 1978): 32.
23. Schmidt's Calculabilities" (Interview with Helmut Schmidt), *Economist,* 6 Oct. 1979, p. 47.
24. From George F. Kennan's famous "X" article, "The Sources of Soviet Conduct," *Foreign Affairs* (July 1947), reprinted in Hamilton Fish Armstrong, ed., *Fifty Years of Foreign Affairs* (New York: Praeger, 1972), p. 205.
25. See note 13 above.
26. "The Atlantic Alliance Needs Leaders Who Face the Facts," *Economist,* 11 Oct. 1980, p. 23.
27. Former French Foreign Minister Jean François-Poncet, as quoted in James O. Goldsborough, *Rebel Europe* (New York: Macmillan, 1982), p. 19.
28. Pierre Hassner, "Western European Perceptions of the USSR," *Daedalus* (Winter 1979): 145.
29. Television interview with Valéry Giscard d'Estaing, February 26, 1980, printed in *Le Monde,* 28 Feb. 1980.
30. As former Chancellor Helmut Schmidt put it in retrospect, "The point is that Jaruzelski . . . was not a man whom Moscow had installed. They didn't like him, they didn't trust him, and deep in his heart he utterly disliked the Russians. He thought it was his national duty to prevent open intervention [by the Soviets] and to act as he did. The tragedy is that he did exactly what the Russians wanted in Poland, and let them escape responsibility for it." Craig R. Whitney, "A Talk with Helmut Schmidt," *New York Times Magazine,* 16 Sept. 1984, pp. 114–118.
31. The long-term exception to this rule has been Romania.
32. As quoted in Werner Holzer, "Es sind auch noch größere Dummheiten im Wahlkampf denkbar" (Interview with Helmut Schmidt), *Frankfurter Rundschau,* 12 Aug. 1980, p. 8.
33. For a theoretical discussion of the "appeasement impulse" built into any alliance—to which I am greatly indebted—see Glenn H. Snyder, "The Security Dilemma in Alliance Politics," *World Politics,* 1984, no. 4.
34. "Personally," recollected Helmut Schmidt, "[Jimmy Carter] was a very nice man. . . . But you couldn't depend on his carrying through what he had agreed with you to do." As quoted in Whitney, "Talk with Schmidt," p. 90.
35. Robert W. Tucker, "The Atlantic Alliance and Its Critics," in Robert W. Tucker and Linda Wrigley, eds., *The Atlantic Alliance and Its Critics,* A Lehrman Institute Book (New York: Praeger, 1983), p. 179.
36. Irving Kristol, "NATO at a Dead End," *Wall Street Journal,* 15 July 1981.
37. Walter Laqueur, "Poland and the Crisis of the Alliance," *Wall Street Journal,* 4 Jan. 1982.
38. Daniel Yankelovich and John Doble, "The Public Mood: Nuclear Weapons and the U.S.S.R.," *Foreign Affairs* (Fall 1984): 35.
39. Ibid., pp. 38–42 passim.
40. "Scandilux" refers to Denmark, Norway, Belgium, the Netherlands, and Luxemburg. The label was invented by the Socialist International to designate a group of NATO countries said to share similar traits and interests that set them off from the other members of the Alliance.
41. Tucker, "Atlantic Alliance," pp. 159–160.

42. As quoted in Don Oberndorfer, "Equipment Is Shipped to Soviets," *Washington Post*, 27 Aug. 1982.

43. "Sortir d'un mauvais pas," (Editorial), *Le Monde*, 16 Nov. 1982, p. 1.

44. Interview with Willy Brandt, November 4, 1981, on Norddeutscher Rundfunk 2 (North German Radio), as quoted from mimeographed record, Federal Press and Information Office, News Department, Bonn.

45. Helmut Kohl, "Die Rolle der Bundesrepublik in der internationalen Politik" (Address to the Chicago Council on Foreign Relations, October 23, 1986); reprinted in Presse- und Informationsamt der Bundesregierung, *Bulletin*, no. 131 (1986): 1103. (Kohl was referring to Soviet–American arms control negotiation.)

46. Helmut Schmidt, from a speech to the Federation of German Newspaper Publishers, November 10, 1981, as quoted in *Süddeutsche Zeitung*, 11 Nov. 1981, p. 1.

47. Even in a more tranquil time, the Carter administration was not pleased by Helmut Schmidt's September 1977 offer to act as a go-between for Washington and Moscow. The president's national security adviser, Zbigniew Brzezinski, recalled that "a responsible and high-level emissary could [have been] useful in contacts with the Soviets, but I warned against using the Germans."
    "Arranging it through the Germans [he wrote in a note to the president] raises questions as to their role and interest in this, and also the question of other allies." Zbigniew Brzezinski, *Power and Principle: Memoirs of the National Security Adviser, 1977–1981* (New York: Farrar, Straus & Giroux, 1983), p. 176. Elsewhere in his memoirs, Brzezinski noted, "The Chancellor was particularly anxious to set up private, direct contacts between Carter and the Soviet leader, with himself as the intermediary. Perhaps one of the reasons why Schmidt's personal criticism of Carter continued and even intensified was that the President did not seize on the concept outright." (p. 307).

48. Whitney, "Talk with Schmidt," p. 114.

49. Paul-Marie de la Gorce, "La politique etrangère de la France entre l'Atlanticisme et le Tiers-Mondisme," *Politique Etrangère*, no. 4 (1983): 896.

50. François Mitterrand, *Ici et Maintenant* (Paris: Fayard, 1980), pp. 241–242, 242–243.

51. As quoted in "Die deutsch-französische Freundschaft hängt doch nicht an einter Tasse Tee" (Interview with François Mitterrand), *Stern Magazine*, 29 July 1981, p. 83.

52. Charles Hernu, "Equilibre, dissuasion, volonté" (Address to the Higher National Defense Studies Institute, November 15, 1983), *Défense Nationale*, December 1983, p. 19.

53. François Mitterrand, from an address before the Bundestag on the occasion of the twentieth anniversary of the Franco-German Friendship Treaty, January 20, 1983, as quoted in Presse- und Informationsamt der Bundesregierung, *Bulletin*, no. 8 (1983): 66.

54. Stanley Hoffman, *Gulliver's Troubles* (McGraw-Hill, 1968), p. 55.

55. As quoted in "Was alle denken," *Der Spiegel*, 24 Sept. 1984, p. 20.

56. Interview with Helmut Kohl, December 18, 1984, on Suddeutscher Rundfunk (South German Radio), as quoted from mimeographed record, Bundespresse- und Informationsamt, Document No. II-1218-5, 19 December 1984.

CHAPTER 2

NATO and Nuclear Weapons

No End of a Lesson

Alliances are the product of two irreconcilable ideas. They represent an uneasy compromise between obligation and sovereignty. Nations in alliance seek ironclad commitments from others; for themselves, they reserve the right to obey only their *sacro egoismo* when choosing between war and peace. Each nation wants unbreakable bonds when its own security it at stake, yet these must be no more than gossamer threads when confederates sound the call to arms. It is easy to see why states are as eager to monopolize control as they are loath to relinquish it to others. To guard against betrayal in the moment of need, they must chain their allies's fate to their own. Yet to evade entanglement in unwanted conflicts, they are equally compelled to loosen the tie that binds.

That impossible ideal was nicely phrased by Prince Bismarck when he sought to inveigle Wilhelm I into a permanent league with Austria. To reassure the reluctant emperor, who did not want to fight Habsburg's battles, Bismarck proclaimed that every alliance has a horse and a rider, meaning a partner who follows and a partner who leads. The flaw in this analogy is, of course, that there are no docile horses when the moment of truth is at hand. Peace suddenly becomes quite divisible, interest replaces obligation, and pledges are dwarfed by brutish calculations of power and vulnerability. Throughout history, all alliances have been haunted by the twin specters of abandonment and entrapment.[1] In the late twentieth century, however, nuclear weapons have transformed the faultline of Alliance divisibility into a gaping fissure.

The Structural Problems of a Nuclear Alliance

The novelty of nuclear weapons stems from the unprecedented speed with which they can achieve unprecedented destruction. With their immense power, nuclear weapons threaten to obliterate the difference between defeat and extinction. In the past, vanquished nations could always hope to survive; to be meaningful today, however, surrender must precede war, not follow it. Since catastrophe might come instantaneously, states may have no room for maneuver and no time for reconsideration. Nuclear weapons favor the offense, and where defenses continue to be weak, miscalculation begets no second chance. Nuclear weapons have literally become the ultima ratio—the last weapons to be used—because they may leave neither users nor targets behind. From this inescapable fact it follows that nuclear alliances, were they to obey only the pure logic of deterrence, rest on the frailest of foundations. Protectors will not make good on their pledges if the price of loyalty is annihilation. By the same token, clients cannot rely on their patron's commitments in the existential crunch. Nor will the strong share control over the ultimate weapon because to do so would be to relinquish to other political communities the decisions over the great power's life and death. *"Le nucléaire,"* as the heirs of de Gaulle are so fond of preaching, *"ne se partage pas"*—nuclear weapons protect only their possessors. Yet mutual help and mutual control are the very glue of alliances. Hence the enduring nuclear dilemmas of the Atlantic Alliance.

There was a time in the distant past when these dilemmas were safely buried. The early fifties were the golden age of NATO, the age of "massive retaliation." Those were the years of an American quasi monopoly in nuclear weapons—when the United States could threaten to rain nuclear devastation on the Soviet Union without fear of retaliation. It was the only time when the United States could safely extend deterrence on behalf of its non-nuclear allies because "assured destruction" remained a one-way menace. Invulnerable to Soviet counterstrikes, the United States did not have to risk Washington for the sake of Bonn, Paris, London, or Rome. Indeed, nuclear weapons could inhibit even the most limited forays because they spelled Armageddon for the aggressor and no risk for their possessor.

Like all golden ages, this one probably never existed. If it happened at all, it spans only a brief and shrouded period: from the early 1950s, when the United States could carry several hundred nuclear bombs into Soviet territory via foreign-based bombers, until about 1957 when the Soviet Union began to deploy long-range bombers of its own. And although it took the Soviet Union another fifteen years to reach parity, American leaders had in fact assumed a condition of mutual vulnerability since the very beginning of the fifties. By 1957, when the Soviets tested their first intercontinental missile, mutual vulnerability was a reality. And should NATO ever dissolve, future historians will undoubtedly mark 1957 as the beginning of its demise. From this time onward, the United States could not avoid the risk of sacrificing its own cities for the sake of Europe's capitals. Its commitment could never again be certain—hence the endless corrosive debates over nuclear strategy that have racked the Alliance ever since.

By 1959, only two years after the Soviets had begun to acquire a rudimentary strategic option against the United States, doubts about America's willingness to unsheathe the nuclear sword for its allies had already seeped into the public record. In his confirmation hearings, Secretary of State Christian Herter conceded that the threat of nuclear strikes on behalf of allies was virtually an empty bluff: "I can't conceive of the President of the United States involving us in all-out nuclear war unless the facts showed clearly that we are in danger of devastation ourselves, or that actual moves have been made toward devastating ourselves."[2] These sentiments were soon shared, though painstakingly suppressed, by Secretary of Defense Robert McNamara. Many years later, McNamara would reveal that he had counseled two presidents, John F. Kennedy and Lyndon B. Johnson, "that they never initiate, under any circumstances, the use of nuclear weapons."[3]

It is perhaps no accident, then, that the first act of the endless Euromissile drama began not in 1979—when NATO launched its fabled "two-track" policy on the development of cruise and Pershing II missiles—but exactly twenty years earlier, in 1959. If the 1979 Brussels Decision was officially aimed at a rapidly growing Soviet SS-20 potential, the problem in 1959 had been the initial installation that year of the SS-20's ancient predecessors, Soviet megaton-warhead missiles code named SS-4 and SS-5. (That force would ultimately number 700.) Then, as in the 1980s, the problem stemmed from Soviet intermediate-range weapons that could hit Europe but not the United States, posing quite clearly a separate threat to Europe, and to Europe (plus environs) only. Then as now, the solution to a mounting Eurostrategic menace was thought to lie in acquiring similar weapons that would be American but somehow distinct from the U.S. strategic arsenal. Thus SACEUR General Lauris Norstad proposed as early as 1959 that NATO acquire a force of mobile, land-based Polaris missiles subject to the joint veto power of the United States and the host country. Rejected after brief debate, the Norstad scheme reappeared a year later in the guise of the ill-fated Multilateral Force (MLF). In turn, that missile-bearing freighter fleet was scuttled in 1965 before it had even left the bureaucratic drawing boards. After a dozen years of quiescence, the same drama would resume, only with different props: SS-20 instead of SS-4 and SS-5; cruise and Pershing II missiles instead of Polaris. In each case the real issue was not strategy but politics.

To be sure, the stage was set each time by bellwether changes in the strategic milieu. At the threshold of the 1960s, the new vulnerability of the United States to Soviet strikes ended the golden age of extended deterrence. And precisely at that moment, as the certainty of the American commitment began to wane, the arrival of the SS-4 and SS-5 missiles added a new dimension to the Soviet threat against Western Europe. (Prior to 1959, the Soviet Union had to rely on slow and vulnerable medium-range bombers.) Finally, European anxieties were sharpened by doctrinal reforms that took due note of America's fall from nuclear grace. Thus, massive retaliation gave way to "flexible response," an American strategy that could hardly reassure the Allies given its novel stress on "pauses" and "firebreaks" during the ominous period between Soviet aggression and the ultimate resort to American nuclear weapons. A conventional-minded doctrine that sought to postpone the nuclear moment of truth as long as possible, this strategy was a rational American response to the lengthening shadow of nuclear vulnerability. But the Europeans were quick to grasp the implications of the new posture; the least trusting souls even suspected that the intent was to limit not only the initial intensity of war but also its geographical scope. Raising the "nuclear threshold"—another key shibboleth of flexible response—would surely lower the price of conventional aggression for the Soviets and increase it for the Europeans. While war might well be contained far from the shores of the United States, Europe could only look forward to the role of battlefield and victim.

An almost identical cluster of troubling changes in the strategic environment would precede the Euromissile drama of the 1970s and 1980s. First, there was the official advent of "parity," as consecrated by the SALT I agreement of 1972. Equal numbers of nuclear weapons on either side added up to a strategic stalemate, reasoned many Europeans; with America's nuclear sword thus neutralized, it could no longer be credibly wielded on behalf of distant allies. Secondly, the shift in the global balance was once more exaggerated by a drastic tilt in the regional distribution of power. A "towering dark cloud" was descending on Europe; Backfire bombers and SS-20 missiles constituted a "massive, unwarranted and unexplained expansion"[4] of Soviet weaponry targeted on Western Europe. Third, just as flexible response had met the new curse of

American vulnerability by engendering a richer array of sub-Armageddon strategic options, American doctrine from the mid-1970s onward would relentlessly search for ways to break out of the debilitating constraints of parity. Escalation had to be carefully controlled, and the new magic words were "selectivity," "precision," and "discrimination." The American response followed smoothly from the premise of parity but, again, many Europeans were not reassured. Where would escalation be contained, if not in Europe? Where would "selective options" be executed (and traded), if not on the Continent?

Though the triggering events in both phases were properly strategic, the debates that would subsequently set Europe against the United States were profoundly, if not exclusively, political in nature. Indeed, all strategic debates in the Alliance have actually been about politics—about power and influence within the Atlantic system, and about Europe's place between the two superpowers. Nor is this paradox so difficult to unravel.

Strategy is about the relationship between (military) means and ends. Yet nuclear arguments revolve around weapons that have never been used since the U.S. lost its nuclear monopoly, that must never be used again, and that are applied to an end (deterrence) that is inherently unknowable. (Only the failure of deterrence could be known.) The universe of strategic discourse is a shadowy one, populated not by terms like *is* or *shall*, but by *might* and *should*. While the debate unfolds in terms of subjunctives and conditionals, what truths there may be lie in guessed intentions and presumed effects. Deterrence is a subspecies of political psychology, if not political faith; hence, all transatlantic disputations about extended deterrence have been marked not by resolution but by endless repetition.

Yet at its core, the debate has been anything but a scholastic luxury, for it proceeds in the grim setting of existential dependence. The Alliance remains essentially a unilateral security guarantee extended by the United States to its European partners. While the West Europeans serve American security interests in many ways, they do not underwrite the inviolability of America's territory and population. For the United States, in fact, the siren song of (nuclear) isolationism, as a theory, has never sounded so alluring as it does today. Vast arsenals of nuclear-tipped intercontinental missiles spell vast reserves of deterrent power. The United States can deter the Soviet Union—as well as any imaginable combination of challengers—on its own. To assure its physical security and the integrity of its national borders, the United States requires neither allies nor foreign bases and bastions. Indeed, alliances probably detract from "pure" security.[5] For it is America's commitments that endanger America's safety. It is Berlin or the Middle East—contested areas that bear the stamp of American commitment without being fully controlled by American might—where confrontation with the Soviets might degenerate into a murderous collision.[6]

In Europe the essence of the American guarantee is expressed in the language of the atom. By extending that guarantee, the United States runs the mortal risk of having to execute a threat that might trigger escalation to megadeath levels. By relying on it, the Europeans run a dual risk of equally catastrophic proportions. On the one hand, they might see the threat exposed as a cosmic bluff; conversely, the threat might be executed such that the Continent serves as the venue and victim of a limited nuclear conflict. For Europe, even a limited nuclear war would be indistinguishable from general war—hence the enduring political nature of the strategic debate. While the perennial vernacular is that of counterforce, credibility, and options, the real question is not about doctrine but about who controls whom. The contest centers not around deterrence and its wherewithals, but around the distribution of risks between the United States and Europe. These are not simply strategic questions, but rather political questions par excellence.

The silent nuclear battle in the Alliance is about influence and insulation. The deadly logic of nuclear weapons bids the United States to tacitly distinguish between its own territory and that of its allies. If deterrence does fail, war must be limited in time, intensity, and space. If there has to be war, it must come to an end before it crosses the nuclear threshold. If war does become nuclear, it must be terminated before it crosses the Atlantic Ocean. The same logic, however, bids the Europeans to deny their patron such freedom of choice. To buttress deterrence, the gulf of geography and sovereignty must be closed. To avoid victimization in a limited war, there must be no exit for the United States. If American strategy has relentlessly searched for additional options, the Europeans have just as obsessively looked for additional chains to keep their protector's fate tied to their own.

Yet this is only half of the dilemma, the other half being the mirror image of the first. The answer to the question, Who controls whom? is complicated by an irreducible ambivalence of interests. While the United States, as the alliance leader, must minimize its risk, it must also maximize its commitment; otherwise, the Atlantic compact would surely unravel. Uncertain protection can only make for uncertain allies, and therefore the United States has regularly responded to disturbances of the "balance of terror" with renewed efforts to restore the endangered "balance of mutual control." At the beginning of the 1960s, one response to the advent of American vulnerability and Soviet Euromissiles (SS-4 and SS-5) was the Multilateral Force, the MLF, which promised the allies a greater say in matters nuclear. At the threshold of the 1980s, reassurance against parity and the Soviet SS-20 came in the guise of Pershing II and cruise missiles. Though clad in the language of strategy, these have been *political* responses to the quite political problem of risk distribution. In the words of Richard Burt when he was Director of Politico-Military Affairs in the Department of State,

The United States took this step [the deployment of new missiles] in the full knowledge that the Soviet Union would most likely respond to an attack on its homeland by U.S. systems in Europe with an attack on the United States. Thus the emplacement of long-range U.S. cruise and ballistic missiles in Europe makes escalation of any nuclear war in Europe to an intercontinental exchange even more likely. This is why our allies asked for such a deployment. This is why the United States accepted it.[7]

Conversely, while the Europeans must maximize "coupling," they must just as strenuously seek to minimize nuclear risks. The "decoupling" instincts of the Europeans have a venerable tradition, too. In 1957 Chancellor Konrad Adenauer politely declined the U.S. offer of Jupiter and Thor missiles capable of reaching the Soviet Union. Though viscerally anti-Soviet and eager to host American tactical nuclear weapons in Germany, Adenauer refused to cross the line that separated the European battlefield from the Soviet homeland. Sanctuary-piercing nuclear weapons are both a shield and a target. By refusing them, Adenauer sent a silent message to Moscow which would be repeated a millionfold by the peace movement of the 1980s: Europe does not want to pay for a nuclear conflict that is not its own.

The curious, but entirely logical, dialectic of coupling and decoupling is just the bottommost layer of the political contest. It pits protectors against clients, and the stakes are the terms of alliance in the shadow of an existential nuclear threat to each and all. The object of this contest is *balance* — between obligation and autonomy, influence and insulation, rewards and risks. On the next level, the contest is about *hierarchy*. The issues are less portentous than nuclear war and peace, but they belong nonetheless to the realm of "high politics" because they revolve around

inherently unequal possessions like primacy, precedence, and prestige—
in short, "positional goods" that cannot be equally shared. The typical
questions are not, Who shall bear the greatest risk? but, Who shall lead?
and, Who shall have a greater say in the conduct of alliance business?

It is a powerful testimony to the *political* nature of nuclear weapons
that this second-level contest should also be articulated in the language
of the atom. Decades ago Britain and France acquired independent deterrents not so much for protection as for prestige. Both nations took
the nuclear road long before he American guarantee had become brittle,
and both saw nuclear weapons as the badge of distinction that would af-
firm their great power status and elevate them over the common herd of
the non-nuclear members of the alliance. In the mid-1950s, when West
Germany asked for American tactical nuclear weapons to add to its own
forces, it did so in part to acquire surrogate nuclear status that would
strengthen Bonn's voice in Alliance councils. The Federal Republic would
later extend a covetous hand toward MLF for the same reason. Conversely, the United States has regularly manipulated access to nuclear
weapons in pursuit of its own hierarchical interests, the MLF representing the most instructive example. Ostensibly responding to a strategic
need, the MLF was in fact launched on a strictly political course. The
missile-bearing freighter fleet was intended to absorb West Germany's
presumed proliferationist ambitions and thus to buttress American control. By forging a new Atlantic connection, the MLF was to undo the
Franco-German entente of the early sixties, which Charles de Gaulle had
hoped to pit against American "hegemony."

On a third level, the nuclear contest is not between allies but between
them and their Soviet opponent. More precisely, the framework is triangular, with Europeans, Americans, and Soviets competing over the
nature of the European order: meaning, the long-term distribution of
power between patrons, clients, and adversaries. Since nuclear weapons
are the supreme symbol of power in the contemporary system, it is again
no accident that the argument perennially revolves around weapons and
strategies, even though the crucial stake—the nature of Europe's order—
is by definition political. And since there are only three players in the
game who by their own actions could change the status quo—the United
States, the Soviet Union, and the Federal Republic of Germany—the cor-
ners of the triangle are essentially represented by Washington, Moscow,
and Bonn.

The power of these three players derives from the critical mass each
brings to bear on the European system. While neither superpower is

strong enough to dislodge the other, both have the (negative) power to transform the system by default, that is, through unilateral withdrawal. Such an event, whatever else it might engender, would spell the end of Europe's bipolar order. Though far weaker than the two superpowers, West Germany—by virtue of its critical weight and geographical position —could theoretically undo the status quo by merely going neutral and could unhinge the balance completely by shifting its allegiance to the Soviet side.

The main thrust of Soviet policy is straightforward enough. The Soviet Union has sought to acquire a predominant position in postwar Europe and, correspondingly, to weaken the American hold on the Continent. Moscow has therefore consistently fought any nuclear arrangements that would undercut its natural geographical advantage (the counterpart of Western Europe's hostage role) or would strengthen the security ties between the United States and its allies (which act to counterbalance Soviet might). Given the Federal Republic's critical role in the European scheme, a related but no less weighty Soviet interest has been to keep nuclear weapons out of West Germany and to keep West Germany out of nuclear weapons. An unbroken line of fierce Soviet hostility runs through contemporary European history, starting from the stationing of American tactical nuclear weapons in the fifties, and continuing toward the MLF in the sixties and INF in the seventies and eighties. Soviet stakes have by no means been on the small side. Indeed, they have been large enough to prompt the Soviet Union to precipitate two of the worst East–West crises in postwar Europe. Khrushchev first tried to dissuade Bonn from acquiring tactical nuclear weapons in 1958; when he failed, there came the long ice age of the Berlin Ultimatum. In the 1980s Brezhnev reenacted the pressure campaign on a Europeanwide scale; when that war of nerves foundered, his successors, Andropov and Chernenko, responded to Pershing II and cruise missiles with a turn toward angry confrontation, including the rupture of all arms control talks. In each case the heart of the matter was not so much the measure of the military balance as the nature of the political order in Europe. The issue was whether the United States and its allies were free to choose the means of their common defense while the Soviet Union claimed precisely the opposite right: a quasi-imperial veto power over the instruments by which the United States would guarantee Western Europe's security.

Yet this is only one side of the problem. The other source of European anxiety flows from the cooperative element in the Soviet–American relationship. The West Europeans, and the West Germans in particular, will always be haunted by the specter of Big Twoism; that ghost arises most naturally when the two superpowers engage in global arms control. In the mid-1960s the West Germans fought a stubborn battle against the Nonproliferation Treaty; a decade later, it was SALT II that seemed to sacrifice their interests on the altar of great power amity. Again, the issue went deeper than fears that the Nonproliferation Treaty would foreclose civilian nuclear power options, or that SALT II would do so in the military arena via "nontransfer" and "noncircumvention" clauses, or that "double-zero" would be the first step toward denuclearization. The central issue was power and influence, and whether the interests of allies would count for more than the claims of adversaries.

To complete the triangle, there is the mixed relationship between Western Europe and the Soviet Union. Since 1957, when Chancellor Adenauer refused to accept American Thor and Jupiter missiles on West German soil, the Europeans have regularly faced a painful trade-off between deterrence and détente. Nor have the Russians ever allowed them to forget the cruelty of their dilemma. Good relations, as proffered by Moscow, carry a price that is set in terms of European nuclear modesty, if not abstention. For the West Germans in particular, nuclear arrangements in the service of extended deterrence pose a direct and fearful threat to their preferred vision of Europe's future. Nuclear weapons, whether tactical or Eurostrategic, whether shared or merely hosted, provoke the Soviets and tighten bipolarity in Europe. As a result, they compress the margins of diplomatic maneuver and reduce access to East Germany and Eastern Europe. For the Federal Republic, at once most vulnerable and most committed to the transformation of the status quo, nuclear choices are in fact choices about Europe's present and future political order. That point was driven home most brutally on the eve of the Pershing II and cruise missile deployment when the Russians threatened "palisades of missiles" in retaliation, which would henceforth separate West Germans from East Germans.

That metaphor merely echoed a larger message: Nuclear weapons are political weapons. As the ultima ratio, they represent the essence of power in the contemporary system, and therefore it is only logical that they serve as the symbols, stakes, and means of a grand political contest that sets patrons against clients, and allies against adversaries. Though perennially articulated in the language of nuclear doctrine and possession, the argument is first and foremost about political relationships. The heart of the matter is not strategy but the distribution of risk, power, and dependence—the very stuff of international politics. If the key issues are political, it should come as no surprise that NATO's recurrent search for hardware schemes à la MLF or INF would add more to the problem than to the solution.

The MLF: A Circle That Would Not Square

When problems recur, it is safe to assume that solutions are either flimsy or misdirected. Already a quarter century ago, the MLF raised many of the painful issues that would return to beset the Alliance in the 1980s. Although the MLF was designed to address a strategic problem—Soviet medium-range missiles posing a separate threat to Western Europe—it was at heart a political instrument of American diplomacy. Set in motion to allay European security concerns about growing Soviet arsenals, the missile fleet provoked fearful disputes about power and primacy within the Western bloc. In the process the MLF would provide a still instructive study in irony. It offered solutions which dramatized dilemmas. Rather than unifying the Alliance, it deepened the internal dissension. And although it was launched to accommodate the presumed wishes of the Europeans, it produced not satisfaction but resentment and hostility among America's intended beneficiaries.

Reading an early postmortem of the MLF impresses the contemporary observer with a haunting sense of déjà vu. "The original proposal for a NATO multilateral force," wrote Henry Kissinger in 1965,

grew out of a military "requirement" which had been generated in accordance with the NATO doctrine prevalent in the late fifties. According to this concept, SACEUR was to have the capability to destroy all weapons aimed at Europe. Thus when the Soviet Union began to deploy large numbers of medium-range ballistic missiles in western Russia, two NATO requirements emerged: a modernization program to replace vulnerable tactical aircraft with missiles and an interdiction mission giving NATO the capability to destroy the Soviet MRBMs.[8]

Yet for several years, pressing strategic logic begat exactly nothing. While a seedling had been planted by SACEUR General Lauris Norstad in 1959, neither Americans nor Europeans were particularly eager to see it grow and flourish. Just as Jimmy Carter would do later, the new Kennedy administration devoted the first two years of its term to exhorting the Europeans to invest in a conventional build-up. Only then might something like a joint nuclear force make any sense. The best description of American interest in the MLF venture was benign indifference, and like Carter's emissaries in 1977 and 1978, Kennedy's diplomats would countenance new nuclear arrangements only in response to a clearly audible

European plea. "Should other NATO nations so desire," declared Under Secretary of State George W. Ball, "we are ready to give serious consideration to the creation of a genuinely multilateral . . . missile force."[9] Whatever the urgency of the strategic rationale for a Euromissile force, both the Kennedy and the Carter administrations simply had different priorities. Kennedy's secretary of defense, Robert S. McNamara, was loath to see another deterrent (besides the British and French ones) disturb his compulsive quest for perfectly centralized control; Jimmy Carter was also not prepared to burden his ambitious arms control project with a weapon as difficult to count and verify as the cruise missile.

Two years into Kennedy's term, the MLF was but a minor American preoccupation that "did not elicit a significant European response." Indeed, "until six weeks before it emerged as the principal objective of American NATO policy, [the Kennedy administration's] highest officials had declared the MLF militarily unnecessary."[10] Here, too, the future would simply imitate the past. Until Jimmy Carter gave his blessing to cruise and Pershing II missiles at the 1979 quadripartite Western summit in Guadeloupe, his spokesmen, from the secretary of defense on down, had continued to denigrate any need for them by pointing to a surfeit of warheads in the American strategic arsenal.

Why, then, did the MLF suddenly leap to the top of the American foreign policy agenda? The strategic facts, surely, had not changed. What had changed with a vengeance was the political setting of the Atlantic relationship. On January 14, 1963, Charles de Gaulle's gathering challenge to American "hegemony" — in the making since his return to power in 1958 — escalated into a dramatic act of defiance. In his notorious press conference, the French president launched a frontal attack on what he called "a colossal Atlantic Community under American dependence and leadership which would soon completely swallow up the European Community."[11] He then proceeded to veto Britain's application for Common Market membership while heaping scorn on the very idea of nuclear integration. If his veto barred from Europe America's faithful British partner (with its power to block de Gaulle's continental ambitions), his attack on the idea of nuclear integration flung an unbearable insult at the very pillar of the McNamara strategy: "centralized control" over the West's nuclear weapons. (That meant, of course, American control, leaving no room for other national deterrents outside the U.S. fold.) The third blow came but a week later when de Gaulle and Adenauer concluded the Franco-German Treaty of Friendship and Collaboration. In the context of provocations past, that compact could only mean the creation of a Gallo-German axis against NATO's patron power across the sea. Adding anxiety to injury were the many hints (some carefully planted by the General himself) of future nuclear collaboration between the two arch-enemies of yore.[12]

With the battle thus joined, the many-flagged missile fleet at last acquired a head of steam. Of dubious strategic value, the MLF suddenly sparkled with enormous political promise. If de Gaulle meant to have his own national deterrent, the MLF would prove to the rest of NATO's members that they need not follow so foolish a path. "Unlike national forces," wrote Robert R. Bowie, the State Department official on loan from Harvard who had virtually invented the MLF, "a multilateral force would not fragment the alliance, but would tend to pull it together." If there was a widening status gap between the nuclear haves and have-nots, then the MLF would "enable the Federal Republic and Italy to have a proper part in nuclear defense without raising the specter of a separate German strategic force."[13] If the Germans were chafing under the yoke of nuclear discrimination, the MLF would "strengthen European cohesion by providing presently non-nuclear powers an opportunity to share in ownership, manning, and control of a powerful nuclear force on the same basis as the other members of that force."[14] If Bonn was anxious about the altogether disconcerting shift from massive retaliation to flexible response,[15] something like the MLF would be the proper means for providing "greater equality, at least for a unified Europe, in the matter of nuclear control."[16] Finally, and most importantly, if de Gaulle was planning to harness West Germany to an anti-American continental combination, the MLF would act as an elegant counter in the transatlantic tug-of-war for Bonn's allegiance. In the words of Kennedy's court chronicler, Arthur Schlesinger, "If de Gaulle meant to make West Germany choose between France and the United States, the MLF, in Washington's view, was the way to make it clear that Bonn would find greater security in the Atlantic relationship."[17]

The 25-ship fleet was thus dispatched on a strictly political voyage. It was launched to harness Germany's presumed nuclear ambitions to a collective enterprise under American leadership. It was to discourage the Allies from imitating the Franco-British quest for a national nuclear defense, the very anathema of McNamara's new doxology. It was supposed to narrow the status gap between those who had already acquired national deterrents and those who were allegedly eager to emulate the performance (even though the West Germans had been bound by sacred treaty since 1954 to eschew all nuclear temptations). At stake was America's primacy in the Alliance, and so the MLF was to buttress centralized control over the ultima ratio under the guise of sharing it; Washington's veto over the actual use of the seaborne missiles was to be retained under all circumstances.

Given its political thrust, the MLF's strategic rationale remained in the dark—and mercifully so. For it was an elaborate piece of diplomatic legerdemain and merely confirmed on all points the long-held French contention. Nations that cannot be expected to commit suicide for one another can hardly be expected to share control over the ultimate weapon with others. But even more fundamentally, the numbers did not add up to a strategic rationale. If the MLF's Polaris missiles were to generate a counterforce capability, why were only 200 projected? The Soviets would eventually array some 700 SS-4 and SS-5 missiles against Western Europe; these could hardly be eliminated with a puny Western force less than one-third as large. If the aim, on the other hand, was not so much a counterforce capability as invulnerability to a Soviet first strike, the freighter flotilla—as opposed to submarines—was hardly an adequate answer. Surface ships cruising in the vicinity of the Continent were only marginally safer than land-based aircraft, which were then carrying the main burden of NATO's deterrence tasks.

Nor did the institutional features of the MLF mitigate NATO's handicap in numbers and location. There was no way the MLF could square the circle of retaining and sharing centralized control. If the MLF could not pose a counterforce threat on its own, it would have to act in conjunction with the American strategic arsenal. In that event, however, why have two nuclear forces—especially if both were subject to American control? And if the MLF was to enhance the endangered credibility of extended deterrence by allowing the Europeans to not only huddle under but also to hold the American umbrella, why the insistence on an undiluted American veto? If the president remained in charge, it was by no means self-evident that he would more readily launch a Polaris missile from one of the MLF vessels off the European coast than the same missile from an American submarine somewhere beneath the ocean.

What if the United States, however, were to relinquish its veto, as some of the more insistent American advocates of the project were hinting and some of the more credulous Europeans were anticipating?[18] The prospect defied the imagination. No nation has ever gone to war on the basis of an allied majority vote; why should they do so now when nuclear weapons had raised the price of misplaced deference to the wills of others by many orders of magnitude? The last thing a great power will yield to others is the decision over nuclear war and peace, and therefore nations which have the ultimate weapons will not share control over them. They may grant to others a veto power over a small part of their nonstrategic arsenal, as the United States has in fact done by agreeing to a "dual-key" rule for some tactical nuclear weapons. They may even deploy their weapons in a manner—for instance, on allied territory close enough to reach the Soviet Union—that increases the risks of nuclear strikes against themselves. Yet they will not allow others to clutch the trigger on weapons which threaten their existence. Conceivably, the United States might have walked away from that bind by simply dispatching the MLF into the sole possession of its European allies. But then the MLF would have been another separate force—anathema to the very purpose of the project, namely, to preempt proliferation and to recentralize control.

Since the MLF could not solve what was in fact the insoluble issue of nuclear control, it certainly could not still the anxieties about extended deterrence that were fueled by the advent of "peril parity" and the doctrinal shift toward flexible response. By the same token, the MLF could not resolve any of the other questions it was designed to address. Since it could not level the irreducible differences between nuclear and non-nuclear powers, it was doomed to only dramatize their inequality. For the nuclear have-nots, the MLF offered merely make-believe control and not, as a result, any incentive to participate. For those who, like Britain and France, already owned nuclear weapons, the MLF was a nuisance that threatened to devalue their national deterrents and their exalted status. The British, held in check by the Anglo-American "special relationship," remained politely indifferent. But the French, correctly reading the anti-Gaullist mission of the MLF, escalated their fire as the Americans pushed for Allied adherence to the scheme. And the smaller nations dropped out one by one.

It was only in the Federal Republic that lukewarm interest changed into avid support. Yet the ultimate irony was that the MLF, launched primarily to reassure the Federal Republic, ended up inflaming every sore point it was intended to soothe. Like tactical nuclear weapons for the Bundeswehr in the 1950s, and INF in the 1980s, the MLF exacted a fearful price within the Alliance, vis-à-vis the Soviet Union, and within the body politic itself.

Because the MLF was America's chosen instrument for prying the Federal Republic from de Gaulle's embrace, it forced Bonn into a nasty choice between its two key allies. These strains were accurately mirrored in the power struggle between the "Atlanticists" gathered around Chancellor Erhard and the "Gaullists" led by his worst intraparty rival, Franz Josef Strauss. The contest over the country's alignment became inseparable from the battle for domestic power. For Ludwig Erhard and his confederates, the ascent to nuclear co-ownership and status, no matter how flimsy, would spell their final victory in the struggle over Adenauer's succession, still undecided since his resignation in 1963. So desperate was Erhard to save his position, along with the sinking missile fleet, that he proclaimed at a Berlin press conference his readiness to sign the MLF treaty as the sole partner of the United States if there were no other takers.[19]

Yet so much eagerness, though prompted by domestic factors, rang the death knell of the MLF. To West Germany's allies, a nuclear axis between the United States and the Federal Republic threatened too much of a German say in matters nuclear; most of them had warily gone along with the MLF precisely to constrain such ambitions. Bonn, the intended beneficiary of the MLF, was now its lonely victim. For in the end the United States defected, too. Since Erhard had beaten back his Gaullist tormentors by presenting himself as the trusty guardian of German–American amity—loosening de Gaulle's embrace in the process—the listing missile fleet was no longer needed to tow the Germans back into the American fold. With the Alliance recentralized and de Gaulle isolated, the MLF would sail onward only to collide with ever larger objectives of American foreign policy.

By 1965 the Soviets had entered the fray as well-equipped combatants. If the United States wanted global arms control, the price of a nonproliferation agreement would be a scuttled MLF. The quid pro quo of cooperation between the two superpowers entailed German abstention from any physical access to nuclear weapons. Nor was President Johnson particularly interested in affronting the Soviets when he was about to escalate the war in Vietnam. By the beginning of 1965, the MLF had become the Flying Dutchman of the Alliance—a testimony to an impossible quest and a ghost of efforts past.

The INF Battle: Allies, Angst, and Arms Control

The story of INF has the same beginning as the MLF story. Once again, the script was written in the language of nuclear weapons and the real plot was about politics—about power and dependence, and about the triangular relationship between the United States, its European allies, and the Soviet Union. Though the props had changed from Polaris to Pershing II and from SS-4/5 to SS-20, the setting of the earlier MLF debate was virtually replicated in the prologue to the INF drama.[20] Like its forebear, the new prologue revolved around a familiar threesome: a deteriorating global balance, a similar trend in the regional balance, and the relation of both to yet another shift in American nuclear doctrine.

By 1975, exactly a decade after the sinking of the MLF, the Soviet Union had surpassed the United States in what was then the accepted currency of global nuclear strength: strategic launchers. (The ratio was 2,537 to 2,142.)[21] The Soviet Union was also about to field a new generation of Eurostrategic weapons capable of hitting Western Europe but not the United States—the Backfire bomber and the triple-warhead, mobile SS-20. Simultaneously, and in response to the new imbalance in strategic launchers, there was another shift in American strategy, this time known as the "Schlesinger doctrine" and named after the secretary of defense in office from 1973 to 1975.

Unlike the McNamara strategy, which, in European eyes, had represented a sudden and calamitous break with the past, the Schlesinger variant raised European anxieties neither directly nor swiftly. Whereas Robert McNamara had ruffled European sensitivities with a set of ex cathedras that downplayed the nuclear response in favor of multiplying conventional options, Schlesinger—perhaps in remembrance of collisions past—came to office stressing instead a richer array of nuclear choices as the proper remedy for strategic parity. If McNamara sought to stretch out the conventional segment of the escalation ladder so as to postpone the nuclear moment of truth, Schlesinger aimed at expanding the spectrum of violence just beyond the "nuclear firebreak." The capability of threatening first use on behalf of allies in a setting of parity required above all weapons that afforded "controlled, selective, and deliberate" options, meaning weapons of precision and tightly limited "collateral damage" that would hit military rather than population targets and thus dispel the specter of mutual suicide.[22] Having paid homage to NATO's ancient orthodoxy, Schlesinger could safely return to McNamara's favorite theme: "the gradual evolution towards increasing stress on the conventional components," and "a diminution of the threat of recourse to nuclear weapons."[23]

What followed exemplified an immutable law of Alliance psychology. Anxieties about deterrence *made in the USA* do not spring full-blown from the depths of Europe's collective unconscious. Instead, it is American doubts, real or exaggerated, that invariably trigger the next anxiety cycle among the European allies. While the seedling is always planted on American soil, the fruits of nuclear discontent will in due time ripen on the eastern shores of the Atlantic. Schlesinger's solutions limned between 1973 and 1975 merely echoed Nixon's classic formulation of the predicament of parity in 1970: "Should a President, in the event of a nuclear attack, be left with the single option of ordering the mass destruction of enemy civilians, in the face of the certainty that it would be followed by the mass slaughter of Americans?"[24]

There was an uncanny parallel to the MLF. Fifteen years earlier, American diagnoses had taught the Europeans to recognize their own nuclear complaints, and it was an American prescription that had whetted European appetites for the proffered cure. And so it was in the case of the 1979 INF decision, whose intellectual (or, more precisely, psychological) origins grew out of the rising debate in the United States about the withering credibility of its nuclear guarantee for Europe. It was not the Europeans but the American secretary of defense who, in 1975, sounded the theme of the "seamless web of deterrence," leaving more suspicious Europeans to wonder whether the web had not been rent, opening gaps of opportunity for the Russians to exploit. In the words of James Schlesinger:

The Warsaw Pact should not be allowed to perceive opportunities for successful military action at any point in the spectrum of potential conflict. A strong deterrent extending across this spectrum will discourage crises or minor conflicts which could escalate. In the event of major conflict, there will be downward pressures to contain the war and move to negotiations, rather than pressures for escalation, if the prospects are dim for successful military action by the Soviets at higher levels.[25]

It was American officials and strategists who, in the mid-1970s, taught the Europeans to appreciate the perils of "gaps" in the deterrence spectrum and the value of "limited nuclear options" and deep-interdiction attacks on the Warsaw Pact's "rear-based forces." It was at this point that congressional pressure forced a searching look at the "pile of junk" (Schlesinger) that the Alliance had for a theater nuclear arsenal: thousands of obsolete, high-yield, short-range, haphazardly guarded, and badly controlled tactical nuclear weapons. Only the gleaming new weapons technologies promised relief—in the form of improved "survivability of these theater nuclear elements" and "reduced yields, special warhead effects such as enhanced radiation [and] improved delivery systems accuracy."[26] NATO was quick to take note of these new vistas, and so the Nuclear Planning Group, meeting in Monterey in June 1975, decided to follow the American lead by pledging to take a sympathetic look at "the implications of technological improvements which might affect NATO's deterrent posture . . . and nuclear capabilities."[27]

The stage was thus set for the entry of the leading dramatis machinae: the cruise missile in the West, followed two years later by the SS-20 in the East. There was nothing in the Schlesinger doctrine that actually foreordained the introduction of cruise missiles; indeed his search for precision and discrimination attached itself to shorter range weapons like the Lance (110 kilometers) and the enhanced radiation warhead, which would leave the Strategic Air Command to take care of "selective strikes" deep within the Warsaw Pact's hinterland. But given the conceptual thrust of the American debate, it would have been a miracle of transatlantic noncommunication if the Europeans had not seized upon the cruise missile as a perfect cure for those NATO afflictions so insistently decried by the American strategic community, both inside and outside the government.

Three factors combined to push the cruise missile to the forefront of European interest. The first was sheer technological promise, a message the Europeans could hardly ignore as they listened to the growing American chorus of praise for a system that Secretary of State Henry Kissinger was apparently willing to bargain away for Soviet SALT concessions. The cruise missile's small size—no more than 6 meters long and 60 centimeters wide—promised concealment, mobility, and hence a dramatic gain in invulnerability. It could not only fly farther than existing long-range systems (NATO's strike aircraft), it could also penetrate the densest air-defense networks along a treetop flight path and still hit remote targets with unprecedented accuracy. Its low price (European experts were fond of quoting a price of $1 million) promised ample procurement as well as relief for finance ministries beset by soaring costs for tactical and strategic air power. Finally, the cruise missile offered the best of all possible deterrence worlds: precise enough to be a counterforce weapon, but not fast enough to pose a first-strike threat.

The second factor stemmed from the logic of American doctrine. If "NATO should have a wide range of nuclear options to provide responses suitable to the provocation,"[28] if deterrence must leave no tempting gaps, then what better way to close them than by way of the cruise missile, which fitted neatly into the gap between battlefield and strategic weapons? If NATO was to "attack WP [Warsaw Pact] theater nuclear forces" and "threaten WP targets of value,"[29] the cruise missile (and an improved version of Pershing I) were virtually predestined to take the place of NATO's vulnerable and obsolete strike aircraft. The main burden of theaterwide deterrence was then being carried by aging attack planes such as the Starfighter and bombers like the Vulcan, first deployed in 1958 and 1960, respectively. The most modern addition to the arsenal was the American F-111, which had entered European service in 1967. All of them relied on airfields that offered prime targets for preemptive destruction; even if they were to survive such attacks, they ran a dwindling chance of completing any offensive missions because of the Warsaw Pact's accelerating investment in air defenses. The rationale for cruise missiles had an air of déjà vu. Here, as in the case of the MLF, the European strategic community willingly accepted the categories furnished by its American counterpart. Only the labels had changed slightly: if the issues then were "invulnerability" and "counterforce," they were now "survivability" and "penetrability."

The third factor in the heightened interest in cruise missiles was also familiar, and the weightiest of them all: Europe's fears about American reliability. It marked the difference between a technical debate and a political conflict, and it exemplified another law of Alliance relations: any dispute over strategy invariably turns into a contest over structure—*structure* being defined as the distribution of power, influence, and control between the United States and Europe. The political phase began not with Jimmy Carter's arrival in the White House—as is frequently assumed—but in early 1975 when the Ford administration and the Soviet Union resumed negotiations on a second SALT treaty. As the Allies looked on from the parterre, the Soviets bestrode the stage—demanding, in effect, a permanent part in the determination of Western security policy in Europe.

Ostensibly only a matter of numbers, the issue actually went to the very core of the European–American relationship. Throughout the SALT I period, from 1969 onward, the Soviets had insisted on a standard of strategic equality which would reserve for them the role of *primus inter pares*. Claiming any weapon as "strategic" that was capable of hitting Soviet territory, they demanded for themselves a total force equal to the combined numbers of American strategic forces, American long-range weapons in and around Europe (the so-called forward-based systems or FBS), and the nuclear arsenals of the French and the British. That equation concealed an insidious choice for the United States and a nasty prospect for the West Europeans. To reassure the latter, the United States would have to pay for European security with its own: by yielding to the Soviet Union a measure of superiority in central systems. Alternatively, if the United States reduced its FBS to retain strategic equality for itself, the bill would have to be paid at the expense of European security. Finally, no matter which way the United States turned, the Soviet Union would end up with a favorable "correlation of forces" vis-à-vis Western Europe because its Eurostrategic weapons—missiles and aircraft targeted on the western half of the Continent—were by definition not part of the global bargain. Incapable of hitting the United States, the Soviet arsenal would nevertheless continue to cast its shadow over Western Europe without any negotiated constraint.

In the SALT I treaty, the United States had resolved this Hobson's choice in favor of the Allies. The tacit bargain left the Soviets in possession of 300 so-called heavy missiles (regarded as a prominent threat to American land-based forces); in return, the Soviets set aside their designs on FBS. As additional incentive, the United States had offered a "noncircumvention" pledge: if the Soviets continued to ignore FBS, Washington would bind itself not to circumvent central ceilings by adding to its own forward-based nuclear forces. It was a problem postponed, not solved.

For when the SALT II negotiations began in earnest in 1975, the Soviets escalated their campaign against the forward-based wherewithals of extended deterrence in Europe. Noncircumvention (meaning the status quo) was not enough. To cement Soviet preponderance in the future, the Allies were to be deprived of the fruits of American nuclear technology, most notably, of the benefits of the cruise missile. To this end, the Soviet negotiators began to press for a nontransfer clause under which either side would undertake "not to transfer strategic offensive arms to other states, and not to assist in their development, in particular, by transferring components, technical descriptions or blueprints for these arms."[30] The implications of this demand were staggering. Its direct consequence would have been the rupture of the Anglo-American special relationship under which the United States had regularly transferred nuclear strategic know-how and weapons (such as the Polaris) to Britain. In the long run, a nontransfer agreement would have been tantamount to a nuclear entente against America's European allies. In effect, the Soviets were trying to harness the United States to the cause of Soviet nuclear primacy in Europe by asking Washington to sacrifice Allied security interests on the altar of superpower arms control.

Enter Jimmy Carter. The Ford Administration, in several proposals to the Russians in 1976, had taken a few hesitant steps on that slippery slope by offering to limit cruise missiles in exchange for limits on the Soviet Backfire bomber.[31] The final offer foreshadowed the notorious "Protocol" of SALT II that would keep European fears galvanized for years to come. The last proposal of the Ford administration was a 600-kilometer-range limit on deployed ground-launched cruise missiles and a 2,500-kilometer-range for test versions. That overture was mercifully closed by the refusal of the Soviets and the approaching presidential elections.

The respite did not last; after Jimmy Carter's arrival in the White House in 1977, the vague specter of superpower collusion would gestate into Europe's classic nightmare. Driven by what the more alarmed Europeans saw as "antinuclear theology," and eager for a rapid breakthrough in SALT II, Jimmy Carter offered the Soviets concessions that made the previous administration look like a shining epitome of Alliance loyalty. For the Europeans the new posture contained a triple anathema. The Protocol banned "cruise missiles capable of a range in excess of 600 kilometers on sea-based or on land-based launchers."[32] There was the return of the ominous noncircumvention clause, even though it was later defused by an "interpretive statement" according to which the provision "will not interfere with continued nuclear and conventional cooperation with [U.S.] allies.[33] Finally, and worst of all, the Backfire bomber—capable of threatening only the Europeans—was simply dispatched as being outside the confines of the SALT II agreement. Whereas the Ford administration had sought to reassure the Europeans by trading cruise missile for Backfire restraints,[34] the Carter administration added (unwitting) insult to injury by declaring the Backfire out of bounds for precisely the wrong reasons: ". . . as long as they are not deployed as strategic weapons."[35]

For the Europeans these priorities were fearfully askew, symbolizing the drastic devaluation of their needs in favor of Big Two collaboration. Carter's arms control policy limited what they regarded as a promise vital to Europe's defenses—the long-range cruise missile. Yet it left unconstrained what they perceived as a grievous threat—the Backfire bomber. Carter's policy seemed to yield to the Russians an ominous hold on the future of the European–American relationship, in the form of the noncircumvention pledge that, in due time, would eat away at the foundations of the protector's guarantee because it tied American hands while leaving the Soviets free to add to their Eurostrategic weapons. Nor were the Europeans assured by the gains the United States hoped to extract from these concessions: a "deep cut" in the Soviet heavy missile force (from 300 to 200, or even 150), which loomed so large in American threat assessments. Previous administrations (Nixon and Ford) had always shouldered that extra burden of threat in order to keep the precious forward-based systems out of the Soviet grasp. Now the situation was exactly reversed. The clients were asked to pay for the security of their patron. Finally, there was no solace in the short duration of the Protocol (until 1981). It was a precedent, and it was practically certified as such at the highest levels of the Carter administration. Asked about the future role of the Protocol, Secretary of Defense Brown responded, "Well, it assures the Soviets these matters will at least remain items for future negotiations."[36]

In short, Carter's SALT policy compromised the very heart of the European–American security bargain. The Backfire became the symbol of threats unshackled, shifting the balance of risk against the Europeans. The cruise missile became the symbol of promises denied, diminishing Europe's weight in the transatlantic balance of prerogatives and obligations. And in the larger realm of East–West relations, where the issue of Europe's order was at stake, the policy foreshadowed not only the denigration of Europe's claims but also a contractually sanctified *droit de regard* for the Soviet Union. Keeping these balances had been the core of the transatlantic relationship, and they were about to be unhinged. That alone would have been sufficient for a full-blown Alliance crisis by early 1977. When the SS-20 began to intrude at about the same time, it provided the most dramatic, short-hand symbol for everything that was wrong in Carter's approach to the Soviets and Europeans alike. To many Europeans his oblivious response to the new Soviet threat proved that the new president was not only erratic and unpredictable, but obtuse as well.[37]

From Decision to Deployment: A Balance Restored

To conclude that the SS-20 (and the Backfire) *drove* NATO's INF project —which is indeed a partial truth—is to believe that symbols determine substance. They do not, and neither did the SS-20 "cause" the decision in Brussels in 1979, even though this mechanistic image has been the preferred version of Allied governments and the premise of all Western arms control offers. That image is nicely reflected in the German term *Nachrüstung* (literally, "counterarmament") and in the credo of the "zero option." Aiming for no missiles on either side implied that Soviet Euromissiles were the only problem—hence a problem bound to dissolve along with their complete liquidation (as offered by General Secretary Gorvachev in 1987).

The heart of the matter lay elsewhere, and properly so. To be sure, the SS-20 did represent a novel and ominous threat. It embodied a three-generation jump over the existing Soviet arsenal. It was solid-, rather than liquid-fueled, mobile rather than stationary, and it carried three warheads (rather than one) over twice the distance covered by the SS-4. Within seven years of its first deployment in 1977, the SS-20 plus its remaining predecessors would almost double the number of Soviet warheads available in the European theater, and the new warheads were three to six times more accurate than the old ones. More importantly, the SS-20 combination of precision, readiness, and invulnerability added enormously to Soviet options. The stationary SS-4 and SS-5 were classic "use them or lose them" weapons. Offering easy targets and requiring many hours of preparation, they had to be fired in toto or not at all, for to launch only a few would condemn the remainder to certain second-strike destruction. By contrast, the relatively invulnerable SS-20 made an excellent warfighting weapon because it could be used or held back according to the needs of the moment. If NATO's flexible response doctrine was based on the ability to control escalation at each and every step, then the SS-20 amounted to a counterdeterrence potential bearing the message that "escalation dominance" had passed to the other side.

Still, the SS-20 provided merely the most conspicuous focus rather than the most crucial factor of the contest to come. The real dispute between the United States and the Europeans from 1977 onward was not over the military but the political balance, not over the terms of deterrence but the terms of alliance. Ordinarily, the "terms of alliance" specify the conditions under which members will come to the aid of each other. In a nuclear alliance, where the use of force is remote and dependence is unequal, the smaller members typically worry about the terms of alliance in a more broadly political sense; they worry about the degree of influence they have over their patron's policy. Months before he gave the speech that is now regarded as the INF equivalent of the book of genesis, Chancellor Helmut Schmidt hinted darkly that "the share of the risks . . . should be justly divided" and that, given parity, strategic nuclear weapons "will become increasingly regarded as an instrument of last resort, to serve the national interest and protect the survival of those who possess these weapons of last resort."[38] Decoded, that message to Jimmy Carter read, "While the reliability of your commitment is declining, our share of the risk is increasing." Instead of solace, the Allies received briefings from two U.S. interagency delegations that merely confirmed their suspicions. According to David Aaron, deputy to National Security Adviser Zbigniew Brzezinski, they brought with them "an optimistic assessment of the balance in Europe." Clearly, "our priorities were on conventional forces at this point." As to the nuclear equation, the American travelers explained that "there were plenty of warheads in our strategic arsenal that could be targeted in the interest of Europeans" and "plenty of earmarked Poseidon missiles" (on American submarines). Moreover, there would be more warheads available since "Britain was about the modernize its nuclear forces." Yet because Schmidt did not worry about numbers so much as about neglect – and especially about Jimmy Carter's SALT priorities and his oblivious response to the SS-20 – "that approach did not work, and so we got the chancellor's speech at the IISS [International Institute for Strategic Studies in London]."[39]

Replete with ponderous circumlocutions, Schmidt's speech was so subtly crafted that it could mean all things to all people. It was certainly too oblique to serve as hard evidence in a political paternity suit that would saddle the chancellor with the progeniture of the INF deployment. Nor were Western Euromissiles the foremost object of his desire.

The strategic portion of the speech contained at least three messages to the United States. Schmidt's first said: "Strategic arms control limitations confined to the United States and the Soviet Union will inevitably impair the security of the West European members of the Alliance vis-à-vis Soviet military superiority if we do not succeed in removing the disparities of military power in Europe parallel to the SALT negotiations." In translation, this meant, "Your SALT policy is self-serving, and it shifts the balance of risk toward Western Europe."

The second message read, "You are ignoring our vital interests." Or, as the chancellor had put it, "SALT neutralizes [American and Soviet] nuclear capabilities. In Europe, this magnifies the significance of the disparities between East and West in nuclear, tactical and conventional weapons. . . . We in Europe must be particularly careful that these negotiations do not neglect the components of NATO's deterrent strategy."

The third message could be read as Schmidt's demand for new long-range weapons. "So long as this [the restoration of the balance through negotiations] is not the case, we must maintain the balance of the full range of deterrence strategy. The Alliance must, therefore, be ready to make available the means to support the present strategy."[40]

The essence of the plea, however, was profoundly political. It was a speech about great power insularity and European dependence, about trust betrayed and loyalty denied. It was a speech about the terms of alliance having turned against the Europeans and about Europe's place between the superpowers being threatened by Soviet intrusion and American indifference. While discoursing about the military balance, Helmut Schmidt was in fact talking about the political balance between the United States, the Soviet Union, and Western Europe. At the same time, he was charging Jimmy Carter with transgression against the three basic commandments of any alliance: you shall not redistribute risks; you shall not separate your fate from ours; and you shall not value the claims of adversaries more highly than the interests of allies.

Throughout the history of the Alliance, the smaller members have habitually articulated their political anxieties in the language of strategy. This pattern should not come as a surprise. Since the American commitment to Europe is ultimately rooted in a nuclear guarantee, any change in American nuclear policy—in the ensemble of arms, arms control, or doctrine—portends an ominous change in the nature of the overall relationship.[41] Nor is Europe's obsession with American strategy devoid of reality. First, familiarity breeds content, and there is safety in the status quo for dependents who cannot determine American policy but must suffer its consequences. Second, American strategy has always changed in response to events that detracted from the solidity of the American commitment—when a deteriorating nuclear balance increased America's own vulnerability. Third, any change in nuclear policy invariably spells a shift in the Soviet–American relationship toward either confrontation or collaboration; neither has ever reassured the Europeans. Finally, strategy is the language of legitimacy. For allies it is a breach of etiquette to proclaim openly, "We do not trust you." Yet it is perfectly legitimate for them to decry lapses in political faith by using the vernacular of doctrinal disputation to discourse on the finer points of nuclear theology.

Since faith was at stake, the Europeans—and the Germans in particular—drew little comfort from the reassurances of the Carter administration that the nuclear balance was stable and cruise missiles were less than miraculous. Throughout 1977 and 1978, Secretary of Defense Brown continued to insist (correctly) that there was no dearth of warheads in the U.S. strategic arsenal. Sufficient to cover any conceivable target of interest in the Soviet territory, they were also numerous enough to counterbalance the Soviet Union's Eurostrategic forces. Nor were there any gaps in the spectrum of deterrence: "The force has the capability to . . . respond at the appropriate level to varied provocations. In particular, we can cover targets of special concern to our allies."[42] He also pointed out that "cruise missiles have become a great preoccupation in Europe; they are seen as perhaps more of a panacea than they really are."[43]

While Brown was justified in deflating exaggerated expectations about the cruise missile, statements such as these (and they were repeated ad infinitum by other spokesmen of the administration) could not soothe European concerns precisely because they took European complaints at face value. The administration's responses were military answers to questions that were only ostensibly about nuclear strategy. What mattered to the Allies was not the military promise of the cruise missile, but the political impact of the promise denied. Indeed, since the cruise missile was but the most dramatic symbol of an entire American policy gone astray, such statements could only inflame European suspicions. Had not Jimmy Carter justified the cancellation of B-1 bomber production in mid-1977 by extolling the virtues of air-launched cruise missiles, which would extend the life of the aging B-52 bomber? If cruise missiles were less than a "panacea," why did the Soviets insist on stringent limitations, while pressing for noncircumvention and nontransfer clauses to boot?

Nations that depend on others for their security worry about their patron's intentions. When trust is low, almost anything can prove what is feared, and almost any issue will do as a test of the entire relationship. The cruise missile was predestined to fill that role to perfection. Because the Carter administration sought to dampen enthusiasm for this remote progeny of the German V-1, the Europeans came to believe ever more fervently in its military promise. Because the Russians sought to block Europe's access while busily adding to their own Eurostrategic arsenals (via the SS-20), the cruise missile assumed a pivotal role in the future of the European balance. And because the United States seemed poised to practice denial in league with the common adversary, the cruise missile would decide the largest question of them all: whether Europe was a subject or an object of great power politics.

Did the Europeans really want new long-range weapons? The question defies a simple answer. On the subministerial level of government, the members of NATO's High Level Group were quick to reach agreement on the principle of deployment—even though the American envoys, following the general direction of the Carter administration, initially approached the enterprise as an exercise in strategic pedagogy rather than in force procurement. Despite American reticence and continued reminders of strategic plenty, an Alliancewide consensus was fashioned as early as April 1978. As one European participant put it, "What emerged was very much European-driven." On the American side, the assessment is similar, though more hedged. "No doubt, what we were hearing was a European demand," and, "It was our perception that the Europeans wanted the hardware."[44]

Yet the actual decision was not made by a group of under secretaries meeting privately, but by their elected political masters in Washington, London, and Bonn when they met with the French president, Giscard d'Estaing, at the Western summit in Guadeloupe in January 1977. Given the upheaval the deployment decision has since caused within the Alliance and within the various body politics, each of the three key protagonists has remained modest about his own contribution—and none of them could be indifferent to the way history is written and rewritten. Jimmy Carter, James Callaghan, and Helmut Schmidt all fell from power before the first missiles arrived in Europe—Schmidt, in part, because of that decision. Both James Callaghan and Helmut Schmidt continued to adhere to it while their own parties—Labour in Britain and the Social Democrats in Germany—turned first against nuclear weapons and then against their party leaders. As the drama unfolded, Callaghan and Schmidt had no incentive to stress the prominent role they had played in the genesis of the INF deployment, and neither did Labour and the Social Democrats as they mounted their strident antinuclear campaigns from the opposition benches.

The Callaghan government had laid out the rationale for deployment as early as August 1978, but the document then dispatched by Defense Secretary Fred Mulley to Harold Brown remains a closely guarded secret.[45] The closest a European government ever came to a public commitment was in a television interview by Defense Minister Georg Leber of Germany in December 1977, and then the commitment was in conceptual terms only. Leber proclaimed that Europe must not be excluded from the options embodied in cruise missile technology. In the face of Soviet Eurostrategic superiority, he stressed the need for "compensatory armament" and suggested that NATO add a "fourth leg"—a continental-range arsenal—to its classic deterrent triad.[46] Throughout 1977 and 1978 Leber kept insisting in private that any range limit for ground-launched cruise missiles below 1,500 kilometers was unacceptable to the German government.

Helmut Schmidt, who for a while had prided himself for being "one of the authors" of the Brussels Decision, would soon come to deny paternity as he was drawn into an ultimately futile struggle for political survival that pitted him against his own party. Queried in 1981, a year before he resigned, about whether the "TNF proposal was a Schmidt idea," he replied that Jimmy Carter had "brought the proposal" to Guadeloupe. "No, it was not my idea. I don't know whose idea it was. . . . I never was enthusiastic about [the idea]. I never was. My idea had been— and I have publicly criticized the Americans for in SALT 2 [sic] not to deal with the question of eurostrategic missiles, as if they didn't matter. This was my idea."[47]

This was a plausible rendering of Schmidt's aspirations—and of his ambivalence. Throughout the two and a half years that led up to the 1979 Brussels Decision, the German chancellor was primarily concerned, if not obsessed, with Carter's indifference to the separate nuclear threat the Soviets were arraying against Western Europe. He worried about the political profits the Soviets would draw from their SS-20 investment ("an instrument of political pressure"[48]) and about the political price Europe would have to pay for Carter's Big Two–oriented SALT posture. Yet he was also haunted by the domestic and détente costs that counter-deployment would exact. He therefore preferred the solution of arms control to arms. His ambivalence was duly noted by Zbigniew Brzezinski on the occasion of the Guadeloupe summit: "Throughout, he was the one who was most concerned about the Soviet nuclear threat in Europe and the least inclined to agree to any firm response."[49]

On the other hand, Schmidt's disclaimers betray an unwillingness to face consequences. With his keen sense for the necessities of political and military balance in Europe, it could not have escaped the chancellor that to will the end was also to will the means. If the political problem stemmed from weapons hoarded by the Soviets (SS-20) and withheld by the Americans (cruise missiles), then the ultimate solution would also have to draw on weapons. Nor has arms control ever restored the balance in the past; at best, it ratifies whatever distribution of military power prevails at the time of agreement. It was wishful thinking to deplore gaps in the spectrum of power without standing ready to close them. It was philosophy without consequences, and it was the logic of that philosophy that demanded a decision.

Nor was the decision at Guadeloupe made for the "wrong"—that is, merely military—reasons. It was a properly political response to a smoldering political failure that had reached its flash point nine months earlier. In the seclusion of St. Simons Island off Georgia, Jimmy Carter had decided in April 1978 against the production of enhanced radiation warheads (ERW), popularly known as "neutron bombs." With that abrupt reversal, an elaborately crafted house of cards—erected on the slenderest of foundations—had come tumbling down. It had been based on the president's emotional revulsion against ERW ("I wish I had never heard of this weapon"),[50] on Western Europe's aversion to shouldering the political costs of deployment, and on the Washington bureaucracy's earnest but haphazard attempt to turn both aversion and reluctance into acceptance. Like all nuclear Alliance issues, the ERW decision placed the worst strains on the Federal Republic. Germany was the natural locus of deployment for an antitank weapon like the enhanced radiation warhead, as well as the perfect pressure point for the Soviet Union. Within the country itself, the neutron bomb offered an ideal domestic weapon for Schmidt's antinuclear and détente-minded rivals within the Social Democratic Party. For the chancellor, these three factors added up to a decision better left to the United States to make.[51] It was a case of a frail commitment meeting with an uncertain demand, and the result was "deferral."

Fettered at home and about to be leashed by the Soviets, Schmidt embarked on an impossible balancing act with regard to INF. To dispel the dreaded specter of "singularity" that would cast Bonn into the unacceptable role of America's continental sword, at least one other nonnuclear state had to accept INF on its soil. To propitiate the Soviets, the chancellor flatly rejected any ownership or control over the cruise and Pershing II missiles to be stationed in Germany. And to propitiate his own party, Schmidt insisted on a "second track" that was to parallel—actually, to precede—the deployment. The long hiatus between the deployment decision and missile availability gave NATO four years to sell its nonexistent weapons in return for the elimination of a steadily growing arsenal of the real SS-20. In the time frame of day-to-day politics, four years approached an eternity. If arms control achieved its purpose, it would serve as a substitute for deployment; if not, arms control might at least provide an alibi for the task that threatened to rend the body politic and to provoke the Soviet Union.

The real risk, however, was that arms control would provide neither substitute nor alibi. If the process of negotiation did not offer a legitimate exit, it could not pacify those who, like the German Social Democrats, had grudgingly accepted the Brussels package only on the assumption that either track would end in nondeployment. If the negotiations did not dispatch the need for the missiles, their failure—conveniently blamed on American "insincerity"—would provide an alibi for rejection. When faced with the reality of deployment at the end of 1983, the Dutch, British, and German socialists responded precisely in terms of this *arrière-pensée*, by opposing the missiles in favor of unconditional negotiations. For them the process was the end, with arms control serving not as a means toward restoration of the military balance but as a symbol of permanent détente. Yet even those who did not carry a hidden agenda were bound to be frustrated. There was no realistic chance that arms control alone could deliver on its loftiest promise and achieve equality at a lower level of arms.

While the West thought in terms of equality—either no missiles or equal numbers for both sides—the Soviet Union hardly countenanced the legitimacy of that principle. Nor could Moscow possibly do so, given the fundamental logic of its Eurostrategic policy in the early 1980s. Indeed, those in the West who believed in the promise of arms control in isolation from arms procurement confronted the Soviets with an impossible (if not impertinent) demand. In its zero-option version, the Western offer was asking the Soviet Union to dismantle an historic strategic advantage over Western Europe.[52] In exchange for giving up a merely potential force—of minor proportions no less (464 cruise and 108 Pershing II missiles)—the United States proposed that the Soviet Union nullify the fruits of its quarter-century quest for strategic superiority on the Continent.

Even in their more modest guises—equal numbers at lower levels—Western arms control proposals aspired to the impossible. As *Pravda* put it on October 3, 1983, the American position was based on the "unacceptable premise that the USSR should reduce its missiles while the United States would deploy its own." To suggest an arms control arrangement whereby one side would increase its strength while the other would diminish his defied both logic and experience. The logic of international politics is based on reciprocity, and it bids each side to yield only assets of equal value. Nor does experience tell a different story. Between nations there are no free gifts; historically, at least, arms control has ratified but never restored the balance of power. In short, those who believed that arms control could solve the problem posed by Soviet arms were asking the Soviet Union not only to accept a net loss of power but to consecrate it by formal agreement as well.

Combining modest means with vast ambitions, the two-track approach was bound for derailment from the very beginning. (And derail it did when the Soviets walked out of the Geneva arms control talks on November 23, 1983, the day the first Pershing II missile components arrived in Europe.) The arms control track aimed at an effortless but fundamental revision of the European status quo in favor of the West. In essence, NATO was asking the Soviet Union to relinquish a quasi-imperial advantage that it had acquired in a fit of American absentmindedness.

In the 1950s the global nuclear balance between the United States and the Soviet Union was virtually identical with the balance of forces in and around Europe. Unable to strike at the Soviet Union directly, the United States had deployed a number of forward-based systems in Western Europe, Turkey, and North America. (These consisted primarily of B-47 bombers and Thor/Jupiter missiles.) Hobbled by similar technological constraints, the Soviet Union counterdeployed Tu-16 medium-range bombers, followed by SS-3, SS-4, and SS-5 missiles.[53] That balance came unhinged when the United States, obeying the logic of technology rather than the (political) logic of reciprocity, started to retire these systems in 1963. With the advent of the Atlas and the Polaris A1, proximity to the Soviet homeland began to spell vulnerability rather than strategic advantage.[54] The last system to be withdrawn was a precursor of the modern cruise missile, the Mace B. Its history is not without irony. A total of 96 Mace Bs were "singularly" deployed in Germany until 1969. With a maximum range of 2,200 kilometers, they could reach beyond Moscow, and they would later become the object of Helmut Schmidt's fond recollections. He claimed, "from hindsight," that the withdrawal of these systems had been ". . . [the] wrong step. They should have been modernized rather than dismantled."[55]

With the benefit of hindsight, he was indeed right to deplore the high political price of technological progress. The withdrawal of American intermediate-range systems did not inspire the Soviets to regard their own Euromissiles as an atavistic luxury. Although their original targets (and raison dêtre) had disappeared, Soviet SS-4 and SS-5 stayed in place. Indeed, shortly after the last Mace B was returned to the United States around 1970, the SS-20 entered development. Also at that time, a substantial portion of the Soviet SS-11 intercontinental missile potential (the commonly accepted figure is 120 with a one-megaton warhead each) was targeted at Europe—complemented by SS-19 ICBMs after 1974. These represented about 10 percent of the total land-based ICBM force as of 1970, and their message was even louder than the signal the Soviet Union sent by its nonreduction of the SS-4 and SS-5. To channel a significant portion of strategic systems into a European mission at a time when the Soviet Union was struggling to achieve global parity, clearly attested "to the very great importance that Soviet military leaders attached to their [theater] posture."[56]

When placed in the proper political context, the numbers may even understate the point. The Soviets were moving to augment (not just to modernize) their Eurostrategic arsenal at a time when the reasons for so doing were palpably declining. While the United States had withdrawn the last of its Euromissiles, the West was moving to deliver the grand prize of détente and Ostpolitik to the Soviet Union. By dint of SALT I, the United States bestowed the badge of parity on the Soviet Union in 1972. During the same year, the Federal Republic ratified what it had resisted for twenty years: the recognition of the German Democratic Republic and the redrawn borders in the East—in other words, a ratification of the Soviet Union's postwar gains in Europe. Subsequently, the 35-nation Conference on Security and Cooperation in Europe (CSCE) reaffirmed what the United States and the Federal Republic had already delivered: the formal acceptance of the status quo. It was that diplomatic constellation that dramatized the political significance of the SS-20 build-up to come.

From 1976 onward, Soviet SS-20 deployments proceeded at an unbroken rhythm of fifty missiles per year. That pace was out of all proportion to what the French and the British were adding to their national deterrents, let alone to the virtual absence of Western INF modernization and the overall decline in Western defense spending throughout the 1970s. From 1969 to the final days of 1983, there was not a single land-based American missile in Western Europe that could strike the Soviet homeland. Nor do bureaucratic inertia or their own modernization needs adequately explain the Soviet procurement pattern. They certainly do not explain the astounding rigidity of the Soviet effort in the face of mounting and audible Western discomfort. Indeed, the Soviets did not react until just before the Brussels Decision of December 1979, and then it was with threats softened only by offers of a freeze that would have cemented an already considerable advantage. In so acting, the Soviets confronted the West with a profoundly unsettling conception of détente. While they were willing to take (and to give) on the level of political and economic détente, they would not yield on military matters, where they enjoyed a powerful and growing advantage.

As a result, the political contest that had rent the Alliance in the early Carter years shifted inexorably into the East–West arena. Having restored the intra-Western balance of risks and control, the Brussels Decision set the stage for a fierce battle over the nature of Europe's order. Once again, Pershing II, cruise, and SS-20 missiles were but the most vivid symbols of the contest. The West was essentially trying to restore the right to equality it had relinquished in a fit of absentmindedness; the Soviet Union, on the other hand, was seeking to reaffirm its quasi-imperial advantage by trying to inflict a massive political defeat on the West. Given the enormity of the stakes, it was clear that arms control was doomed to failure.

The issue was the inequality of the strategic relationship between the Soviet Union and Western Europe, and the political perceptions such a "favorable correlation of forces," to use the Russian vernacular, would engender among the European members of NATO. Also at stake was the nature of the relationship between the United States and its European allies. By claiming that the United States had no right to deploy certain categories of weapons in the service of extended deterrence, the

Soviet Union was in fact challenging the very core of that relationship while demanding for itself a veto power over Western defense choices. The entire postwar order in Europe depends on America's commitment to unsheathe its nuclear sword for the sake of its allies. That foundation would surely crumble if the Soviets were allowed to determine the means by which the United States will uphold its security guarantee for Western Europe.

A steadily growing SS-20 potential was the military counterpart of nontransfer and noncircumvention clauses in the context of SALT. If the former increased the separate threat to Western Europe, Soviet insistence on the latter sought not only to deny compensation to the Europeans but also to accentuate the political separation of the United States and its allies. To succeed on both fronts would advance some long-held Soviet objectives: to sow doubts about the solidity of America's security pledge; to divide allies from allies; and to gain a commanding position on the Continent from which the Soviet Union could dictate the terms of the relationship to them all.

The issue, then, was an ancient Soviet policy that, in contemporary parlance, goes by the name of *decoupling*. Its objects were to dramatize Western Europe's hostage role and to deny the United States the means by which its countervailing power could be inserted into the European balance. That this was the essential thrust of Soviet policy emerges clearly from all Soviet arms control proposals in the four years between the Brussels Decision and the start of deployment in late 1983.[57]

The Soviet Union shifted from a refusal to negotiate, to offers of freezes and moratoriums; from freeze to limited withdrawal; from withdrawal to partial launcher reductions; and then from launcher to warhead cuts. The best offer, made in October 1983, was a limit of 140 SS-20 missiles — 22 launchers less than the total of 162 French and British missiles the Soviets had regularly defined as a benchmark for Eurostrategic equality. That figure also promised a substantial reduction from the 243 SS-20 missiles then stationed west of the Urals. Yet it was precisely this flexibility that underlined the essential point, and one from which the Soviets never budged: there could be no deployment of American weapons.[58] Nor did the public diplomacy offensive unleashed by the Soviets in Western Europe have any objective other than the total collapse of the deployment track. In essence, the Soviet Union sought to gain on the streets what it could not hope to achieve at the Geneva bargaining table: "the preservation of the equality principle," which in Soviet eyes meant "renouncing the deployment of new American intermediate-range missiles in Western Europe."[59]

In keeping with time-honored practice, Soviet efforts were concentrated on West Germany—the country at once most dependent on extended deterrence and least able to bear the political costs of deployment. If war broke out, the Federal Republic "did not have the slightest chance of survival."[60] Even short of war, West Germany would have to pay in the precious coinage of détente and national aspirations. According to Andropov, "Relations between our two countries will be bound to suffer," while the two Germanys would have to "look at one another through thick palisades of missiles."[61] Soviet blandishments were also focused on the Federal Republic. In the summer of 1980, at the height of Soviet-American tension over Afghanistan, Brezhnev rewarded Schmidt's détente-minded mission to Moscow with a promise to engage in INF arms control talks, something the Soviets had heretofore rejected. After Helmut Schmidt's fall from power in the fall of 1982, Soviet leaders would regularly host prominent Social Democrat visitors, always dispatching them homeward with the gift of tantalizing but vague concessions. And they would continuously remind the West Germans of their stake in détente. "We would like the Federal Republic to display its own self," said Foreign Minister Gromyko just prior to the critical March 1983 elections, "to be guided by its own interest and to yield to foreign influences if they do not meet these interests, the interests of maintaining good relations with the Soviet Union."[62]

That was continuity par excellence. The Federal Republic is the fulcrum of the East–West balance in Europe; even a minor shift in the position of West Germany threatens a major, if not total, shift in the European balance. Accordingly, the Euromissile battle was but the third act in the oldest of Europe's postwar dramas, with Germany representing both the stage and the prize. In the early 1950s the Soviets had tried to forestall the Federal Republic's inclusion in the Western coalition with offers of neutralization-cum-reunification. In the late 1950s they mounted a massive pressure campaign—which escalated into the Berlin Ultimatum—to keep American battlefield nuclear weapons out of German hands. Twenty years later the Federal Republic found itself once more at the fulcrum of the balance and in the spotlight of Soviet–American rivalry. It was in Germany where the fate of the INF deployment was going to be decided.

At stake were the terms of the postwar European order; in the end, strategy was completely dwarfed by politics denuded of all its finery. The basic issue was no longer military rationales enveloped in the subtleties of nuclear technology, but a raw test of wills. Would the Soviet Union impose its quasi-imperial conception of security on NATO's nuclear arrangements? Or would the Alliance live up to its raison d'être and deny the Soviet Union the great political advantage that flows from its geographical position and superior might?

Deterrence and the European Order

The Soviet Union lost a momentous battle of wills when the first Pershing II components arrived in Germany on November 23, 1983. To conclude that politics had corrupted strategy, that an uncertain military rationale had been needlessly transfigured into a grand political principle, is to ignore the political nature of all strategic disputes in Europe—indeed, to ignore the importance of politics as such. Politics is about power, and a test of wills is nothing but a nonviolent verdict on the balance of power among nations. It is a test of strength short of war, and to yield to great pressure even in peacetime is to yield on the very raison d'être of alliance, which is to maintain freedom of choice and to deny an opponent the political fruits of his military power.

Nor did NATO engage in the test for frivolous reasons. If it had failed to respond, the Alliance would have conceded what it was founded to prevent: the conversion of a surfeit of Soviet strength into political dominance. As in clashes past, the missile issue was but a reflection of the larger conflict in and over Europe. Perhaps the conflict could have remained latent—if the West had solved its internal nuclear problems at an earlier stage, or if the Soviet Union had confronted the Alliance with a less expansive notion of its own security. Yet once Moscow set out to undo the Brussels Decision, the question was not, Shall we deploy? but, Shall we submit? To defer on a question of nuclear weapons was no trivial matter. It meant submitting on a fundamental of the military balance: namely, America's countervailing strength as the basic condition of Europe's postwar order.

It is easy to denigrate the military arguments in favor of the INF deployment. The rationale promulgated by Western governments is that it was necessary to "counter" the Soviet SS-20 build-up. But if "counter" meant "counterforce," then 464 slow-flying cruise missiles were inadequate for the task of destroying over 300 SS-20 missiles capable of reaching into Western Europe. If "counter" merely referred to a numerical equivalent, 572 Western systems were also no match for more than 1,200 warheads on Soviet SS-20 and SS-4 missiles. Nor were these numbers sufficient to regain escalation dominance. For that purpose, 2,000 systems (as initially envisioned by Pentagon planners) would have been closer to the mark, and then only in the context of restoring American strategic superiority. Another rationale focused on selective options (to be executed with precision-delivered warheads in the 10–60-kiloton range), but that rationale concealed a debatable premise: that selective strikes could be credibly threatened and victoriously traded when escalation dominance was no longer in Western hands.

Another major rationale concerned survivability and penetrability. Cruise missiles will evidently have an edge over attack aircraft for some time to come. Even the most modern Soviet surface-to-air missiles depend on line-of-sight target acquisition, and that is a difficult if not futile task in the face of missiles approaching at the treetop level. "Look down, shoot down" airborne systems have a better chance at interception, but still have the problem of discrimination—how to distinguish between "clutter" and a diminutive aggressor flying close to the ground. (Future versions of the cruise missile will include stealth technologies and radar-confusing countermeasures.) And effective defenses against Pershing II missiles, once they are launched, are still an ambition rather than a reality.

The question of survivability produces even more ambiguous answers. Almost half of the cruise missiles and all of the Pershing II missiles were assigned to six bases close to Warsaw Pact territory.[63] None of them—including those missiles stationed in Italy and Britain—could survive a nuclear "bolt out of the blue." Yet that is a hypothetical scenario. In reality, there would be some time for dispersal, and once mobility is assumed, Soviet planners would have to allocate a great number of warheads to destroy them. They would have to contend with twenty-nine flights of cruise missiles (consisting of four transporter-launchers with four missiles each) and thirty-six Pershing II platoons (with three missiles each). These would be either concealed (especially the cruise missiles with their off-the-road transportability), or in motion. If in concealment, they could not be targeted with precision (unless there was perfect, real-time intelligence on the ground). If in motion, they would also require saturation bombing. In either case, the Soviets might have to expend a very large number of warheads per launch group, which does not promise a very attractive force-exchange ratio.[64] On the other hand, mobility and camouflage are constrained by the dense habitation patterns of Western Europe (as well as by the Pershing's dependence on presurveyed launch sites). If survivability had been the dominant criterion, NATO should have dispatched its missiles to sea.

Nor is the argument from the premise of extended deterrence wholly plausible if—as many critics have done—its most obvious element is stressed: the matter of credibility. Capable of striking the Soviet Union,

American missiles on Allied territory pose an ancient dilemma. An American president would not launch them more readily than strategic weapons unless he could be sure of not having to pay the price of an intercontinental exchange. Yet even if he were so reassured, his allies would not be, for it is they who provide the theater of limited nuclear war.

Such an assessment derives, however, from a narrow view of extended deterrence. Being a psychological process, deterrence must properly be located in the head of the would-be aggressor. What are the Soviets' calculations as they contemplate an attack on Western Europe? Pershing II and cruise missiles embody four sobering characteristics. They are land-based, long-range, American, and "strategic," by Moscow's own definition. Literally placed in the path of any Soviet advance, they cannot be circumvented. Capable of reaching Soviet territory, they cannot be ignored. And thus, they must be destroyed. Yet these are American weapons, and like all U.S. forces in Europe, they narrow the gap of sovereignty and geography; they serve notice that the United States cannot claim indifference to an aggression against its allies. Most importantly, however, these missiles are *strategic,* by the Soviet Union's own reckoning. In attacking Western Europe, they would have to attack not only American conventional forces but also part of America's strategic arsenal.

Accordingly, the geographic distinction between Pershing II and Minuteman III pales, as does the distinction between American and European territory. Since the Soviets could not hope to preempt all of the Europe-based systems, they must countenance the possibility of being hit in return. If they must anticipate American strikes, they could not confine their salvos to America's Europotential only — aiming, as it were, at their adversary's switchblade while leaving his sword intact. At least, this is not how the Soviets see their predicament. As they have put it themselves,

It ought to be quite clear that . . . any preemptive nuclear strike is senseless unless it destroys or at least substantially weakens the strategic nuclear potential of the other side's retaliatory capability. . . . A first strike in Western Europe would have no sense from any point of view, for it would only expose our country to riposte by an absolutely intact U.S. strategic arsenal.[65]

In other words, the Soviets must attack the entire panoply of the United States if they want to strike at Europe. Raising the specter of all-out war, such a decision is approached with exponentially greater caution than a war that would promise to be limited to Europe. In this seamless web linking regional and global conflict lies the very essence of extended deterrence.

It is therefore misleading to question the military rationale of the Euromissiles—that they are either too slow (the GLCM) or too fast (the Pershing II); that they are too few (to yield "real" options) or too many (to avoid provoking the Soviets); that they can do too much (inflict strategic damage) or too little (against the mobile SS-20). The point is that cruise and Pershing II missiles are political weapons. They were intended to provide additional reassurance, not additional military options. Their mission was not to destroy military targets but to pierce territorial sanctuaries. They were the paradoxical answer to the problem of parity. For the sake of extended deterrence, the United States had to become absolutely vulnerable once it was no longer absolutely invulnerable. In the golden age of extended deterrence, complete immunity to Soviet strikes made for the complete credibility of America's threats. As one dwindled, so did the other—posing the ultimate risk of abandonment in a war that might start as well as end in Europe. Hence the relentless European search for "coupling," which is just another word for homogenizing the risks and extending vulnerability westward. Nor is it so paradoxical for the weak to seek safety through the exposure of the strong. If a client can deflect threats to himself onto his protector, he reaps a triple gain. He limits his patron's choices; he forces the patron to accept all dangers as indivisible; and as a result of these two consequences, he can signal to their common adversary, "If you attack me, you unleash global war."

The ultimate logic of the Euromissiles was the destruction of sanctuaries. If all are going to be entangled in war, all are going to be equally vulnerable. If all are equally vulnerable, all will be equally safe. Threatening Soviet soil while forging a solid escalatory link to America's strategic arsenal, these missiles point both ways, as it were. Euromissiles are poised to carry nuclear destruction into the territory of both superpowers, promising to defy any traditional distinction between "small" and "big" wars; that is the murderous foundation on which the safety of lesser allies thrives.

It is hard to exaggerate the political, if not historical, significance of the missile deployment. By stationing Pershing II and cruise missiles in Western Europe, the United States accepted a burden that few great powers have wittingly shouldered in the past. The United States allowed its allies to shift part of the common existential risk from their territories to its own. In turn, the Europeans paid a heavy political price in the currency of domestic cohesion rent and diplomatic opportunities forgone (vis-à-vis the East). Were the costs too high? Not if they are measured against the stability of the European order, which the Alliance was founded to maintain on Western terms. The missiles may have changed only a small feature of the military milieu, but the political consequences are far larger than their numbers would suggest. By accepting extra risks, the United States reaffirmed the security bargain struck in the aftermath of World War II. By resisting domestic disaffection and external pressure, the Europeans reminded the Soviet Union that its definition of "equal security" had spelled neither equality nor security for the western half of the Continent. By meeting these respective challenges, the United States and Europe restored some crucial balances that had been endangered by American neglect and by Soviet insistence on a controlling voice in the European order. On March 15, 1985, the Belgian parliament approved the immediate deployment of sixteen cruise missiles, over the dissenting votes of Socialists, Communists, Greens, and the Flemish, as well as Walloon, nationalists. One year later, on February 28, 1986, the Dutch legislature ended six years of agonizing domestic debate by also deciding in favor of the deployment scheduled to begin in 1988 — over the opposition of the Labor party (PVdA). The Belgian and Dutch commitments had been in doubt ever since the Brussels Decision in December of 1979. In the end they did follow the lead of the three large host countries: Britain, Italy, and West Germany. That outcome suggested that the center continued to hold, which is no small achievement in an age of nuclear parity that is said to pose mortal dangers to the health of alliances.

Nor did the deployment destroy the prospects of arms control, as the Soviets were pretending when they walked out of the Geneva negotiations in 1983. Negotiations resumed in 1985. By the time President Reagan and General-Secretary Mikhail Gorbachev met at the Reykjavík Summit in 1986, the Soviets had even accepted the fabled zero option proposed by the West in November of 1981, which foresaw the total elimination of medium-range missiles in Europe. Though the comprehensive arms control package was rent asunder in the last hour of the Hofdi House meeting, Gorbachev resurrected the "zero solution" on February 28, 1987, by offering to negotiate on long-range INF independent of all other issues, such as the Strategic Defense Initiative. It could fairly be concluded that the Soviet Union's failure to gain a veto power over Western defense choices had played a key role in its change of heart. Victorious in the great test of wills of the 1980s, the Alliance had evidently forced a recalculation of Soviet strategy. Instead of threatening a "dense palisade of missiles," Gorbachev invited the West Europeans to join him in the "common house of Europe." A benign vision, it did not seem to change the basic game of Soviet Westpolitik. Gorbachev's call for a new European architecture echoed Soviet appeals of the 1950s for "denuclearization" and "collective security" arrangements, which would have consecrated the Soviet Union's natural preponderance while either diminishing or excluding the American presence as the extracontinental balancer.

And so there is no end to the lesson. By the time The Hague conclusively reaffirmed the Dutch commitment, in the spring of 1986, NATO's nuclear drama had merely come full circle—not to an end. Precisely at that moment, the stage was set for a replay of the drama with different props and actors. Ronald Reagan—who had used Jimmy Carter's SALT II agreement as the very symbol of the U.S. fall from power—was now eager to crown his second term with a sweeping arms agreement that would include "deep cuts" on the strategic level and the total elimination of INF on the European level. As a result, Reagan began to raise the same anxieties that had set the Allies against Jimmy Carter a decade earlier, which triggered the tortuous process of resentment and reassurance that would eventually culminate in the deployment of cruise and Pershing II missiles.

Though the zero solution had been agreed policy since November 1981—when President Reagan first raised it to the level of official, NATO-wide proclamation—the European allies were not assured, and predictably so.[66] To denude Western Europe of American missiles viewed by the Soviets as strategic, would be to withdraw the great political prize the Europeans had gained from deployment: the fusion—symbolized by land-based, long-range weapons—of European and American strategic space. Having committed themselves to the zero option as a palliative to the antinuclear protest movement, the West European governments could hardly attack the president directly only five years later. But the unanimous message emanating from London, Paris, and Bonn virtually echoed what Helmut Schmidt had said to Jimmy Carter in 1977.

In the voice of the French foreign minister, Jean-Bernard Raimond, "A negotiation that would lead to the total elimination of U.S. nuclear arms in Europe, without remedying the imbalance in the conventional and chemical arms area, would be dangerous for the security of the continent."[67] The former West German chief-of-staff, Wolfgang Altenburg, speaking as chairman of NATO's Military Committee, put it more bluntly: "We need armaments which undercut any Soviet assumption that Europe's security might be decoupled from America's strategic nuclear potential."[68] Just as Helmut Schmidt had worried about regional imbalances being dramatized by global agreement (in SALT II), the Germans now worried about the possibility that a zero balance on the INF level would expand the threat on the short-range nuclear and conventional levels.

At the bottom of the ladder, the Soviets had meanwhile assembled some 900 shorter range missiles (FROG/SS-21, SCUD-B/SS-23, and SS-12/22, with ranges from 80 to 900 kilometers), which could handle many of the targeting tasks previously assigned to the SS-20. And for the West Germans, a 120-kilometer missile stationed in East Germany was hardly less worrisome than an SS-20 fired from the distant reaches of the Soviet Union, because *both* could hit West German space. Hence Defense Minister Manfred Wörner's double plea: A conventional balance had to *precede* zero on INF; and there would have to be nuclear compensation for cruise and Pershing II missiles—in the form of an enlarged short-range panoply and airborne or sea-based U.S. nuclear weapons.[69]

In the aftermath of Reykjavík, Chancellor Kohl traveled to the United States, where he virtually repeated Helmut Schmidt to drive home an ancient German message: "The vision of a denuclearized world, which emanates from President Reagan's Strategic Defense Initiative and which is mirrored in Secretary-General Gorbachev's [Reykjavík] proposal, would fundamentally change current alliance strategy at the expense of the Europeans, unless the givens were transformed—like the enormous conventional edge of the Soviets."[70] He was followed by the French prime minister, Jacques Chirac, who demanded: "An agreement on medium-range missiles must not undercut the overall balance of nuclear forces, and must not award an advantage in short-range missiles" that would negate the value of an INF accord.[71]

That was continuity par excellence. Like Schmidt a decade earlier, Kohl and Chirac were reasserting Western Europe's classic anxiety, what amounts to the basic law of European defense: Stabilizing any one level of the deterrence structure through arms control magnifies imbalances on the next level below, diminishing West European security. And like Schmidt, Kohl exhorted the United States to not shift the balance of risks against its European allies. If Schmidt had reacted to SALT II as a threat to the Eurostrategic balance, his successors worried about an INF accord that would either dramatize disparities on the shorter range level (SRINF, with a range of up to 1,000 kilometers) or lead to a SRINF agreement that would first accentuate the imbalance on the tactical-nuclear level and then the oldest imbalance of them all: the conventional-geographical one. "An agreement on weapons with a range from 500 to 1,000 kilometers only," said Chancellor Kohl, "would neglect precisely those weapons that threaten our country above all,"[72] meaning thousands of battlefield and shortest-range forces that are destined to explode in Germany, and in Germany only. And on the conventional-geographical level lurked the oldest specter of them all: a Europe eventually denuded of American nuclear weapons. These had been inserted into the balance decades ago to fuse Europe's and America's strategic fates, hence to deny the Soviet Union the dominance normally conferred by superior conventional might and natural geographic advantage. And quite logically, the Soviet Union had, from the 1950s onward, never ceased to insist on the denuclearization of NATO's defenses in order to unshackle its conventional strength from the debilitating constraints posed by American nuclear weapons.

Nor had Gorbachev's disarmament-minded policy really changed another ancient Soviet game. Although by 1987 he stood ready to dispense with a large armory of INF and SRINF in the context of the "double-zero" solution, the basic thrust remained a veto over NATO's nuclear choices in the service of extended deterrence. And so the United States was asked to practice self-denial in ways that recalled the "non-transfer" and "non-circumvention" clauses tabled by the Soviets in the 1970s. The United States was to forego the option of converting its Pershing II into a shorter-range version (e.g., a Pershing Ib) for potential deployment by the West Germans whose 72 Pershing Ia with American warheads were rapidly approaching obsolescence. Neither was the United States to retain the option of converting land-based cruise missiles into a sea-borne type, hence to put some wherewithals of extended deterrence out to sea. These conditions echoed the oldest demand in the Soviet repertoire—for a Soviet *droit de regard* over Western security policy, a claim that was the central stake of the great Euromissile battle of the early 1980s.

Finally, the West Europeans were not heartened by the process that had brought the "zero solution" and denuclearization visions to the fore again—the progeny of precisely that "Big Twoism" that had obsessed Helmut Schmidt prior to his legendary 1977 speech before the I.I.S.S. in London. Citing European anxieties about superpower summitry, French Prime Minister Jacques Chirac dramatized the oldest of Europe's traumas: Once more "decisions vital to the security of Europe could be taken without Europe really having any say in the matter."[73] That was, is, and will be the core of nuclear conflict between America and its allies, and it will continue as long as Europe's dependence endures.

Notes

1. This distinction was borrowed from Michael Mandelbaum, *The Nuclear Revolution: International Politics Before and After Hiroshima* (Cambridge: Cambridge University Press, 1981).
2. Senate Committee on Foreign Relations, *Nomination of Christian A. Herter: Hearing*, 86th Cong., 1st sess., 2 April 1959.
3. Robert S. McNamara, "The Military Role of Nuclear Weapons," *Foreign Affairs* (Fall 1983): 79. Publicly, however, McNamara faithfully stuck to alliance orthodoxy. A "large-scale Soviet attack on Western Europe . . . would compel us to respond immediately with whatever force was needed to halt the onslaught, even with tactical nuclear weapons, if necessary." In addition, "The defense of Europe against an all-out Soviet attack, even if such an attack were limited to non-nuclear means, would require the use of tactical nuclear weapons on our part." House Armed Services Committee, *Hearings on the Defense Program and 1964 Defense Budget*, 88th Cong., 2d sess., 27 Jan. 1963, pp. 56–58.
4. The alarm was first sounded by Fred C. Iklé, then director of the Arms Control and Disarmament Agency (ACDA), in an address before the Town Hall of California, August 31, 1976. As quoted in David Binder, "U.S. Aide Accuses Soviet on New Missile," *New York Times*, 1 Sept. 1976, p. 2.
5. Robert W. Tucker discusses the logic of nuclear isolationism (which he does not accept) in "Containment and the Search Alternatives: A Critique," in Aaron Wildavsky, ed., *Beyond Containment* (San Francisco: Institute for Contemporary Studies Press, 1983).
6. In the language of popular fantasy, this point was driven home by the American television film. "The Day After," aired in late 1983. The nuclear war that obliterated the movie's fictional Kansas town did not start with a bolt from the blue but followed escalation of a conflict in Central Europe.
7. Richard Burt, "NATO and Nuclear Deterrence" (Address at a conference of the Arms Control Association, Brussels, September 23, 1981), reprinted in Marsha M. Olive and Jeffrey D. Porro, eds., *Nuclear Weapons in Europe* (Lexington, Mass.: D.C. Heath/Lexington Books, 1983), p. 111.
8. Henry A. Kissinger, *The Troubled Partnership* (New York: McGraw-Hill, 1965), p. 128.
9. George W. Ball, "NATO and the Cuban Crisis" (Address to NATO Parliamentarians Conference, Paris, November 16, 1962), *Department of State Bulletin*, 3 Dec. 1962, p. 835.
10. Kissinger, *The Troubled Partnership*, pp. 130, 141.
11. *Major Addresses, Statements and Press Conferences of General Charles de Gaulle* (New York: French Embassy Press and Information Division, 1965), p. 214.
12. With some imagination, de Gaulle's blandishments in the early 1960s could have been construed as an invitation to the Germans to participate in the development of the *force de frappe*. On September 7, 1962, during a visit to West Germany, de Gaulle pleaded for a "solidarity of our weapons": "Armament . . ., in order to be effective, requires . . . that scientific, technical, indus-

NATO AND NUCLEAR WEAPONS / 89

trial and financial means and capabilities be utilized whose borders become more extended every day. France and Germany can assure themselves these means of power the more they can unite their capabilities." Address to the Academy of the Federal Armed Forces, September 7, 1962, as translated from Presse- und Informationsamt der Bundesregierung, *Bulletin*, no. 168, (1962): 1427.

During his January 14, 1963 press conference, de Gaulle replied to a question about German nuclear weapons: "It is up to Federal Germany to say what it wishes and to conduct its own policy. . . . It is evident that there is close solidarity between the defense of Germany and that of France, but each country is master of its own house, and I shall not answer for the German Government." (*Major Addresses* p. 221.)

13. Robert R. Bowie, "Strategy and the Atlantic Alliance," *International Organization* (Summer 1963): 730.
14. Dean Rusk, "Toward a New Dimension in Atlantic Partnership" (Address in Frankfurt, October 17, 1963), *Department of State Bulletin*, 11 Nov. 1963, p. 730.
15. Adenauer's defense minister, Franz Josef Strauss, had argued, "We have reasons to believe that the New Look [sic] of the American defense conception—the strengthening of conventional forces and the simultaneous raising of the nuclear threshold—will be interpreted, if also fallaciously, by Khrushchev as a renunciation of the nuclear deterrent strategy." As quoted in Walter Gong, "Der Minister, Berlin und die Bombe," *Die Zeit*, 1 September 1961, p. 3.
16. Bowie, "Strategy," p. 728.
17. Schlesinger, *A Thousand Days*, pp. 744-5.
18. Bowie, "Strategy," p. 728. The German defense minister, Kai-Uwe von Hassel, proclaimed at one point, "For the purpose of effective deterrence, I do not consider the unanimity principle acceptable in the long run." Address to the Western European Union (WEU), June 6, 1963, reprinted in the document collection, *Deutschland und die Welt* (Munich: Deutscher Taschenbuch-Verlag [dtv], 1964), p. 438.
19. "Erhard erwartet Chrustschow Ende Januar in Bonn," (Report on the Chancellor's press conference of 7 October 1964) *Frankfurter Allgemeine Zeitung*, 7 Oct. 1964.
20. Originally known as LRTNF—long-range theater nuclear forces—the weapons of contention were rechristened INF—intermediate-range nuclear forces—by the Reagan administration in 1981.
21. International Institute for Strategic Studies, *The Military Balance, 1977-1978* (London: IISS, 1977), p. 80.
22. James Schlesinger, *Report of Secretary of Defense to the Congress on FY 1976 and Transition Budgets, FY 1977 Authorization Request and FY 1976-1980 Defense Programs.* 5 Feb. 1975, p. I-16.
23. As quoted in Richard Burt, *New Weapons and Technologies: Debate and Directions*, Adelphi Papers, no. 126 (London: IISS, 1976), p. 21.
24. Richard M. Nixon, *United States Foreign Policy for the 1970s: A New Strategy for Peace*, Report to the U.S. Congress, 18 Feb. 1970, pp. 54-55.
25. James R. Schlesinger, *The Theater Nuclear Posture in Europe: A Report to the U.S. Congress in Compliance with Public Law 92-365*, April 1, 1975, p. 11. Mimeo.

26. Ibid., pp. 20–21.
27. "NATO Nuclear Planning Group Communique," NATO Press Service, Brussels, 17 June 1975.
28. Schlesinger, *Theater Nuclear Posture*, p. 15.
29. Ibid., p. 13.
30. Senate Foreign Relations Committee, *SALT and the NATO Allies: A Staff Report to the Subcommittee on European Affairs*, 96th Cong., 1st sess., Oct. 1979, p. 30.
31. For details of the Ford proposal, see the excellent study by Charles A. Sorrels, *U.S. Cruise Missile Programs* (New York: McGraw-Hill, 1983), ch. 6 (especially pp. 155–156), and Robert J. Art and Stephen E. Ockenden, "The Domestic Politics of Cruise Missile Development, 1970–1980," in Richard K. Betts, eds., *Cruise Missiles: Technology, Strategy, Politics* (Washington, D.C.: The Brookings Institution, 1981), p. 396–7.
32. For the text of the "Protocol," see *Department of State Bulletin* 79, no. 2028 (Special Issue, "Vienna: SALT II Agreement) (July 1979): 44–45.
33. For the full text of the statement of June 29, 1979, see U.S. Senate, *SALT and the NATO Allies*, pp. 36–37.
34. In congressional testimony, Secretary of State Henry Kissinger recounted: "In the negotiations conducted by the Ford Administration, proposed restrictions on cruise missiles were made conditional on comparable restrictions on the Backfire." Senate Foreign Relations Committee, *Hearings on the SALT II Treaty*, part 3, July–August 1979, pp. 169–70.
35. Harold Brown, "Defense Planning and Arms Control" (Address at the University of Rochester, April 13, 1977), as quoted in Sorrels, *U.S. Programs*, p. 156.
36. As quoted in Sorrels, *U.S. Programs*, p. 232 no. 69.
37. In the German case, anxiety was compounded by sheer resentment. A few months into his term, Carter had managed to affront Bonn across the full gamut of its policy. Carter's human rights forays threatened to disturb the carefully designed circles of German Ostpolitik. His antiproliferationist campaign against a multibillion-dollar complete-fuel-cycle sale to Brazil appeared to threaten the Federal Republic's leading position in nuclear technology. Carter's insistence that Germany act as a "locomotive" in the world economy (through domestic inflation) was a frontal assault on German economic orthodoxy. Nor were the Germans assured by PRM-10, a Presidential Review Memorandum leaked to the press in August 1977 that suggested NATO troops might have to fall back to the Rhine before regrouping for a counterattack against the invasion armies of the Warsaw Pact.
38. Helmut Schmidt, Address at the Ministerial Meeting of the North Atlantic Pact, May 10, 1977, reprinted in *Survival* (July/August 1977): 177–178.
39. David Aaron, interview with author in New York, 15 Feb. 1984.
40. Helmut Schmidt, "The 1977 Alastair Buchan Memorial Lecture," October 28, 1977, reprinted in *Survival* (January/February 1978): 3–4.
41. During the transition from massive retaliation to flexible response, Henry Kissinger observed, "Many of our Allies . . . cling to the status quo as the best guarantee of our reliability. Unilateral change of our strategic views has a symbolic quality for them. If we are able to alter our views about strategy, might

not the same be true of other commitments?" Kissinger, *The Troubled Partnership*, p. 98.

42. Harold Brown, *Department of Defense Annual Report, FY 1980*, 25 Jan. 1979, p. 79.

43. House Subcommittee on Defense Appropriations, *Hearings on Department of Defense Appropriations for FY 1979*, part 2; 8, 9, and 14 Feb. 1978, p. 715; Sorrels, *U.S. Programs*, p. 196.

44. Interviews with the author in Washington and London, November 1981.

45. For a report on the episode, see John Barry, "Labour and Cruise," *Sunday Times*, 6 Feb. 1982, p. 17.

46. As recounted by the interview, Lothar Ruehl, in his article, "Der Beschluss der NATO zur Einführung nuklearer Mittelstreckenwaffen," *Europa-Archiv* (April 1980): 102.

47. Helmut Schmidt, in a discussion with visiting American journalists, Chancellor's Office, Bonn, October 29, 1981, as quoted from the written English record provided by the Press and Information Office of the Federal Government, pp. 13 and 20.

48. Helmut Schmidt, "A Policy of Reliable Partnership," *Foreign Affairs* (Spring 1981): 747.

49. Brzezinski, *Power and Principle*, p. 295.

50. As quoted in ibid., p. 304.

51. Even so, the American decision was carefully hedged. The United States would authorize production of ERW, then offer arms control to the Soviet Union and deploy ERW only once such talks had failed. In addition, there was the "nonsingularity principle" that required at least one other European country to host ERW. Uncharitably, Brzezinski noted, "Schmidt had obviously maneuvered to make the decision appear as a purely American one." Ibid., p. 306.

52. On November 18, 1981, President Reagan offered to forego deployment in exchange for the dismantling of some 500 SS-4, SS-5, and SS-20 missiles. Department of State, *Current Policy Documents*, no. 346, 18, Nov. 1981.

53. For a detailed history of Soviet deployments, see Stephen M. Meyer, *Soviet Theater Nuclear Forces*, Part 2, *Capabilities and Implications*, Adelphi Papers, no. 188 (London: IISS, 1984), pp. 1–19.

54. The Atlas was a land-based intercontinental ballistic missile, and the Polaris A1 was a sea-launched ballistic missile.

55. "Schmidt's Calculablities" (Interview with Helmut Schmidt), *Economist*, 6 Oct. 1979, p. 49.

56. Meyer, *Capabilities and Implications*, p. 21.

57. For a concise analysis of the INF negotiations through late 1983 (when they ruptured), see Jed C. Snyder, "European Security, East–West Policy, and the INF Debate," *Orbis* (Winter 1984).

58. Hence it was only logical that the legendary "walk in the woods" solution, sketched by negotiators Yuli Kvitsinski and Paul Nitze, was disavowed in Moscow. The exploratory draft foresaw equal limits of seventy-five launchers for each side. Since each cruise missile launcher carries four GLCMs, while SS-20 came with a triple-warhead, that scheme would have given a small

warhead advantage to the West (300 to 225), counterbalanced by a Soviet monopoly on ballistic missiles.

59. TASS commentator Nikolai Sergeyev, "Gelegenheit zu Verhandlungen darf nicht versäumt werden," *Neues Deutschland*, 28 Nov. 1979.

60. Radio Moscow, December 18, 1979, as quoted in *Monitor* (Bonn), 19 Dec. 1979.

61. Chairman Yuri Andropov during his talks with Chancellor Helmut Kohl in July 1983, as quoted by Serge Schmemann, "Soviet Invokes German Partition in Warning Kohl on New Missiles," *New York Times*, 6 July 1983.

62. Andrei Gromyko, in a press conference in Bonn, January 18, 1983, as quoted in Dusko Doder, "Russia Seems to Favor German Nationalism if Armed Against U.S.," *International Herald Tribune*, 8 Feb. 1983.

63. Three bases for 108 Pershing II missiles are in southwest Germany; one cruise missile base each are in the Federal Republic, Holland, and Belgium (with a total of 192). Farther afield, 160 cruise missiles are assigned to England (Greenham Commons and Molesworth), and 112 to Italy (Comiso).

64. For some calculations of the force-exchange ratio, see Meyer, *Capabilities and Implications*, pp. 42–43. On the basis of a 40-kph travel speed for NATO launch vehicles and a 30-minute Soviet response time, the Soviets might have to target 48 warheads on each of the 65 launch groups, which comes to a total of 3,120.

65. "The Threat to Europe" (Moscow: Progress, 1981), p. 20.

66. For concise summaries of European worries at the beginning of 1986, see "US N-missiles plan welcomed by Nato allies," *Financial Times*, 25 Feb. 1986, and "Regierung sieht deutsche und europäische Interessen gewahrt," *Frankfurter Allgemeine Zeitung*, 25 Feb. 1986.

67. As quoted in Pierre Lellouche, "Let's Go Slow on 'Zero Zero'," *Newsweek*, 17 Nov. 1986, European edition, p. 20.

68. As quoted in "Die Nato sucht nach Ersatz für die Pershing," *Frankfurter Allgemeine Zeitung*, 5 Dec. 1986, p. 2.

69. As reported in "Kohl ist mein Partner, Kollege und Freund," *Frankfurter Allgemeine Zeitung*, 22 Oct. 1986, p. 1.

70. Helmut Kohl, Address to the Chicago Council on Foreign Relations, October 23, 1986, reprinted in *Bulletin*, no. 131 (1986): 1103.

71. Jacques Chirac (on the eve of his departure for the United States), as quoted in Jim Hoagland, "Chirac Asks U.S. Not to Let Pact Imperil Europe," *International Herald Tribune*, 30 March 1987.

72. "Erklärung des Bundeskanzlers," 15 May 1987. *Bulletin*, No. 46, 20 May 1987, p. 423.

73. As quoted in "Chirac Calls on Western Europe to Draw Up Own Security Charter," *International Herald Tribune*, 3 Dec. 1986.

CHAPTER 3

Peace and Populism

As the 1980s began, an old specter returned to haunt Europe – the specter of neutralism and nuclear pacifism. Most notably in the Continent's northern, Protestant parts, a thriving peace movement, flanked by the churches and Socialist parties, set out to batter the foundations of established security policy. In terms of noise and numbers, the domestic war over Euromissiles was the most spectacular upheaval in postwar European history. No conflict in this generation has torn at NATO's social fabric as fiercely as the battle over its 1979 decision to station some 500 cruise and Pershing II missiles on European soil. Millions of demonstrators massed in the towns and cities of Western Europe to block their deployment. The battle pitted old against young, Right against Left, leaders against followers. From the Netherlands to Norway, from Great Britain to Germany, the Brussels Decision would drive center-left parties toward the outer fringes of the political specturm. At least one government – Helmut Schmidt's in Bonn – fell largely because its leader could not stem the revolt of his own cohorts against nuclear weapons. It was the most impressive display of populist muscle in the postwar era.

Though the immediate targets were the accoutrements of extended deterrence, the attack would soon transcend the issues around neutron bombs and nuclear missiles. Suddenly, Western Europe seemed poised at a historical double-divide. One was a crisis of belief that found its

---

The terms *populist* and *populism,* as used in this chapter, should not be confused with the meaning derived from American history, where *populist* denoted a member of the American People's Party (1891–1904), advocates of free coinage of gold and silver, public ownership of utilities, and government support for agriculture. *Populism* is used here more generally, denoting the pursuit by self-selected bodies of political goals outside – and against – the institutions of representative government, using the tools of grass roots and protest politics (demonstrations, mass marches, blockades, etc.), that is, "mobilization from below."

outlet in the impulse of neutralism—the temptation to opt out, to refuse moral and political choice, and to ignore the reality of power in international affairs. It was not policies that hung in the balance, but their premises: the bond between Western Europe and the United States; the commitment to self-defense; indeed, the very idea of alliance as a freely chosen form of political community.

The other divide was marked by a crisis of political institutions. Many observers were quick to surmise that the antinuclear movement of the 1980s presaged something more fundamental than yet another cycle of nuclear anxiety, that it was more than just a rerun of the "Ban the Bomb" movement of the late 1950s. As one British commentator put it,

Pandora's Box has been opened. For good or ill, nuclear strategy in Europe has been a "leadership decision," taken by an informed few—a tiny nuclear elite—on behalf of an only-intermittently-interested many. . . . That no longer applies to Western Europe. The Pandora's Box of the nuclear age is public participation in nuclear policy-making; and the true message of the protest movement . . . is that the lid has opened.[1]

In other words, by the beginning of the 1980s, Western Europe was apparently caught in the midst of a true sea change, and the new nuclear politics, far from merely echoing the revolt of the late fifties, in fact betrayed a secular transformation that was here to stay. According to this widespread view, Western elites had finally lost their authority over national security policy, the last bastion of a disembodied *raison d'état*. The ramparts of the last arcanum had apparently crumbled before the onslaught of democracy's triumphant forward march. And the people, spearheaded by a militant protest movement, were about to outflank the institutional procedures of representative government and gain a permanent veto power over their nations' security policies.

Yet during the last days of 1983, the first missiles arrived on schedule in Britain and West Germany; in 1985, and 1986, the Belgian and Dutch parliaments approved the deployment of cruise missiles on their countries' soil. Compared to the din of the demonstrations, the installation of these missiles lacked even the minimal punch of a decent anticlimax. It was almost a nonevent, which stood in bizarre contrast to firmly embedded expectations. Had not the more venturesome spokesmen of the German peace movement promised to make the country "ungovernable"? What about those resolute women who had ringed the British cruise missile base at Greenham Commons with their bodies? Why did democratic governments coldly ignore a clamorous vox populi, not to mention the pollsters who had regularly reported hefty majorities against the deployment?

This chapter will analyze the battle and seek to explain why the peace movements of Western Europe failed in their announced goal, which was to block the deployment of intermediate nuclear forces (INF) in the five host countries: Britain, West Germany, Italy, the Netherlands, and Belgium. Second, it will address a larger question: Did the rise of the peace movement actually signal the transformation of West European politics? Was it just another "cyclical burst"—or a "secular break" with the traditional routines of governance? Had Western Europe's leadership elites lost their sway over national security policy?

Finally, what are the implications for the future of the Alliance? Does the 1980s protest movement presage the severance of those ligaments that have held the transatlantic compact together for decades—or was the revolt inspired by more limited objectives? In other words, was the target of discontent the deployment of nuclear weapons—or was it the tie to the United States? Was the target NATO itself?

Public Opinion and Public Policy

During the denouement of the Euromissile crisis in November of 1983, as the West German parliament delivered a solid vote in favor of the government's nuclear choice, only a few hundred demonstrators had gathered to mount a last minute vigil around the Bundestag. It was a far cry from the tens of thousands who had beleaguered Bonn in the fall of 1981 and the summer of 1982. Powerless to affect the vote inside, the protestors managed to score but one noisy point when, in desperation, they set off an air raid siren somewhere in the neighborhood. Unwittingly though, the helpless screech of the siren did make a point about the nature of Western politics that was all too often forgotten during the headier days of the peace movement: the distinction between moods and majorities, between the "input" of populist politics and the "output" of representative government.

Though shaken and occasionally demoralized, the established political institutions of Western Europe would hold their own because they were facing populist movements, not popular majorities. That many thoughtful observers would equate one with the other and proceed to write the obituaries for representative government, highlights a unique (and deceptive) advantage of modern protest movements. Their best allies are not the masses but the ersatz forces of mass participation—opinion research and television. Opinion polls tend to eclipse the classic mediating institutions; television magnifies the drama of dissent; both of these great accelerators of contemporary politics have given rise to the beguiling impression that the traditional democratic process has been replaced by a *plébiscite de tous les jours.* But even though the demonstrators habitually dominated the headlines and the television screens, their compatriots looked elsewhere during election time. In the crucial contests of 1983 (and again in 1987), it was Helmut Kohl and Margaret Thatcher who won at the polling booths, not their peace-minded rivals on the Left who had gambled on the antinuclear and anti-American sentiments of their electorates. Nor were the voters confronted with fuzzy choices. Germany's Christian Democrats and Britain's Conservatives had openly campaigned on a promissile platform. And the Left on either side of the Channel had left little doubt that it was out to derail the deployment.

The verdict of the ballot box should not have surprised anybody—least of all the professional pulse-takers who had little trouble in extracting antimissile pluralities, if not majorities, from their quarry. In Britain half of those polled were against the "government's decision to allow the American government to base cruise missiles on British soil." In West Germany the margin was 39 to 29 percent. In Belgium 42 percent opposed and 26 percent supported "the installation of American missiles on its territory." In the Netherlands the opposition added up to a strong majority, with 68 percent rejecting and only 28 percent affirming the siting of cruise missiles in their country.[2]

Yet here again, the most hackneyed truth about polling reemerged with remarkable consistency: the answer is shaped by the question. Strong resistance to the missiles was registered only when the respondents were confronted with a crude yes/no alternative. Nor is this a startling outcome, since nobody, European or American, looks forward to receiving new nuclear weapons on *his* soil. Indeed, when the question is posed in such bald terms, opposition turns into a veritable avalanche. A West German sample was asked, "Assume, new missiles were to be stationed *in your area.* Would you agree, or not?" Eight out of ten did not.[3]

Once the question becomes more complicated, and the respondent is allowed to "cue" on items other than just missiles, there is an almost total reversal of sentiments. In 1982 a Europeanwide poll posed the following query: "The countries of Western Europe and NATO are generally on the right course now, trying to negotiate arms reduction in Geneva, but also planning to deploy Pershing IIs and cruise missiles if the USSR does not reduce its own nuclear threat." Predictably, six out of ten Britons, almost 70 percent of West Germans, one-half of the French, 57 percent of the Italians, six out of ten Dutch, and 66 percent of the Belgians, opted for "agree."[4]

Did they do so because the wording was so suggestive? Perhaps. But there were two other twists to the question that were at least as crucial. First, the respondents were not faced with a simplistic choice between *Yes* or *No* to new missiles, let alone to nuclear weapons in their own backyard. Second, the query was framed within a wider political context. When missiles are linked to such "good" things as *NATO* and *negotiated reduction* and to such "bad" things as *Soviet nuclear threat*, nuclear weapons become part of a larger web of interests which reveals weights and priorities—and thus, a more complex picture of attitudes.

Within the wider fabric, strands such as *Soviet threat* and *alliance* regularly dwarf the more ambivalent thread of aversion to (new) nuclear weapons. Throughout Western Europe, the attachment to NATO remained as strong as ever during the battle over the Euromissiles. Even in the supposedly most antinuclear country—the nation whose name was appropriated to designate the dread disease of neutralist pacifism as *Hollanditis*—approximately three-quarters of the population preferred NATO membership to withdrawal. The number of those who affirmed the need for America's participation in Europe's defenses even increased slightly, to 62 percent in 1982. Nothing could dramatize the resilience of the Alliance fabric more vividly than another Dutch poll in 1982, which revealed that less than three out of ten would advocate leaving NATO even if the Alliance "holds on to nuclear weapons." Finally, nuclear pacifism, no matter how strident, was tempered by a strong dose of Calvinist realism. Thus, six out of ten Dutch attributed Europe's peace in part or in toto to the existence of nuclear weapons, and more than half believed that, come what may, "we shall have to learn to live with nuclear weapons."[5]

The peace movement failed to convert moods into majorities because antinuclear sentiment—no matter how widespread in countries like Holland or Norway—was but one among many in the cluster of attitudes people bring to bear on foreign policy and defense, and it was by no means the decisive one. Yet there was a more profound reason for the ultimate stultification of the antinuclear rebels. It is hard to harness the tide of popular disaffection if the masses do not care. Though the very epitome of brooding terror, nuclear weapons apparently do not terrorize enough to rouse the populace from its habitual lassitude in matters of defense and security policy. The public opinion experts label this phenomenon, *low issue salience* which, in turn, breaks down into the triptych of indifference, ignorance, and immunity.

In the fall of 1981, a West German sample was asked to respond to NATO's two-track approach, which foresaw negotiated reductions but also Western deployment of cruise and Pershing II missiles if arms control talks failed. About four in ten were favorably disposed, and about 20 percent were against NATO's two-track strategy. The most striking figures emerged from the rest of the sample, revealing a solid block of ignorance and indifference. Exactly 40 percent admitted that they either "did not know" or "did not care."[6]

The following fifteen months witnessed the grand flowering of the West German peace movement. According to the spokesmen of the Krefeld Appeal—a loosely bound umbrella organization of ecologist, church, and antinuclear groups—several million signatures were amassed on petitions against NATO's missile plans. In the fall of 1981 and the summer of 1982, hundreds of thousands marched on Bonn to protest the deployment. Prominent figures of political and moral authority—like the former chancellor, Willy Brandt, and many Protestant theologians—added their voices to the growing chorus of resentment. Key segments of the German media, both print and electronic, provided an ever increasing barrage of antinuclear fire, lavishly interspersed with nationalist and anti-American code words. And in 1983 the West Germans were asked once more to respond to the same question about the two-track decision, phrased as in 1981. The average voter was not impressed. He responded virtually as he had two years earlier, give or take a couple of percentage points. In other words, one and a half years of militant, nationwide agitation had done nothing to change the attitudes of the populace at large. Four out of ten still displayed either ignorance of indifference, signaling an astounding degree of immunity to the passions of the self-selected few.[7]

No less astounding was the protest movement's inability to implant its own conception of the real threat into the collective consciousness of the West German populace. Asked in 1982 whether the "stationing of American missiles" had made the "likelihood of an attack" greater, or whether "our security [had in fact] been improved," 22 percent opted for "greater likelihood of attack." Almost twice as many (42 percent) thought, however, that security had improved, and 32 percent believed that the missiles simply made no difference. In 1984, after the first batch of missiles had arrived and two years of activism had run its course, there was again virtually no change. If anything, trust in the missiles had increased—close to half of the sample felt that the accoutrements of extended deterrence *made in the USA* had actually enhanced German security.[8]

While concerns about nuclear weapons rose dramaticallly thoughout Western Europe in the early 1980s (when measured in isolation from other worries), such concerns remained too weak to galvanize a truly mass-based revolt. Perhaps the most fascinating evidence for the low salience of nuclear weapons emerges from a poll taken in an obscure town tucked away in the southwest corner of the Federal Republic. In the fall of 1983 pollsters descended on Schwäbisch-Gmünd to plumb the community's nuclear angst. The town was chosen for good reasons. It shares the neighborhood with an American army base that was being readied at that time to receive a detachment of Pershing II missiles. The German peace movement and Soviet public diplomacy had targeted the Pershing II as a particularly lethal affront to the Russian homeland and, hence, as a prime target for Soviet nuclear strikes. Predictably, close to 60 percent of the town's inhabitants opposed the deployment. But then the field workers asked another question. Would they—the presumptive victims—also "actively support" the peace movement. Only 15 percent replied that they would.[9]

The low import of nuclear weapons characterized the pattern throughout Western Europe. In the ranking of concerns, unemployment ran far ahead of any other worry for 60 to 80 percent of all respondents. Conversely, nuclear weapons were relegated to fifth place in France and Italy, and to fourth place in Britain. Only in Germany, the Netherlands, and Norway did nuclear weapons edge up to second place. Yet even in Holland and Germany, nuclear weapons were separated by a gulf of twenty-one and thirty-five percentage points, respectively, from the over-arching issue of unemployment.[10]

More significantly, the rank order of concerns reveals a striking reversal when respondents are asked to list their worries as factors in their voting behavior. Invited to relate their sentiments to political choice, the supposedly Hollanditis-infected Dutch dropped "new nuclear weapons in the Netherlands" to fourth place—after unemployment, social security, and crime.[11] These responses dovetailed nicely with the outcome of the 1982 election. The spearhead of the Dutch antinuclear revolt, the Inter-Church Peace Council (IKV), had urged the populace to treat nuclear weapons as the supreme issue of the campaign and to vote for the parties of the Left. Yet it was the Christian Democrats and the right-of-center Liberal party (VVD), who garnered a majority in the Second Chamber. The West German pattern was no different. Prior to the 1983 federal election, four issues emerged as the decisive ones: unemployment, social security, inflation, and the national debt. Conversely, foreign policy had sunk to the bottom of the agenda.[12] And the Social Democrats, after a hapless campaign of antinuclear and nationalist shibboleths, were left with their worst result since 1961.

In short, nuclear weapons were not a winning issue in Western Europe. At worst, they actually paved the road to electoral defeat, as in Britain where Labour emerged from the 1983 contest with its worst ballot showing since 1918. Old-time partisans deserted Labour in droves, and those who did so were more likely to mention defense as a crucial issue than were Labour loyalists. They were also much more supportive of cruise missiles and the British national deterrent than the stalwarts who voted their party affiliation. In other words, "those sticking with Labour did so despite Labour's defense policy; those deserting Labour did so, at least partly, because of the policy."[13]

The Correlates of Crisis

The "Great Atlantic Crisis of the 1980s" was neither a crisis of public opinion nor of democratic governance. Public opinion, though distinctly shaken by nuclear weapons and visions of war, did not rally around the banners of the militant few. Nor did the institutions of representative government, though rattled, succumb to the clamor of the streets. On its own, the peace movement could not even hope to translate noise into the necessary numbers. And where its voice was amplified by the traditional parties of the democratic left—as in the inverted Arc of Angst that stretched from Britain via the Low Countries and Germany into Scandinavia—the offensive ground to an abrupt halt at the polling booths. At the end of the day, every Labour (or Liberal) party that had sought to absorb or outflank the protest movement ended up not in power but on the opposition benches.

The foundations did not crumble, and the consensus did not truly unravel. Mass opinion veered neither toward neutralism nor pacifism. As measured on a "better red than dead" scale, the West Europeans turned out to be only slightly less defense-minded than the United States. Vast majorities continued to favor resistance over surrender in Britain, Holland, and West Germany—precisely those countries thought to be most thoroughly infected by the bacillus of Protestant angst. To round out the surprise, among the large countries moral lassitude seemed to have spread farthest in France, the least "civilian" and most Catholic of the continental powers. (See table following.)

Resist or Surrender?

Question: "Some people say that war is now so horrible that it is better to accept Russian dominance than to risk war. Others say that it would be better to fight in defense of [name of country] than to accept Russian domination. Which opinion is closer to your own?"[a]

	Responses		
Countries	Better to Fight	Better to Accept Domination	Don't Know
United States	83%	6%	11%
Switzerland	77	8	15
Great Britain	75	12	13
Germany	74	19	7
Netherlands[b]	73	18	9
France	57	13	30
Denmark	51	17	32
Belgium	45	14	41

Source: Gallup Political Index no. 259, March 1982.

a. The question referred to a hypothetical Soviet attack on the Netherlands and posed the alternative between "resistance" and "nonresistance."

b. Data for the Netherlands gathered by U.S. International Communications Agency (USICA) in October 1981.

Nor were the correlates of crisis adequately captured by labels such as *neutralism* or *anti-Americanism*. Large majorities continued to favor membership in NATO, and the strength of devotion was again highest in the Arc of Angst where Hollanditis had allegedly taken its largest toll: in Norway, the Netherlands, and West Germany.[14] As for opinions of the United States—which was offering to the world at the turn of the decade a vexing image of weakness and willfulness—there was some decline in sympathies. Still, favorable opinion of the United States held at a high level; again, it was highest in West Germany (73 percent), where the foundations of Atlanticist orthodoxy were seen to be shifting more rapidly than anywhere else.[15] Conversely, favorable opinion of the Soviet Union ranged from 11 percent in Belgium to 20 percent in the Federal Republic.[16]

In other words, anti-Alliance, pacifist, or pro-Soviet sentiments were not the correlates, let alone the causes, of the malaise. Was it then just a tempest in a transnational teapot? While there was less than met the eye (and the headlines), the public opinion data merely limn the limits, albeit sturdy ones, of crisis. The significant indices of trouble lay elsewhere, and they were more specific. First, aversion centered not on the Alliance but on its nuclear wherewithals. Second, the source of fear and loathing was not the United States (anti-Americanism), but rather American policies—which, as Cold War II unfolded, were battering the tranquility of the détente that Europeans had come to accept as a permanent fixture of their lives. Hence the third area of angst: ballooning visions of war as the West Europeans reacted anxiously to the rumble of great power conflict.

Nuclear Weapons

Western Europe has lived with the accoutrements of extended deterrence since the late fifties, when the first generation of intermediate-range missiles (Thor and Jupiter) and tactical nuclear weapons arrived by the thousands. Their installation on West European soil triggered the first antinuclear movement. After the weapons were safely ensconced, the *Kampf dem Atomtod* ("Fight Nuclear Death") and Ban the Bomb movements in Germany and Britain evaporated with nary a trace. Public anxiety dwindled, and for almost a generation nuclear strategy stayed confined to the inner sancta of a small transatlantic coterie of experts and officials. That phenomenon recalls an adage of the economists, "Old taxes are good taxes." Once nuclear weapons are absorbed psychologically, once they are hidden in remote silos or on isolated bases, they become "good"—that is, nonoppressive—weapons.

A quarter century later, a new generation of nuclear weapons—neutron bombs, Pershing II, and cruise missiles—forced itself once more into the collective consciousness of the West; suddenly, Western publics were again confronted with the murderous premises of their security. Nor was Western Europe the only victim of nuclear angst. European anxieties were loudly echoed by the citizens of Utah and Nevada—staunchly conservative and defense-minded all—when they were asked to accept MX missiles on their soil. And thus Jimmy Carter's favorite basing scheme (200 MX missiles shuttling back and forth between 2,400 launch points) foundered largely on the fears of those who lived next to the potential targets of Soviet saturation bombing. The moral of this transnational tale need not be belabored. Nobody likes nuclear weapons, least of all when they are about to transform one's own habitat into a magnet for nuclear strikes. And nobody likes to be reminded of the fact that our security rests on weapons which might obliterate our society and every person in it in a matter of days, if not hours.

Hence, it was not NATO that drew hostility but its nuclear weapons; not the arsenals of yore but the latter-day descendants, Pershing II and cruise missiles. (Indeed, had the cause of rebellion been nuclear weapons per se, NATO's 6,000 "old" tactical nuclear weapons would have been a far more appropriate target of criticism because they are designed to explode, not in the distant reaches of the Warsaw Pact, but on or over densely populated home ground.) Public opinion data tend to confirm what plausibility suggests. While faith in nuclear deterrence remained high,[17] and pressures for unilateral removal remained low,[18] hostility to nuclear weapons rose sharply whenever the question cued on the dual stimulus of *new missiles* and *your neighborhood*. When the issue was posed thus, eight out of ten West Germans opposed deployment—the largest anti-INF majority ever registered in Western Europe.[19] Similarly, on a "better red than dead" scale, the will to resist dropped dramatically whenever nuclear weapons were factored into the query. In the Netherlands, willingness to fight fell by seventeen points, from 73 to 56 percent.[20] In the Federal Republic the plunge was even more drastic. If almost three-quarters of the population would choose defense rather than Soviet domination when no nuclear cue was given, there was a striking reversal when nuclear war was posited as the price of freedom; in the shadow of the atom, only 30 percent would "defend democracy" while 45 percent would "above all avoid nuclear war."[21] Finally, there was a distinct increase in unconditional hostility to nuclear weapons, in the wake of NATO's Euromissile decision. In 1972 only 36 percent of a Dutch sample had agreed completely with the statement, "The use of nuclear weapons is not acceptable under any circumstances, not even if we are attacked with nuclear weapons ourselves." By 1983 that proportion had grown to 45 percent.[22]

Anti-Americanism

While the penchant for equidistance between the superpowers increased during the early 1980s, that did not happen because the United States itself had fallen into disrepute. Nor was the Soviet Union suddenly viewed as a benign denizen of the Continent; indeed, perceptions of Soviet threat were generally on the rise. Least of all was there any new readiness to dispense with the United States as the security lender of last resort. The meaure of disaffection was at once more subtle and more dramatic, centering on Western Europe's refusal to accept American policies as the epitome of wisdom and prudence.

The deterioration of the U.S. image proved most drastic among its British cousins, America's tacit or formal comrades-in-arms since the War of 1812. If expressions of confidence and doubt in American "ability to deal wisely with present world problems" were about evenly balanced in 1977, the gap had grown to an astounding forty-six percentage points by 1983.[23] In the Netherlands distrust of American ability to deal responsibly with the world increased from 37 percent in 1977 to 50 percent in 1981.[24] After a massive survey of available Western European data, a recent Atlantic Institute study concludes, "There exists a profound concern about the United States, and levels of trust seem to have dropped to the lowest point since the Second World War."[25]

The Fear of War

Waning faith in American judgment and leadership correlated well with another significant index of anxiety: the increasing fear of war. In Britain concern about a future troubled by global conflict shot upwards by twenty-four percentage points right after the invasion of Afghanistan, driving popular pessimism to the record level of 69 percent. As compared to 1963, the expectation of a nuclear war soared by 33 points. In the spring of 1980, 75 percent of the French believed that "the present international situation carries the risk of a world war." In West Germany almost seven out of ten thought in 1981 that peace in Europe had become "less secure"; as many people in the Netherlands felt, in the same year, that the danger of war had increased over the previous decade.[26]

Together the "three fears"—of new nuclear weapons, American policy, and war—provided a fertile substratum for the peace movement of the 1980s. In their own ways, each of these anxieties reflected the same message, and one that was not without irony. The pillars of certainty, nuclear deterrence and alliance with America, had suddenly revealed their dark side: behind the reassurance and stability lay dependence and danger.

The impending arrival of a new generation of land-based missiles thrust the irreducible dilemma of contemporary defense to the forefront of public consciousness. Nuclear weapons not only buttress deterrence, they also drive home the fatal consequences of its failure. "Old" nuclear weapons, even though half-forgotten, suggested a sturdy shelter; "new" nuclear weapons reminded their beneficiaries that they, the protected, are also the potential victims, that the shelter may double as a target of deadly attack. Nor is it an accident that democracies like the end (deterrence) but loathe the means (nuclear weapons). As the philosophes of the Enlightenment and their nineteenth century sociologue heirs had dimly foreseen, democracies are indeed pacific in their basic disposition. Martial virtues and a high level of societal mobilization—meaning, the subordination of the self for the sake of the collective—do not flourish among those who sanctify the principles of life, liberty, and the pursuit of (individual) happiness. Security through deterrence may thus be ideally suited to the democratic ethos. Based on machines rather than men, and on weapons that are distant, silent, and ostensibly unusable, deterrence promises safety without blood, sweat, and tears. That promise is brutally shaken when new weapons intrude on the mind, cutting through what was thought to be the impenetrable barrier between "deterrence" and "warfighting"—driving home the fact that we might, after all, brandish what must never even be unsheathed.

To make matters worse, these new weapons were not even the object of sovereign choice, and thus anxieties about nuclear weapons were compounded by anxieties about their provider. As with the ultima ratio, the West Europeans had come to view the United States as the silent and undemanding guarantor of their blessed state. Dependence, though profound, did not grate as long as the patron power remained modest in its claims for tribute. That would change radically when Jimmy Carter II turned against Jimmy Carter I after the invasion of Afghanistan, and when Ronald Reagan came to power in 1981 by repudiating both. Protection, which had seemed to be extended gratis, suddenly exacted a nasty price as the United States sought to drag Western Europe into a conflict with the Soviet Union they were loath to accept as their own. Every token of fealty the United States demanded seemed calculated to increase the risk of war. The politics of denial—embargoes, credit cut offs, and diplomatic boycotts—threatened to rob the West Europeans of the civilian means by which they had hoped to domesticate Soviet military might. The rhetoric of confrontation and the reality of rearmament (especially via European-based nuclear forces) sliced into the tranquility of the Continent from an opposite direction—by provoking the Soviet Union. That the Europeans would blame the United States (as evidenced by the dramatic drop of confidence in its "ability to deal wisely with present world problems") rather than react to the relentless build-up of Soviet power in the previous decade, is hardly surprising.

Nations that depend for their security on others want the best of all possible worlds. The Europeans want full protection but minimal risks; they endorse the end—the credibility of American power—but not necessarily the means—the reassertion of American power, be it in the form of Euromissiles or confrontationist policies toward the Soviet Union. Both of these actions fueled tensions, not only by puncturing the quiescence the Europeans had come to take for granted during the 1970s, but also by accentuating their dependence on a suddenly unpredictable ally whose moves they could not control.

Moreover, there was a conspicuous difference between Cold War II and its precedent in the forties and fifties. In those days an expansionist Soviet Westpolitik, though conducted from a position of military inferiority, evoked fear, anticommunism, and Alliance cohesion. The reverse was true of the 1970s and beyond. Although European public opinion took due notice of the impressive growth of Soviet military might, that perception simply did not sharpen the sense of physical threat, because the Soviet Union took care to flex its muscle softly, if at all, when making moves on the European chessboard. It was the United States that manifestly attacked the status quo as it sought in the 1970s to reverse its long decline from power. And the Soviet Union, having reaped the fruits of détente precisely because it had dispensed with the cruder means of exerting pressure, could pose as the defender of the status quo and as the innocent victim of the American call to arms.

Theories of Revolt

Many theories have been advanced to explain the purported "collapse of the defense consensus," the sudden specter of "Atlantis lost," and the apparent "democratization of national security policy." The previous analysis suggests a sense of caution; anxieties about nuclear weapons, American intentions, and the danger of violent conflict certainly enriched the soil where insurrection flourished. Yet, at the worst, the consensus frayed only on the edges, and revolt did not spread beyond the militant few. The puzzle in need of solution is not located in any genuine mass movement; the revolt did not even sweep the entire length and breadth of the half-continent. The problem is a more limited one, and it has two aspects. Geographically, the assault on orthodoxy acquired its strongest momentum in the Arc of Angst linking Britain, the Low Countries, West Germany, and Scandinavia. (By contrast, it proved weak in Italy and impotent in France.) But politically, the rise of the peace movement posed a serious challenge only where its cudgel was taken up by the established parties of the democratic left. Which raises the question of geography, from another angle. Why did Labour in Britain, the SPD in Germany, or the PvdA (Labor) in Holland turn the cause of the peace movement into its own? Why did the Socialist parties of France and Italy coldly ignore the temptations of pacifism, neutralism, and anti-Americanism?

In noting the geographical impact of the peace movement and the stark differences between the Protestant North and the Catholic South, it is tempting to assign a key causal role to religion. Indeed, in the Netherlands and the Federal Republic the Protestant churches have been in the vanguard of the protest movement, and in Germany in particular, prominent Protestant theologians have been eager to lend the cachet of religious authority to the political cause. On the basis of these facts, it seems fitting to conclude that Protestant political culture has served as the motor of revolt, driven by guilt unrelieved by confession and penance; the precedence of conscience over authority; a critical stance vis-à-vis the demands of the political order; and, lastly, what Max Weber calls the "ethics of pure conviction" (*Gesinnungsethik*).[27]

But the religious factor raises too many questions to be able to serve as the answer. It does not explain why in Holland there is a strong link between Protestantism, church activism, and the peace movement, while all churches have by and large stayed out of the fray in Protestant Britain. It does not explain why the American bishops, rather than the spiritual leaders of the Protestant majority, have become the fiercest critics of nuclear orthodoxy in the United States. Nor does the religion factor shed much light on Belgium — with its tiny Protestant minority — where protest activity was not only high but apparently so effective as to stalemate a succession of governments on the INF issue. In Scandinavia, the bastion of Lutheranism, the church was hardly in attendance wherever the antinuclear faith was preached; in other countries, particularly in Denmark, the most spectacular actions of the movement were spearheaded by women's groups. In West Germany — which is almost evenly divided between Catholics and Lutherans — Protestant churchmen and theologians played a prominent role in the peace movement, but the connection between Protestantism and protest is by no means clear. The pious, in fact, tend to be quite heretical when contemplating the antinuclear catechism. With respect to the correlates of crisis (for example, support for the peace movement, or hostility to nuclear weapons), the most religious tend to be the least infected by the spirit of protest. Among regular churchgoers, only 36 percent view the peace movement as "necessary"; among those who attend "seldom or never," sympathy leaps to 54 percent. The rejection of nuclear weapons is similarly skewed: 39 versus 57 percent.[28] Finally, the most vivid message of skepticism emerges from the Netherlands, the country that serves as the paradigm of the Protestant/protest connection. It turns out that it was not the Roman Catholic population that was most critical of the Inter-Church Peace Council—the avant-garde of the Dutch peace movement—but rather the Calvinists, who Max Weber portrayed as the very embodiment of the Protestant ethic.[29]

The Protestant connection frays even more when placed into a wider context. Polls show that, ironically, the Protestant paradigm fits the Catholic South more closely in many respects than it does the North. Pacifist sentiments, as measured on a "better red than dead" scale, are significantly higher in France and Italy than in Germany, Great Britain, and Holland.[30] Nuclear pacifism—defined as the readiness to relinquish nuclear weapons unilaterally—grips Italy much more tightly than it does Britain, Germany, the Netherlands, and Norway; it reaches record levels in Spain, the most Catholic country of them all.[31] In 1981, at the height of the war scare, many more Italians (55 percent) than Dutch (36 percent) were categorically opposed to the use of nuclear weapons.[32] Again in Italy, the unconditional refusal of INF was significantly higher than in the Netherlands.[33] And neutralist sympathies flourished most strongly in France, rather than in the Arc of Angst.[34]

Yet France and Italy—where popular sentiments are measurably more "Protestant" than in the Protestant countries—happened to be the strongholds of Atlantic orthodoxy. In Italy antinuclear protest remained too fitful to amount to a real campaign; in France it was barely audible; and in both countries socialist (or socialist-led) governments acted as sturdy guardians of NATO's missile plans. This double paradox—the gap between Catholic faith and "Protestant" beliefs, and between popular opinion and governmental behavior—must discredit even further any theory that would equate denomination with destiny.

Nor do other macrosociological explanations, such as age, fare much better. It is undeniably true that protestors tend to be young, but it is not true that the young are all protestors. Where generational data exist, the old can rarely be distinguished from the young. In West Germany, for instance, opposition to "new missiles" is practically identical across the full spectrum of age groups. A similar pattern holds true for the other correlates of crisis: defense spending, the "importance of [maintaining] good relations with the East," perceptions of the Soviet military threat, the necessity of NATO, and (with a bit more variation) the fear of war.[35]

In Britain attachment to NATO varies between the ages only by decimal points, as does the desire for "greater accommodation with the USSR."[36] The young score higher on the correlates of crisis only if a third factor intervenes: a high level of education. That link, however, is neither new nor specific to the situation of the 1980s. As observed by one who has studied the Campaign for Nuclear Disarmament (CND), the British peace movement of the 1950s, "Higher education has something of a radicalization effect on those who experience it," and "young CND supporters [are] characterized by their success in the educational system."[37] Higher education also meets a crucial condition of activism: ample discretionary time, which distinguishes students from those who are fettered by the responsibilities of work and family.

Nor is it clear whether nuclear weapons are a unique cause of youthful disaffection. Successive generations of West European students have taken to the streets for a succession of causes: nuclear weapons in the 1950s; the Vietnam War in the 1960s; civilian nuclear power in the 1970s; nuclear weapons again in the early 1980s; once more nuclear plants in the mid-1980s, especially after Chernobyl. And throughout the 1980s, protest has fastened onto a variety of less portentous issues: Palestinian rights, American "imperialism in Central America," or acid rain. In West Germany those who fought pitched battles against nuclear power plants, airport runways, and Pershing II missiles during the past decade, redeployed in the mid-eighties to defend the nation's forests against the *Waldsterben*, literally, the "dying of the woods." Perhaps, then, the true message of the antinuclear revolt is not that the Pandora's Box of populism has been cracked open for good, but that a permanent, free-floating protest potential may exist that attaches itself to issues as they come and go.

If neither religious denomination nor generation can adequately account for the rich variety of reactions to nuclear weapons, could the facts of possession provide the answer? Perhaps it was not nuclear weapons per se but *foreign* nuclear weapons in particular that inflamed passions in the Arc of Angst, while sparing those who, like the French, harbored neither American troops nor their nuclear arms. Michael Howard has written that the discontent of democracies may derive from the distance that separates modern European society from those who are charged with its protection. The "divorce of the bourgeoisie and their intelligentsia from the whole business of national defense" has given rise to the belief "that peace is a natural condition threatened only by those professionally involved in preparations for war." As a result, "the military become the natural target for the idealistic young. And how much more will this be the case if those military are predominantly foreign; if the decision for peace or war appears to lie with a group of remote and uncontrollable [American] decision-makers whose values and interests do not necessarily coincide with one's own?"[38]

This insight may explain why the French—blessed with a *force de frappe* (since 1960) and the absence of American troops (since 1966)—have turned a deaf ear to the clamor of the peace-minded. But it does not explain why the non-nuclear Italians have generated very little protest, remaining content to shoulder the burden of additional American missiles and to act as the paragon of Atlantic Alliance virtue. Nor does it account for the case of Britain, the second oldest nuclear power, where "the majority of [the peace movement's] active supporters are opposed to British possession of nuclear weapons of *any description,* whether independent or as part of Britain's NATO commitments, whether land- or sea-based."[39]

Party and Populace

Sociology, it appears, does not fully explain politics. Theories that focus on sweeping background variables, such as religion, age, or (nuclear) dependence, may elucidate dispositions. But they obscure the primarily political nature of revolt and the "intervening variables" of institutions, leadership, and, above all, political parties—the crucial nexus between opinion and policy. Protest movements do not spring full-blown from the depths of an angst-ridden collective unconscious, nor do they flourish in a political vacuum. In addition to fundamental dispositions, there must be leadership and organization to harness psychology to power. Hence, we must look at the politics behind the populism, and that question looms all the larger in view of the original puzzle: why did similar moods lead to different manifestations? Indeed, the paradoxical question ought to be posed more sharply still. Why did France and Italy remain virtually untouched by the tide of revolt, even though pacifist, neutralist, and antinuclear sentiments were measurably more virulent in those two countries than in the North? Conversely, why were the northern countries—where public opinion would confound the Cassandras—swept by waves of militant protest that reached all the way into the established party system?

A fascinating clue emerges from the survey data. Wherever the grand totals were disaggregated to find links between sociological status and political sentiment, it was not religion, age, sex, or class but party preference that served as the best predictor of national security attitudes. In Britain, between thirty and forty percentage points separated Conservative and Labourite responses on such items as "unilateral abandonment of all nuclear weapons," "US missile bases in Britain," and "canceling the Trident missile system."[40] In the Netherlands the "removal of nuclear weapons from Dutch territory" polarized Social Democrats (PvdA) and the right-of-center Liberals (VVD) by a staggering margin of forty-eight points.[41] In West Germany almost twice as many Greens as Christian Democrats refused "new missiles in the FRG," and the gap between the latter and the Social Democrats measured twenty-six percentage points.[42] In Italy, by contrast, there is no such polarization between PSI (the Socialists) on the democratic left and the Christian Democrats (DC). On "confidence in the US political system," DC and PSI partisans are separated by only seven percentage points; the same slender gap obtains between the supporters of INF deployment in either camp.[43] Visible differentials (in the range of twenty points) emerge not between PSI and DC, but between PSI and the Communists. A similar pattern holds true in France.[44]

What does this clue indicate? It points to a powerful link between party preference and political attitudes. More concretely, it reveals that the sentiments of the faithful move in tandem with the policies and pronouncements of their parties. Where the democratic left—as in the North—became radicalized, so did its adherents. Where the Socialists—as in France and Italy—acted as prophets of the Atlanticist creed, their followers professed opinions that were hardly distinguishable from the attitudes of the Right. Yet the numbers do not resolve the more important problem of discerning cause and effect. Has the rank and file imposed its will on the parties, or vice versa? Do parties react to shifting demand curves for political goods, or do they in fact create their own demand by mobilizing their partisans? In short, who leads and who follows? Is it "mobilization from below" or "mobilization from above"?

These questions do not lend themselves to rigorous proof, but a number of reasons suggest that the marketplace of political ideas is dominated by the producers rather than the consumers. In the first place, it is the very raison d'être of parties to stake out positions that will draw the undecided to their cause, that is, to create a supply that will galvanize demand. Secondly, it would be surprising to witness a reversal of this pattern in, of all places, the highly specialized submarket of national security policy. The rank and file is least likely to rush to the vanguard when it comes to defining new demands on an area as arcane as nuclear strategy.[45] Such doubts are reinforced by a third factor—the low salience of national security policy in the collective consciousness of the West European public. If the peace issue distinctly remained a minority concern—too weak to throw elections or to harness a mass movement—it is difficult to see how irresistible demands from "below" would have forced the parties into a change of course. Conversely, it should be expected that the faithful look to their parties for guidance precisely on items, like security, that they habitually ignore. Fourth, and perhaps most important, the battle over peace engulfed the leadership of key Socialist parties in the North *before* it spilled out into the public realm. Where it did not, as in Italy and France, partisan polarization and peace-minded militancy remained virtually negligible.

Hence, we must look not only at the actors in the populist drama but also at the authors of the script that shaped the terms of the debate long before the play became a noisy free-for-all. In the Federal Republic, the Netherlands, and Great Britain, the established parties of the democratic left began to push nuclear weapons to the front of the stage while the activists were still demonstrating against nuclear power plants. The German peace movement's date of conception is probably July 17, 1977, when the SPD's secretary-general launched his famous assault against enhanced radiation (ER) weapons: "Is mankind turning mad? . . . Our scale of values has been turned upside down. The objective is the preservation of matter; mankind has become a secondary consideration. . . . The neutron bomb symbolizes the perversion of thinking."[46] It was a deliberate call to arms, directed as much against Helmut Schmidt (in power since 1974) as against Jimmy Carter, and dedicated as much to détente with the Soviets as to undercutting the ascendancy of the middle-of-the-road Schmidt wing within the party. The battle against nuclear weapons—first against ER projectiles, then against INF—began as a power struggle within the party itself long before the huge peace marches of 1981 and 1982 would converge on Bonn. It was spearheaded by those who, like Willy Brandt, Herbert Wehner, and Egon Bahr,[47] saw neutron bombs, Pershing II, and cruise missiles as a grievous threat to arms control, détente, and Ostpolitik. Domestically, they hoped once more to convert the battle against nuclear weapons into ballots during the 1980 election, and thus reenact the successful strategies of 1969 and 1972. Within the party, the nuclear issue would also help to reshift the balance of power leftward and toward Willy Brandt, who had been forced to yield the chancellorship to Helmut Schmidt in the wake of the Guillaume spy scandal in 1974.[48]

The pattern that would subsequently unfold within the SPD was emblematic for its sister parties in northwestern Europe. Played out on a populist stage, the antinuclear drama acquired its unique resonance in the Northern Tier because it embroiled the large political parties, which had played leading, if not dominant, roles in government throughout much of the 1970s. Its protagonists were neither young nor of the grass roots, but rather professional politicians who sought to rouse and ride forces that promised victory in the battle for domestic power. The moral of that drama echoed what a CND veteran had to say about the role of Labour in the first British peace movement. Unilateralist sloganeering was but a "means of covering up a struggle which has very little to do with disarmament or defense and a great deal to do with an internal struggle for power."[49]

And so it was one peace movement later. In Britain the standard bearers of the Labour left, Anthony Wedgwood-Benn and Michael Foot, began to wield the antinuclear cause against the ancien régime of the former prime minister, James Callaghan, after Labour's defeat by the Conservatives in the summer of 1979. At that point the British peace movement was only embryonic — a loosely led band of thousands, but eagerly nourished by the Labour left as it mustered its forces against the Callaghan wing. CND demonstrations had featured prominent Labour leaders in profusion, and at the end of 1980 the veteran unilateralist Foot emerged as the victor in the battle for Labour's leadership. Concurrently, the party adopted unilateral nuclear disarmament as a key platform plank. In West Germany Helmut Schmidt fought a protracted but losing war that began in earnest in the early days of 1979 — almost a year before NATO's missile decision, which is widely, but inaccurately, portrayed as the fountainhead of the revolt. The contest ended with Schmidt's ouster from the chancellorship in the fall of 1982. In early 1983 the ascendancy of the "National Left" was complete. The SPD launched an election campaign that reverberated with anti-American overtones (the key slogan was, "In the German Interest") and left no doubt that the party, if victorious, would block the deployment of INF.

It is this dynamic of large party radicalization, absent in Italy and France, which must explain why the peace issue entered the mainstream of electoral politics in the North. Having been captured by their left wings, these parties were destined to lose their hold on power and then, freed from the responsibilities of governance, to move even more rapidly toward the extremes of the political spectrum. As a result, the democratic left legitimized and amplified fundamentalist dissent, endowing the movement of the militant few with a derivative weight it could not have mustered on its own. Nor did the peace movement even remotely approach such an exalted position in Italy and France, where the Socialist parties obeyed a very different compass.

In moving sharply leftward, the democratic left of the Northern Tier was responding to three factors. The first stems from its changing internal sociology. As the skilled workers — the traditional mainstays of La-

bour and the social democratic parties—moved toward *embourgeoisement*
and then out, the university educated activists of the sixties' generation
moved in. They had come to political consciousness in the battle for the
university and against Vietnam, and they had fought an establishment
that was pro-America, pro-NATO, and pro-defense. Embarked on a "long
march through the institutions,"[50] the heirs of 1968 would naturally turn
against the icons of their elders. Nurtured on a decade of détente, they
could easily ignore the building blocks of military power that underlie
Europe's astounding postwar stability. They saw the West, and especially the United States, as an instigator of international tension, and the
Soviet Union as the hapless victim of Western encirclement. They saw
alliances and nuclear weapons not as inhibitors of armed conflict but as
its most likely cause. And to wrest power from the Schmidts and Cal-
laghans meant appealing to those who had moved from the radical university circles of the 1960s into the caucuses and convention halls of the
seventies and eighties.

It is these subinstitutions of Labour, SPD, and PvdA that control the
main channels of advancement: a seat in the party executive, and nomination for Parliament. The Dutch case is probably paradigmatic: "PvdA
voters are more 'conservative' than PvdA members. . . . PvdA delegates,
who decide the rank order of candidates for the Second Chamber [i.e.,
position on the party's slate] want to express the more leftish view of
the party's members, . . . elected PvdA parliamentarians are more to the
right than PvdA Council members, and . . . PvdA ministers are further
to the right than PvdA parliamentarians."[51] Such a setting is certain to
throw up radical candidates and to force their rivals into a more extreme
stance.

The peace issue, nurtured by real fears of nuclear weapons and war,
thus dovetailed nicely with the ongoing passage of power from the postwar leadership to the generation of the forty-year-olds. To these two fac-
ets—the setting and the sentiments—a third should be added: the pseudo-
populist flavor of the television age, which tempts aspiring politicians to
travel outside the institutional avenues of power and appeal directly to
the populace at large. This was the road the New Left took throughout—
sometimes even against their own mentors, as in Britain when Neil Kinnock replaced Michael Foot only three years after the septuagenarian Labour leader had routed the moderate Callaghan forces.

If the dynamics of recruitment and intraparty advancement made for
radicalization, the second and third factors might explain why the process unfolded most swiftly in the areas of foreign and defense policy.

Why would the northern Socialist parties commit themselves so whole-heartedly to a minority quest, which proved to be a losing issue to boot? One answer is surely, *faute de mieux*. The 1970s had been the Social Democratic Decade in terms of both power and policy. In the Northern Tier the 1970s were marked by the ascendancy of the democratic left, which would rule alone or in coalition for most of the decade. On the policy front, the decade was characterized by the rapid expansion of the state's role in the national economy, generally financed by either real or inflationary growth. Giving to Peter without taking from Paul, governments had apparently resolved the ancient conflict between private prosperity and public welfare, between defense spending (which would rise) and social spending (which would rise even faster). At the threshold of the 1980s, however, that strategy had reached a double dead end. Long-term economic decline not only reimposed the nasty choices of yore, but it also robbed the democratic left of yesterday's winning campaign issues. No longer the guarantors of seemingly endless growth, none of the Socialist parties that had presided over the onset of the worst recession in postwar history could run on its economic record, let alone against it by preaching the conservative virtues of belt-tightening and budgetary restraint. The lack of domestic campaign alternatives thus combined naturally with instinct and ideology to push the peace-cum-détente theme to the fore. By default, it was the best campaign banner available; in times of economic contraction, such a policy had the additional advantage of circumventing the welfare/warfare state dilemma by legitimizing defense, rather than domestic, spending cuts.

The third factor was perhaps the profoundest of them all because it may well betray a more lasting transformation of West European domestic politics. The Cold War decades had been dominated by the Conservatives. The center-right's Socialist rivals had entered the corridors of power after a long and painful adjustment process that required the repression of ancient pacifist inclinations, as well as making a commitment to NATO and nuclear weapons. Neither the SPD nor Labour, to name but the two most important parties, had ever been comfortable with that role. Nor had they ever forgotten a basic lesson of the cold war—that it is Conservative parties, oriented toward defense and alliance, that profit from a tense climate in East–West affairs. Détente, arms control, and East–West amity thus reflect more than simply ideological predilections; they provide the vital setting for Social Democratic parties to rise to power—and subsequently flourish. Hence, the democratic left fastened on the peace issue not only for lack of potent domestic alternatives but also for reasons of power and self-legitimization. To have sailed with the prevailing wind — which, by the turn of the decade, blew cold from Washington as well as from Moscow — would have meant competing on the "wrong" platform, that is, on the issues of military strength and anti-Sovietism. These issues were triply unpromising. They would have required slicing into an already stagnating social and welfare budget; they were the natural and more credible preserve of the Right; and they would have amounted to an ex post facto admission that a decade of social democratic détente policy had failed to deliver on its lofty promises.

By the mid-1980s the Socialist parties of the Northern Tier were again confronted with the ancient conflict between sect and church, between doctrinal purity and the messy compromises of power. Yet the return to "Bad Godesberg"[52] promises to be lengthy, given the rout of the moderates, the attempt to co-opt ecologists and peace activists, and a far from completed recruitment process that attracts to the fold not the heirs of Gaitskell, Callaghan, and Schmidt but the younger admirers of Brandt, Kinnock, and his German doppelganger, Oscar Lafontaine.[53]

The change can be described in broader terms by analyzing the shifting relationship between the democratic and communist left. During the Cold War decades, communism marked the unbreachable limits of legitimacy, separating permissible dissent from collaboration with an inimical superpower. The success story of alliance with America and the era of conservative ascendancy cannot be explained without considering the domestic impact of anticommunism, which targeted "the enemy" both within and without. That binding consensus stigmatized not only Communist parties — even large ones like the PCF and PCI — as agents of a foreign power, but it also tainted as handmaidens of Bolshevism those Socialist parties that would follow their traditional instincts and plead for disengagement, neutralization, and nuclear disarmament. To drop that burden and gain electoral respectability, the democratic left had to become holier-than-thou in matters of defense and foreign policy and eschew even the most fleeting association with communist cohorts and causes. The obsessive fear of contamination explains, for instance, why the German Social Democrats swiftly abandoned the first peace movement (1957–58) after a short-lived attempt to turn the popular revulsion against tactical nuclear weapons into a springboard for governmental power. To futher objectives that were insistently pursued by the Soviet Union and its domestic surrogates was at that time the sure road to electoral disaster. Or as Herbert Wehner, the long-term parliamentary leader of the SPD put it in retrospect, it was dangerous to "rouse moods and mobilize people with whom Social Democracy could not continue to make

common cause after a certain point and who would obstruct even further its access to the so-called common man."[54]

Today, after a decade of détente, both the external and internal threat
have lost their sting, and anticommunism is no longer the great polarizer
(and arbiter) of West European politics. Where once there were impenetrable barriers between the democratic and communist left, there are
now regular contacts, flanked by ad hoc cooperation. Members of both
sides have freely mingled in the peace movement, although neither ever
managed to gain control over this many-feathered flock. The most telling
transformation has occurred in the realm of policy. Previously loath to
lay claim to objectives even remotely like those of the Soviet Union, the
Socialist parties of Britain, Germany, and the Scandilux countries have
rallied around positions that do not echo but do resemble Soviet prefer-
ences, to wit: hostility to Western INF deployment; proposals for nuclear-free zones; attachment to a no-first-use strategy; opposition to the
Strategic Defense Initiative (SDI); criticism of American arms control
postures; the refusal to confront the Soviet Union over Afghanistan and
Poland; and a general disposition to impute either benign or defensive
motives to Soviet policy.

The great exceptions to this shift have been the Socialist parties of
France and Italy. It is that fact, rather than religion or opinion, that must
explain why their Socialist-led governments have ignored the temptation of populist pacifism and have steered a course that either equals (as
in Italy) or exceeds (as in France) the alliance-minded fervor of the moderate right. The key differences relate to phase and position in the electoral system. Unlike their counterparts in the North, the Socialist parties of Italy and France had captured governmental leadership only at
the beginning of the 1980s, when the promise of détente and East–West
harmony had begun to pale and attention had turned to the rise of Soviet power, Afghanistan, Poland, and, as in France, the belated discov-
ery of the Gulag. And unlike their northern confrères, they had to acquire power in a two-sided battle—against both the bourgeois right and
the communist left (the latter being strong in the South but puny in the
North). The dual rivalry informed a strategy that would push the southern Socialists inexorably toward the center, where they could draw votes
from the Right while denying them to the Communists—by posing as
the trusty guardians of political resolve and military strength.

The key to the politics of populism lies in the nature of the political
system, the arena where parties compete for power and position. The
decisive difference between the stalwart South and the Arc of Angst is
the presence or absence of large but marginalized Communist parties

and the impact of each, respectively, on the strategies of the democratic left. The northern Socialists could drift leftward to absorb or co-opt (and thus legitimize) the forces of protest—to harness a "majority to the left of the CDU/CSU," as the SPD chairman, Willy Brandt, put it—because they did not run the risk of being tainted by association. There was no powerful domestic rival even further to the left who would force them to demonstrate impeccable Atlanticist credentials. And once the Cold War in Europe was ostensibly over and no more than a troublesome obsession of Reaganite America, the Soviet Union no longer functioned as an equivalent source of discipline from the outside. Indeed, after a decade of détente that had favored the ascendancy of the social democratic left, Moscow had ceased acting as the pole of repellence; it had in fact become the legitimate and indispensable partner in cooperation.

Conversely, the French and Italian Socialists could move to the right and ignore the populist road to power because their Communist adversaries were trapped in what the Italians call the "majority zone"—the consensus-bound area which promised a share in power after decades of isolation. Although among the most dogmatic of Western Europe's Communist parties, France's PCF had swallowed pride and principle in 1981 to gain four cabinet posts in Mitterrand's Socialist regime. Chained to governmental discipline, the French could not, and dared not, rouse the faithful in the service of anti-Americanism and neutralism, let alone rouse them against nuclear weapons, the shiny symbol of French *gloire* and great power status. And since most of the French peace movement was virtually a subdivision of the PCF, its voice was not only timid but also discredited.

The same pattern obtained in Italy, even though that country was anticipating the placement of foreign missiles on its soil and not a national *force de frappe*. Bettino Craxi's Socialists could comfortably don the mantle of stout-minded Atlanticism because their left flank was secure against a Communist assault. Eager to break the burdensome connection to Moscow, Enrico Berlinguer's CPI had long before embraced the Alliance, refusing to countenance "any unilateral action, whether with regard to disarmament or our stable ties to the Atlantic Pact."[55] Nor did the PCI dare to mobilize its considerable potential in the streets in order to shake the government's INF commitment—for fear of losing the aura of respectability it had labored long and hard to acquire. Brushing aside the call of the French Communists to join a "unified peace movement," the PCI occasionally sounded more resolute than the social democratic parties of the North. Or as one member of the Central Committee observed, the deployment of Euromissiles was "theoretically possible," and the party's approach to this question was based on the "necessity for a balance of forces and equal security."[56]

The moral of this story lies in the power of political structures. Indeed, there can be no other lesson when similar societal dispositions throughout Western Europe produce such different political manifestations in different countries. When the same fears and resentments draw the established Left in the North toward the vortex of protest, while pushing its southern counterpart toward stout-minded Atlanticism, attention must perforce shift from society to the polity. Why are certain "inputs" sometimes transmitted and amplified, when at other times they are deflected and contained? Short of a real revolution – which dispatches the problem of political structures along with the structures themselves – social minority movements depend for their growth on the political setting in which they arise. Hence, we must ask why established political leaders take up certain cudgels at certain times to clobber and cow their opponents. And given the stark differences between the Southern and the Northern Tier, which cannot be explained adequately by religion or by any other sociological background variable, the answer must be sought in the political milieu where elites (and counterelites) compete for power and position.

That milieu yielded options to the democratic left of the North which it denied to the Socialists of the South. The social democratic parties of the North could move to the left because that terrain was not contaminated by the presence of powerful Communist parties. Nor were they deterred from occupying that space, as they had been in the distant past, by the Soviet Union. After a decade of détente, contacts with Moscow no longer spelled the kiss of death but, to the contrary, promoted electoral profit for those parties that sought to position themselves as trusty guardians of East–West amity in Europe. There was thus little danger in trying to outflank or absorb the forces of fundamentalist protest. Yet in the process of embracing the cause of the peace movement, the social democratic left ended up enlarging it.

Conversely, the nature of the party system in the South foreclosed such a strategy; in Italy and France the Socialists were neither forced nor tempted to move left because their Communist rivals were loath to lose whatever respectability they had gained in thirty years of tortuous adaptation. As a result, peace-minded agitation remained in Italy and France but a pale copy of the real thing. The moral of the story is that, in Western Europe at least, politics matters more than populism. Throughout the North as well as the South, the crucial issue was not peace but power; and that, in fact, is the name of the democratic game.

Democracy and Defense: Lessons from History

Waning by mid-decade, the peace movement of the 1980s had been but another cyclical burst, echoing the upheavals of the 1950s. Twice, then, the postwar polities of Western Europe were shaken by militants who sought to exorcize nuclear weapons, if not to undo the alliance that had elevated those weapons to the ultima ratio of Western security. When organized disaffection recurs, it raises the question of times and circumstances. When does peace become an issue in the political market place? Why do peace movements arise, and why do they disappear?

To begin with, there is a distinct generational flavor to antinuclear protest. While the young—as the opinion data reveal—are not protestors, the protestors tend to be young. The peace movements of the fifties and eighties are separated by a quarter century, and perhaps it is no mere fluke that this period spans the normal generational cycle of twenty-five years. Every generation must come to grips with nuclear weapons on its own; in both eras, a new generation had to learn to live with "the bomb" that could not be banished from the earth but might one day incinerate it. To accept the terrifying paradoxes of deterrence—that more is never enough, that we must threaten to condemn the world in order to save it— goes against the very grain of post-Enlightenment teleology, which sees all problems as temporary and all evils as mere stepping stones on the path to ultimate salvation. Perhaps, then, it should come as no surprise that the more privileged, university-sheltered young—whose very lives are progress incarnate—should regularly revolt against so powerful a symbol of doom as nuclear weapons.

But moods, whether among the young or the old, do not for movements make. As in any uprising, there have to be tangible trigger events that convert a vaguely felt malaise into the push and pull of personal revolt. A sense of crisis must prevail before people start voting with their feet, and there were three crisis factors present at the beginning of both antinuclear waves.

First, both peace movements were preceded or accompanied by momentous shifts in the nuclear balance. Soviet rocket threats against Paris and London during the Suez Crisis of 1956 were the early harbingers of a new age; one year later the West would learn that the Russians had launched their first intercontinental ballistic missile ahead of the United States. Before 1957, massive retaliation had been a one-way threat only— the comfortable monopoly of the United States. After 1957, Western societies were suddenly brought face to face with their own vulnerability to the nuclear firestorm—a fact that Soviet statements and demarches (combined with multimegaton weapons demonstrations) rarely failed to press home during the headier days of the "missile gap."

What Suez and Sputnik did for the first peace movement, the relentless Soviet build-up during the 1970s did for the second. Matched by the breathtaking expansion of the Soviet strategic arsenal, the three-generation jump from the half-forgotten SS-4 and SS-5 to the SS-20 missiles in the European theater conveyed the dreadful message that all of Western Europe, though a serene island of seemingly permanent détente, was in fact an immovable target and a hostage to Soviet nuclear might.[57] That sense of victimhood may explain the curious psychology of displacement that informed so much of the peace movement's analysis. To imbue the Pershing II with a greater threat than the SS-20, to condemn Reagan rather than Russia, and to turn against Western "decapitation weapons" instead of their precursors in the East, was not a flight of curdled fancy but an act of propitiation that took due notice of the realities of power. In the years of Western neglect (the last American Euromissile, the Mace-B, had been withdrawn in 1969), the Soviets had assembled a counterdeterrence panoply in Europe that was virtually indistinguishable from a first-strike threat. In such a setting, it was rational to be irrational—to depict the West as the "aggressor," to espouse the moral superiority of self-denial, and to avoid any provocation that might unleash the ire of a superior adversary.

Rapid technological change and the shift from older to newer, more "usable" weapons yielded a second trigger event. We live most comfortably with the bomb when we are allowed to forget its existence. The less visible its means, the larger loom the benefits of deterrence. Forgetfulness and repression cease to function, however, when new weapons intrude on the mind. In the late 1950s the deployment of American medium-range missiles (Thor and Jupiter), as well as thousands of tactical nuclear weapons, literally brought the abstractions of deterrence down to earth. It was no accident that the first peace movement flourished most in West Germany. A country the size of Oregon, the Federal Republic came to host more nuclear weapons per square mile than any other nation in the world. And the bulk of these tactical weapons were short-range—destined to devastate the defender's land, not the aggressor's.[58]

Similarly, at the threshold of the 1980s yet another generation of nuclear weapons punctured the veil of repression that is normally kept lowered over matters like death, taxes, and the accoutrements of "mutual assured destruction." Many of the new weapons entering the arsenals of the eighties were smaller and more accurate, hence, ostensibly more "usable"; "warfighting" and "prevailing" suddenly seemed to have edged out "deterrence" as the doctrine of the day. Neutron bombs, Pershing II, and cruise missiles abruptly reminded the Western Europeans that nuclear terror was the price of an unprecedented peace-cum-prosperity; that survival—in Churchill's legendary words—was indeed the "twin brother of annihilation." Anxieties triggered by the arrival of new weapons combined easily with fears about their purveyors; from there it was but a short step to the sheer paranoia in the attitude that the United States was no longer Europe's loyal guardian but in fact a coconspirator bent on turning the Continent into the "shooting gallery of the superpowers."[59]

The third crisis factor precipitating the new peace movement was political, and perhaps the most important of them all: the breakdown of détente, that is, the collapse of moderation between the two superpowers and their angry resort to confrontation. New generations of nuclear weapons terrify because they suddenly cast a glaring light on the murderous premises of our security. Any surge in Soviet power awakens us to our ever present vulnerability to nuclear extinction. But sharply deteriorating East–West relations add urgency to the renewed angst. Rightly or wrongly, democratic societies instinctively recoil from the sound and fury of international tension because they habitually equate the noise with the real war.

By 1957 the vaunted post-Stalin "thaw" had segued into an offensive phase in Soviet diplomacy—a policy that Nikita Khrushchev's own colleagues would condemn as "adventurist" when they toppled him in 1964. That phase began with a campaign of threats against the nuclearization of NATO, especially against the Federal Republic, which was about to acquire American tactical weapons for its armed forces. The threats escalated in 1958, when Khrushchev flung down his Berlin Ultimatum, and reached a flash point in 1961 when American and Soviet troops confronted each other across the Berlin Wall. The culmination was the Cuban Missile Crisis of 1962, which pushed the two superpowers to the brink of global war. These were the halcyon days of *Kampf dem Atomtod*, Easter Marches, and the Campaign for Nuclear Disarmament—it was a very good time for proclaiming the moral superiority of "redness" over "deadness."

A similar chill descended at the beginning of the present decade, which was ushered in by rattling events like the Iran hostage crisis, the Soviet invasion of Afghanistan, and the war of nerves over Poland. The Euromissiles intruded on the Western psyche precisely at a time when the strategic arms control talks (SALT II) ended in frustration and the détente of the 1970s was giving way to Cold War II. Slicing into Europe's tranquility from many directions, these events seemed to make war more likely, inevitably deflecting attention from the obvious sturdiness of the "balance of terror" toward the unthinkable consequences of its collapse. It did not matter that nuclear weapons had kept the peace for almost forty years. Indeed, the very success of deterrence in keeping the great powers on their best behavior was now seen as the greatest danger in it, as many in the West succumbed to proof-by-reverse-induction: fail it must because it had endured so long.

Twice in the postwar era, peace movements were spawned by strikingly similar events: the thudding arrival of new weapons systems, the darkening shadow of Soviet power, and the deepening chill in East–West relations. History, then, suggests why protest movements are born. But why and when do they disappear?

To begin with, protest movements fail because they fail. Behind this tautology lurks a congenital problem of all anti-institutional politics. Social movements try to mobilize maximum numbers at maximum speed, and thus they become a motley crowd. Pastors and pacifists, Reds and Greens, Leninists and idealists are all factions; they do not a coalition make. For a while they manage to submerge their ideological differences for the sake of the great single issue—in this case, the battle against cruise and Pershing II missiles. But when that overriding objective is frustrated —as it was when the first missiles arrived at the end of 1983—the problem of organization returns with a vengeance.

The response to the first setback is the communal huddle and collective soul-searching. Where did we all go wrong? Not so far behind this question comes the intramural reckoning, the not so friendly squaring of accounts. Who "lost" the battle? The third stage brings the bitterness and break-up as the diverse factions, faced with their clashing needs, either withdraw to the intimacy of their individual folds, or, conversely, strike out to impose uniformity by trying to capture the entire movement.

Unlike political parties, populist groupings are not equipped to survive out in the cold—which explains why, for instance, the German Greens still exist as a political force while the German peace movement had virtually disappeared by the mid-1980s. Established parties are geared for a life in opposition. They have organizations that have been in place since time immemorial. They have a base, and they dispense patronage and positions to their cohorts. Even after defeat in a national contest, they can seek cover in local and regional power bastions, to regroup for the counterattack four years later. For entrenched political parties, defeat does not spell the end but a new beginning.

Not so for ad hoc aggregations like peace movements. How do they inspire their supporters and gain new recruits after failure? If the call to stop the missiles did not rouse the masses yesterday, will the call to stop the next batch prove more persuasive tomorrow? Especially when the television cameras, their old but fickle allies, have turned relentlessly toward the next newsbreak that promises, once more, to change the course of history. The worst enemy of grass roots movements is not the Establishment, but boredom. Another mortal threat emanates from precisely those political parties that are trying to co-opt or outflank them. Parties embrace issues to win, even though they might continue to cling to them long after their sterility has been revealed at the polls. Yet in the end, that grip must be loosened; parties, unlike movements, are in the business of politics for the power and not the principles. In West Germany the first peace movement was doomed when the SPD, after a disastrous defeat in the crucial regional election of North Rhine–Westphalia, forsook the antinuclear cause and embarked instead on the road to Bad Godesberg. In Britain the Campaign for Nuclear Disarmament shrank into a sect when Labour abandoned unilateralism in favor of Harold Wilson, who became prime minister in 1964.

Such structural handicaps are compounded by external threats. Peace movements, as history also suggests, are not hardy perennials. To flourish, they require quite specific soil and climate conditions. Around 1963 the first antinuclear movement in Europe had vanished virtually without a trace. The Cuban Missile Crisis of the previous year was an obvious watershed. To the rattled Western mind, the happy outcome at the brink was doubly reassuring. It revealed that statesmen laboring under the shadow of the apocalypse do not behave as fecklessly as did their forebears in 1914. The outcome also revealed that, in spite of Sputnik and Soviet missile threats, the nuclear balance had not tilted in favor of the Soviet Union. To those who would have yielded to Khrushchev's gamble in Cuba and Berlin, for survival's sake, it demonstrated that it helps to be strong when moving toward the edge of the nuclear unknown.

With the global balance so palpably restored, the fear of nuclear weapons rapidly receded throughout the West. The new weapons became old weapons and were forgotten once more. But there was a third factor, perhaps the most reassuring of all, that helped to pacify ruffled sensibilities: the global détente that followed the reassertion of Western strength in Cuba and Berlin. In the wake of deadly confrontation, the United States and the Soviet Union took their first steps toward taming the menace of the atom by linking Washington and Moscow through the vaunted "Hotline" in 1962, and by concluding a limited test ban treaty in 1963.

Modest as they were, these steps soothed the sting of nuclear anxiety. They symbolized the power of political action over brooding terror. If the weapons could not be banished from the earth, they might at least be rendered impotent. And the lesson transcends the events of yesteryear. Precisely because nuclear weapons cannot be exorcized, they require not only a stable balance of power but also a doctrine of salvation. Arms control and détente, no matter how sterile when measured against the enduring facts of power and conflict, have provided that doctrine – a vital myth that injects reassurance into an intractable reality. The peace movement of the 1980s could not have flourished had it not been for the decline in superpower moderation that accompanied the frightening surge in the quantity and quality of nuclear weapons. On the other hand, the movement would not have receded as quickly without the return of a calming moderation in the tone and discourse of international politics by the mid-1980s.

Democracies are not oblivious to the claims of a strong defense; indeed, as the experience with two peace movements shows, the faith in deterrence is as likely to wane when the West appears weak as when military plenty becomes a purpose unto itself. Nor is it the weapons as such that make for angst. The first peace movement vanished precisely at the time when not only the United States but also Britain and France were in the midst of a resolute strategic build-up in the aftermath of the Cuban Missile Crisis. The implements of Armageddon were hardly being buried at this point. The arms race was moving along at a brisk pace in the 1960s, and the number of American warheads reached its peak in 1967. What *did* change in 1962 – what sapped the élan of the first peace movement – was the change in the global political climate toward safety rather than terror, détente rather than conflict. Assurance, then, is not the enemy of arms but their vital ally. And thus, antinuclear revolts, no matter how fleeting, carry an abiding message. Democracies want their rivalries to be regulated, and they prefer big sticks that come with restrained language. They are not enamored of the drumbeat of rebellion – but in the shadow of the atom, they do like a quantum of solace.

Notes

1. John Barry, "Just Who Is Deterred by the Deterrent?" *London Times,* 18 Aug. 1981.
2. Kenneth Adler and Douglas Wertman, "Is NATO in Trouble? A Survey of European Attitudes," *Public Opinion* (August/September 1981).
3. From a poll conducted by Second German Television (ZDF) in the summer of 1983, as quoted by Elisabeth Noelle-Neumann of the Institut für Demoskopie

in Allensbach, West Germany, in her article, "Drei Viertel gegen die Raketen-stationierung?" *Frankfurter Allgemeine Zeitung*, 16 Sept. 1983, p. 11 (emphasis added).

4. Poll conducted by SCOPE of Lucerne, Switzerland, commissioned by *Time* Magazine, and published in *Time*, 31 Oct. 1983.

5. For all Dutch data cited in this paragraph, see David Capitanchik and Richard C. Eichenberg, *Defence and Public Opinion*, Chatham House Papers, no. 20 (London: Routledge & Kegan Paul, 1983), ch. 4, "The Netherlands," pp. 31, 33. This book is a very useful brief overview of public opinion data in Western Europe. For the most exhaustive, most recent, and most carefully analyzed survey of Western European opinion, see Gregory Flynn and Hans Rattinger, eds., *The Public and Atlantic Defense* (Totowa, N.J.: Rowman and Allanheld, 1985). It covers Britain, France, West Germany, Italy, the Netherlands, and the United States.

6. Poll commissioned by *Der Spiegel*, executed by Emnid, and cited in *Der Spiegel*, 2 Feb. 1983. The exact wording of the question was not revealed. The interviewer explained the substance of the two-track approach and then confronted the respondents with four alternatives. The exact breakdown was 36 percent "in favor"; 21 percent "against"; 12 percent "does not interest me"; and 30 percent "have not made up my mind yet."

Apparently the wording matters a great deal because various polls have revealed much more powerful support for NATO's Brussels Decision.

Respondents were asked: "The so-called NATO double-decision has been around for a while. With that decision the NATO countries agreed, on the one hand, to counter the Soviet intermediate-range missiles with comparative missiles of their own in Central Europe, on the other, to launch disarmament negotiations with the Soviet Union. On the whole, is this double-decision a good thing or a bad thing?"

	May 1981	*Jan. 1982*	*Dec. 1982*	*Aug. 1983*
Good thing	53%	52%	51%	49%
Bad thing	20%	22%	25%	23%
Undecided	27%	26%	24%	28%

Source: Noelle-Neumann, "Drei Viertel...," p. 11.

7. Responses in favor of the two-track decision even rose by two percentage points to 38 percent. Opposition increased from 21 to 22 percent, 11 percent were "not interested," and 28 percent were undecided. Emnid/*Der Spiegel* poll, see note 6.

8. The numbers for 1984 were 22 percent (likelihood greater), 48 percent (security improved), and 28 percent (no difference). Poll conducted by Emnid, as cited by Gebhard L. Schweigler, "Anti-Americanism in Germany," *Washington Quarterly* (Winter 1986): 81. For a concise analysis of the available surveys and the rejection of the "radical break" hypothesis, see Hans Rattinger, "Change and Continuity in West German Public Attitudes on National Security and Nuclear Weapons," *Public Opinion Quarterly* (Fall 1987).

9. Institut für angewandte Sozialwissenschaft (Infas), "Die politische Stimmung in Schwäbisch Gmünd im September 1983," (Bad Godesberg: Infas, 1983), as cited in *Der Spiegel* no. 42, 1983, p. 59.

10. Atlantic Institute, ed., *Security and the Industrial Democracies: A Comparative Opinion Poll* (Paris: Atlantic Institute–Lou Harris, 1983), p. 5.
11. Flynn and Rattinger, *Atlantic Defense*, p. 231 table 6.10.
12. "Polit-Barometer," as broadcast by Second German Television (ZDF), 7 Dec. 1983.
13. Ivor Crewe, "Britain: Two and a Half Cheers for the Atlantic Alliance," in Flynn and Rattinger, *Atlantic Defense*, pp. 25–26.
14. For Norway, (72 percent in favor of membership), see Flynn and Rattinger, *Atlantic Defense*, p. 309 table 7.12; for the Netherlands (72 percent in favor), see ibid., p. 267 table 6.42; for the Federal Republic (78 percent in favor), see Capitanchik and Eichenberg, *Public Opinion*, p. 65 table 9.
15. Gallup Poll of March 1982, as summarized in *Newsweek*, 15 March 1982, European Edition, p. 13.
16. Ibid.
17. More than five out of ten West Germans agreed with the proposition that "an attack by the East can best be prevented by deterrence." Elisabeth Noelle-Neumann, "Ein großer Teil der Bevölkerung bleibt stanfest," *Frankfurter Allgemeine Zeitung*, 30 Oct. 1981, p. 11 table 2.
18. Almost six out of ten Dutch opposed the unilateral removal of nuclear weapons from their territory in 1981. Flynn and Rattinger, *Atlantic Defense*, p. 253 table 6.30.
19. See note 3 above.
20. Flynn and Rattinger, *Atlantic Defense*, p. 234 table 6.14.
21. Noelle-Neumann, "Ein großer Teil...," p. 11 table 4.
22. Flynn and Rattinger, *Atlantic Defense*, p. 235 table 6.15.
23. Twenty-four percent expressed "very great" or "considerable" confidence; 70 percent had "little," "very little," or "no" confidence. Norman L. Webb and Robert J. Wybrow, "Friendly Persuasion: Advice from Britain," *Public Opinion* (February/March 1983): 13 fig. 1.
24. Flynn and Rattinger, *Atlantic Defense*, p. 263. See also data published in *De Volkskrant*, 6 March 1982, indicating that 55 percent of the respondents had become more critical of the United States than a few years before.
25. As a cautionary note, the editors add, "Unfortunately, this is another case in which earlier data are sparse, and it is impossible to know whether the figures are really more dramatic, or whether it just seems as if they must be. What one can say, however, is that this time, it is less U.S. reliability and more U.S. political judgement that is being called into question." Flynn and Rattinger, *Atlantic Defense*, p. 376.
26. Figures taken from Flynn and Rattinger, *Atlantic Defense*, p. 22 table 2.6; p. 23 table 2.7; p. 77; p. 123 table 4.11; and p. 229.
27. It should be noted, however, that Lutheranism—by far the majority denomination of Protestantism in West Germany and Scandinavia—has an ancient tradition of "render unto Caesar" submission to the claims of the state. The antiauthoritarian cast of "pure conviction" is not a distinctive trait, historically, of German Lutheranism. Like the Vatican, the Lutheran church concluded an early peace with the Hitler regime, and today many pastors in the peace movement present that dark chapter as a reason (or a rationalization) for their contemporary activism.

28. Flynn and Rattinger, *Atlantic Defense*, p. 159 table 4.36 and p. 163 table 4.38. As a note of caution, it should be added that these figures do not distinguish between Catholics and Protestants. Since Catholics attend church far more frequently than Protestants, the sample might be biased in favor of Catholics who also tend to be more conservative and authority-prone than their Lutheran brethern.

29. Thirty percent of Dutch Catholics disagreed with the IKV, but so did 53 percent of the Calvinists. Jan Siccama, "The Netherlands Depillarized: Security Policy in a New Domestic Context," in Gregory Flynn, ed., *Overlooked Allies: The Northern Periphery of NATO* (Totowa, N.J.: Rowman and Allanheld, 1985), table 3.6.

30. Seventy-five percent in Britain, 74 percent in West Germany, and 73 percent in the Netherlands would prefer armed resistance to peace and Soviet domination; in France, only 57 percent and in Italy only 48 percent would so choose. *Gallup Political Index*, no. 259 (March 1982). For Dutch data, see U.S. International Communications Agency (USICA) survey, October 1981.

31. Attitudes were measured by asking respondents to choose among various statements about nuclear weapons. The strongest antinuclear statement— "Give up all nuclear weapons regardless of whether the Soviet Union does" —was chosen by 35 percent of Italians and 55 percent of Spaniards. The figures for West Germany, Britain, the Netherlands, and Norway were 23, 17, 25, and 15 percent, respectively. Atlantic Institute, *Industrial Democracies*, p. 9.

32. Flynn and Rattinger, *Atlantic Defense*, p. 95 table 3.20, and p. 235 table 6.15. These polls were conducted on a national level only and, thus, are not identically worded.

33. In early 1981, 54 percent of Italians were unconditionally opposed to INF deployment, even though the question merely posed Europe in general as the hypothetical locus of deployment. At the same time, only 46 percent of the Dutch were thus opposed, even though the questions specifically cued on "deployment in the Netherlands." Since hostility to INF rises in response to the stimulus of geography ("in *your* country/area"), the Italian poll probably underestimates the level of anti-INF attitudes. For the Italian data, see Flynn and Rattinger, *Atlantic Defense*, p. 192 table 5.16. For the Dutch figures, see *Haagsche Courant*, 26 April 1981.

34. In March 1981, USICA tried to measure neutralism by posing the following question: "Do you think it is better for our country to belong to NATO...or would it be better for us to get out of NATO and become a neutral country?" Large majorities in the Protestant tier opted for alliance. In France, however, opinion was almost evenly divided between alliance (45 percent) and neutrality (40 percent). Adler and Wertman, "Is NATO in Trouble?" p. 10.

35. Flynn and Rattinger, *Atlantic Defense*, p. 164 table 4.39; p. 159 table 4.36; p. 157 table 4.34; p. 166 table 4.40.

36. From a chapter appropriately entitled, "Great Britain: Generational Continuity" by Peter Fotheringham, in Stephen F. Szabo, ed., *The Successor Generation: International Perspectives of Postwar Europeans* (London: Butterworth, 1983), p. 95 tables 4.4 and 4.5.

37. Frank Parkin, *Middle Class Radicalism: The Social Bases of the British Campaign for Nuclear Disarmament* (Manchester: Manchester University Press, 1968), pp. 171, 173.
38. Michael Howard, "Reassurance and Deterrence," *Foreign Affairs* (Winter 1982/1983): 316.
39. Ivor Crewe, "Britain: Two and a Half Cheers for the Atlantic Alliance," in Flynn and Rattinger, *Atlantic Defense*, p. 29 (emphasis added).
40. Flynn and Rattinger, *Atlantic Defense*, pp. 60–63 table 2.28.
41. Ibid., p. 250 table 6.25.
42. Ibid., p. 164 table 4.39.
43. Ibid., p. 210 table 5.46, and p. 207 table 5.40.
44. Ibid., p. 94 table 3.9 (measuring attitudes on "neutralism").
45. In the Netherlands, for instance, almost half of all respondents felt that laymen were not equipped to deal with the issue of removing nuclear weapons from the country. See Flynn and Rattinger, *Atlantic Defense*, p. 239.
46. Egon Bahr, "Ist die Menschheit dabei, verrück zu werden?" in the SPD paper, *Vorwärts*, 21 July 1977, p. 4.
47. Respectively, the chairman, parliamentary leader, and secretary-general of the SPD.
48. Günter Guillaume was an official in the Chancellor's Office when he was exposed as an agent of the East German State Security Service.
49. "The Meaning of Aldermaston," *New Statesman*, 31 March 1961, p. 101, as cited in Leon V. Sigal, *Nuclear Forces in Europe: Enduring Dilemmas, Present Prospects* (Washington, D.C.: The Brookings Institution, 1984), p. 93.
50. Thus arose a famous slogan of the German New Left. For an elaboration of the West German case, see Josef Joffe, "Is Schmidt's Party Over?" *New Republic*, 2 June 1982.
51. Siccama, "The Netherlands Depillarized," p. 137.
52. Bad Godesberg was the site of the legendary SPD convention in 1959 where the party shed its residual Marxism and moved toward the embrace of NATO and its nuclear strategy.
53. Anti-NATO and antinuclear, the relatively young prime minister of the Saarland was one of the key contenders for the leadership of the SPD after the Brandt era, which ended with his resignation in 1987.
54. As quoted in Günter Gaus, *Staatserhaltende Opposition: Gespräche mit Herbert Wehner* (Hamburg: Rowohlt, 1966), p. 26.
55. Romano Ledda, "Les propositions du PCI pour la paix et pur le développement dans le monde." *Les Communistes Italiens* (October 1981), as quoted in Jean-François Bureau, "La contestation des armes nucléaires et les partis politiques en Europe de L'Ouest," in Pierre Lellouche, ed., *Pacifisme et dissuasion* (Paris: IFRI, 1983), p. 194.
56. Paolo Buffalini, as quoted by John Vinocur, "Rome and Bonn Appear to Ease View on Missiles," *New York Times*, 16 Jan. 1983.
57. The SS-4 and SS-5 were liquid-fueled, stationary, and equipped with a single warhead. The SS-20 is solid-fueled, mobile, and carries a triple-warhead.
58. In the summer of 1955, 1.7 million West Germans were "killed" and 3.5 million "incapacitated" during the NATO war game, "Carte Blance"—the simu-

lation of a tactical nuclear war in Central Europe. Three years later, "Carte Blanche" provided the German peace movement with one of its most powerful arguments. During the parliamentary debate on West Germany's acquisition of nuclear delivery vehicles, Helmut Schmidt used language that presaged Egon Bahr's attack on the neutron bomb nineteen years later: "Do you remember the NATO maneuvers *Carte Blance* and *Black Lion?* There is a new [nuclear] staff exercise going on at present—this time called *Blue Lion.* I have been told that the officers . . . were reduced to tears [while thinking about] the day-to-day consequences of the reality behind the exercise." *Verhandlungen des Deutschen Bundestages* (the official proceedings of the West Germany parliament), 22 March 1958.

59. Thus arose the memorable phrase by the former SPD mayor of West Berlin, Pastor Heinrich Albertz, at a Bonn rally on October 11, 1981. For the entire speech, see *Frankfurter Rundschau*, 12 Oct. 1981.

CHAPTER 4

Conventional Deterrence

Postwar Europe is an island of astounding stability. Violence has rent outlying areas (for example, when Turkey invaded Cyprus in 1974), and the Soviet Army has repeatedly moved against members of its own bloc. Since 1945, however, not a single shot has been fired between the great powers or between their alliances, and four decades later, the Continent could look back at a period of peace longer than any other in the annals of European history. (The previous record was the thirty-nine-year period between Napoleon's final defeat in 1815 and the outbreak of the Crimean War in 1854.) For a state system that had almost destroyed itself during the "Second Thirty Years' War" between 1914 and 1945, such tranquility betrays a surprising break with the past. The achievement looms even larger when one recalls not only Europe's traditional penchant for force, but also the myriad of unresolved conflicts left in the wake of World War II.

Stability and its Discontent

Surely, Europe's postwar stability does not rest on the acceptance of the status quo. The Continent is divided between two antagonistic blocs. Their frontiers touch in the heart of Germany, a nation that has served as either the arena or the source of great power conflict for centuries past and that, even today, is saddled with a revisionist legacy. Rivals for power, the two blocs are also governed by inimical ideologies and regimes. While the nation-states of Western Europe no longer harbor territorial ambitions, there is hardly a country in Eastern Europe whose borders remained intact after the cataclysm of World War II. Tensions between regime and nation have regularly erupted in violence. And most of East

European countries continue to grapple with nationality problems within and outside their frontiers.

Yet there is peace, which has jelled into ultrastability, and into a paradox to boot. Why should the postwar order endure in the face of so many smoldering challenges? Since it does endure, what are the ligaments of the status quo?

The first factor of stability is the projection of the two once remote superpowers into the heart of the Continent. Order, though not always in harmony with the aspirations of the lesser powers, has become the counterpart of partition. By extending its sway as far as its armies could march, the Soviet Union has built an imperial (and pontifical) domain that has suppressed revisionist instincts and repeated national revolt — from East Germany in 1953 to Poland in 1982. By protecting Western Europe against itself and the hegemonic ambitions of the Soviet Union, the United States has fashioned a voluntary equivalent of empire: a security community where old rivalries persist, but where the use of force is no longer just another political tool.

The second pillar of stability is an unprecedented concentration of peacetime military power on either side of the divide. By fielding about a million troops each in Central Europe, the two alliances have raised the price of conquest enormously. More importantly, however, huge and well-equipped forces-in-being perpetually evoke in the mind of the would-be aggressor the absolute certainty of vast damage. In 1914 the German general staff could still believe in the promise of a lightning strike westward that would reap victory before the cumbersome Russian war machine was fully mobilized. Until 1942, the Wehrmacht could sweep across much of Europe because none of the Third Reich's enemies were prepared for war. Today, however, even a latter-day Schlieffen or Hitler would be intimidated, because the costs of miscalculation loom so unequivocally large.

Third, there is the presence of nuclear weapons — a bottomless reservoir of destruction that has virtually eradicated the distinction between aggression and suicide. Evoking the specter of instantaneous megadeath, nuclear weapons have not only raised the costs of war exponentially but have also created a terrorizing taboo against the use of force of any kind. Real confrontations have been exceedingly rare. And where they did arise — as during the Berlin Crisis — not a single shot was fired, even though battle-ready Soviet and American troops stood almost eyeball-to-eyeball when the Berlin Wall went up in August of 1961. In this encounter, as in other moments of great tension, nuclear weapons imposed a degree of caution on the United States and the Soviet Union that, historically, has not been a distinguishing trait of great powers.

Of course, why something did *not* happen—a war, for instance—can never be proven. Yet it stands to reason that nuclear weapons are an integral element of Europe's unprecedented stability. It stands to reason that thousands of so-called tactical nuclear weapons on the Continent, backed up by the vast strategic arsenals of the two superpowers, have imposed a surfeit of prudence on their possessors. It is not the sudden gift of wisdom but sheer fear which has kept the alliances on their best behavior in Europe. Though unproven, it seems quite clear that the awesome might of the atom has played a central role in keeping Europe an island of peace while the world outside the sway of this balance of terror has been racked by some 150 violent conflicts and wars since 1945.

Yet this astounding stability has bred its own discontent. Instead of counting their blessings, Europeans and Americans alike have begun to look with renewed anxiety at the pillars of their common security. Indeed, if sheer volubility were the true measure of anxiety, the contemporary debate on Alliance strategy might lead an innocent observer to surmise that Western security in Europe hangs by the slenderest of threads. Why else would so many insist on radical reform—be it in the name of "striking deep" or "defending in depth," of "conventional deterrence" or "conventional retaliation," of nuclear "no-first-use" or, perhaps, "no-use-at-all"?

Given the sturdiness of the European order, it could not be the impending collapse of NATO's forward defense in Central Europe that inspires the insistent search for doctrinal relief. Quantitatively, the Alliance is no more outmanned or outgunned than in years past. Nor is the political climate in Europe worse than in the forties through the sixties; if anything, it is more benign than in the Cold War decades.

Of course, it is not NATO's strategy as such that has fallen on hard times, but first and foremost the nuclear premise of that strategy. Nuclear weapons have been the core and ultima ratio of Western strategy in Europe; if there is anything that unites all the critics it is their conviction that the Alliance should, and can, wean itself from what is said to be an excessive reliance on the atom. The leitmotiv of criticism is the stress on conventional weapons, whether for the sake of deterrence or repellence. The variations on this theme are myriad. There are those who believe in the virtue of "no-first-use," and those who believe in the promise of "emerging technology" (ET). Some would either defend or attack in an extended space; others would seek to deter the Soviet Union by threatening "conventional retaliation." Yet antinuclear sentiments are the common bias of the critics, transcending politics and ideology. This aversion is hardly surprising at the present juncture in Alliance history.

It is no accident that the strategic debate should have unfolded in the setting of an unprecedented societal challenge to the mainstays of Western defense. The antinuclear revolt that drove hundreds of thousands of demonstrators into the streets and squares of Western Europe during the early 1980s did not achieve its immediate objective: to derail the deployment of Pershing II and cruise missiles, which began on schedule at the end of 1983. But the counterelites who sought to rouse popular anxieties about the policies of Western Europe governments scored, perhaps, a more profound victory. Though they did not carry the day, the peace movements of the Northern Tier (along with the social democratic left) succeeded in imposing their own terms on the political debate. Their conceptual—or more precisely, psychological—victory became amply evident when the defenders of the orthodox consensus themselves were forced to assume the burden of proof; when governments everywhere began to legitimize their military decisions not in terms of security but in the vernacular of arms control and disarmament; and when the strategic community on either side of the ocean embarked on an ardent search for non-nuclear alternatives for Western defense.

Some of the roots of discontent are, of course, older than the peace movement. NATO's hallowed flexible response doctrine, ratified in 1967, is premised on Western escalation dominance—and those halcyon days are irretrievably past. The Soviet Union's relentless build-up toward parity and beyond has blunted America's nuclear edge while sharpening its exposure to Soviet strategic nuclear strikes. Moscow's parallel quest for superiority on the theater level—with the SS-20 at one end of the spectrum and a new generation of more precise, shorter range missiles at the other—has yielded to the Soviet Union a counterdeterrence panoply that all but constitutes a first-strike threat. Together, these two trends have spawned two predictable sets of anxieties among Western elites.

On the American side of the Atlantic, the Soviet Union's impressive nuclear investment has inevitably increased the price of America's nuclear guarantee to its European clients. Extended deterrence *made in the USA* now carries unbearable risks for its providers, and one would not be far wrong in surmising that the widening American search for conventional options is also an unspoken attempt to lower the existential price of Alliance leadership. Nor should this come as a surprise. If the United States must court suicide to make good on its nuclear pledge to the Allies, it can hardly be faulted for seeking to postpone the nuclear moment of truth as long as possible.

European concerns are more ambivalent. On the one hand, the where-withals of extended deterrence are no source of comfort. Nuclear weapons on their soil, as the West Europeans were amply reminded in the course of the Euromissile drama, are both a shield and a magnet; the western half of the continent will be the first (if not only) nuclear battle-field and victim if deterrence fails. On the other hand, the Allies have never been soothed by the prospect of an extended conventional defense either; in their hearts, West Europeans are as repelled by such notions as "pauses" and "firebreaks" as Americans are naturally attracted to them. (From an American vantage point, a European war that cannot be de-terred should at least stop at the other Atlantic shore.) The Europeans have recently come to look more kindly on conventional options, but only as long as they buttress the credibility of the nuclear threat. Their enthusiasm will surely wane once these options proliferate into a substi-tute for nuclear deterrence.

The zeitgeist of the 1980s, fortified by the din of the demonstrations, has merely suppressed, not buried, the second half of the classic Euro-pean dilemma. Conventional defense, shunted aside like an unwanted child since the grandiose but unmet Lisbon force goals of 1952, began to look good because the nuclear orthodoxy looks so grim when contem-plated through the prism of societal dissent. Enter the dazzling prom-ise of emerging technology, and the stage was set for a curious, but not quite accidental, convergence between the moralists and the technolo-gists—between those who would wish away nuclear weapons and those who would wish them good speed because there are better and smarter weapons on the shelf or in the pipeline.

If nuclear weapons, with their immense killing power, can command neither Soviet respect nor popular consent, why not rely on the surgical precision of conventional weapons rather than on sheer nuclear destruc-tiveness? High tech conventionalism appeals to liberals because it veils the grisly face of nuclear war, and to conservatives because it might lift some restraints on the forbidding use of any force. Conventional deter-rence appeals to Europeans because it might pacify their rattled elector-ates, and to Americans because it might loosen the fateful link between European and global war. In short, conventionalism has cast so wide a spell because it promises to slice through many nasty dilemmas both old and new; and it looks cheap to boot because manpower will always be more costly than microchips. Can the promise live up to the problem?

No-First-Use and the Political Role of Nuclear Weapons

The root of the most harrowing Western security dilemma in Europe lies in the fact that only nuclear weapons can deter nuclear weapons. This may be a truism, but it defines the ironclad parameters of Europe's defense choices; the sustained Soviet build-up in the European theater has done nothing to loosen those limits. The dilemma cannot be cracked by a peace movement that simply wishes to exorcise nuclear weapons, nor by high tech wizardry that would try to circumvent the quandary by deep interdiction or high-speed maneuver. At best, NATO could (and should) mute its dependence on nuclear weapons, and this—the idea of no-first-use (NFU)—is precisely the much debated prescription of the *Foreign Affairs* "gang of four": Messrs. Bundy, Kennan, McNamara, and Smith.[1] These authors, all former public officials, fall neatly in between the antinuclear activists and the technology-minded conventionalists. If their hearts are with the antinuclear critics of NATO's strategic orthodoxy, their memories are those of prominent decisionmakers who used to stand at the very core of that tradition. As a result, their proposal is suffused with a vexing ambivalence toward nuclear weapons. A shaky compromise between possession and abstinence, the no-first-use idea merely limns what ought to be starkly etched: implications of staggering proportions.

For NFU proposes to do away with the very mainstay of NATO's strategy in Europe: the launching of nuclear weapons as a deliberate escalatory response to a merely conventional Soviet aggression. NFU, then, embodies a sweeping policy of self-denial because it would bid the Alliance to not engage in nuclear strikes under any circumstances save one: the first use of nuclear weapons by the Warsaw Pact (WTO). NFU would enjoin NATO to *accept defeat in a conventional war rather than resort to nuclear weapons in order to reverse the verdict of the non-nuclear battle.* What might be the consequences of such a posture?

No-First-Use or No-Use-At-All?

A pledge like no-first-use signals a nation's or an alliance's intent as to its choice of weapons in the event of war. Yet any declaration of intent among nations, and certainly one like NFU, raises a critical problem: by itself, such a declaration is meaningless, if not pernicious. The Soviet Union pledged adherence to NFU in 1982.[2] In the words of the Soviet defense minister, Dimitri F. Ustinov, "Only extraordinary circumstances—a direct nuclear aggression against the Soviet state or its allies—can compel us to resort to a retaliatory strike as a last means of self-defense."[3] Shortly after Foreign Minister Andrei Gromyko had pronounced his country's NFU pledge before the United Nations, Ustinov wrote: "[NFU] means that in the preparation of the armed forces, still more attention will now be given to the task of preventing a military conflict from growing into a nuclear one. These tasks in all their diversity are becoming an integral part of our military activities."[4]

Did this statement signal a fundamental reorganization in tactics, equipment, and doctrine? According to an authoritative Soviet observer, Mikhail Milshtein, the practical effects of the advertised NFU posture were far more modest. "In order to implement the commitment," wrote Milshtein, "a strict regimen has been established for tightening still further the control over nuclear weapons to ensure that there is absolutely no possibility of unauthorized launching of nuclear weapons of any kind, tactical or strategic."[5] In other words, the Soviet NFU pledge seems to mean precious little above and beyond what in fact both superpowers have been trying to do for decades—to impose control systems on their armed forces that would militate against the unauthorized or accidental use of nuclear weapons.

In all other respects, the Soviet NFU proclamation has not been followed by the appropriate doctrinal, tactical, and practical reforms. Indeed, the opposite is the case. Soviet doctrine continues to stress the need for decisive strikes, both conventional and nuclear. Surely, the Soviets would hope to win a war in Europe before it goes nuclear; yet whatever their NFU statements might presage, virtually all of the their military exercises continue to reveal the classic pattern of massive nuclear operations on well-nigh all levels of conflict. In fact, precisely around the time they made their NFU pledge, the Soviets introduced three new nuclear artillery systems into Central Europe that, by dint of their forward position, do not appear to be ideal second-use weapons.[6] Nor does their relentless missile build-up in Europe—especially with a new generation of shorter range missiles, the SS-21, SS-23, and SS-22, moved forward into Czechoslovakia and East Germany in the mid-1980s—indicate that the Soviets are about the forsake the atom in their planning for war.[7]

The point is not their hypocrisy (on which the Soviets have no monopoly) but the vacuity of any verbal pledge, no matter how solemnly uttered. Nations plan for war not by listening to their opponent's commitments but by looking at his capabilities. As long as NATO has nuclear weapons in the field, they might be used. As long as they might be used, those weapons must be destroyed—by conventional means if possible, by nuclear means if necessary. A no-first-use vow on the part of NATO, therefore, does not change the basic intention of Soviet planners: to eliminate the Alliance's nuclear weapons *before* they are used.

At the opposite extreme in the spectrum of possibilities, a Western NFU declaration might actually be pernicious—if in fact it did change Soviet risk assessments. The key (though unstated) implication of the NFU idea advocated by the four American former officials—whose *Foreign Affairs* article gave rise to the NFU debate—is that the Alliance must accept defeat in a conventional war rather than resort to the ultima ratio of nuclear weapons. The prescription is clad in absolute terms: "Even the most responsible choice of even the most limited nuclear action to prevent even the most imminent conventional disaster should be left out of authorized policy. What the Alliance needs most today is . . . a clear-cut decision to avoid nuclear actions as long as others do."[8]

Such an injunction is more than a mere variation on NATO's prevailing doctrine, as it may well end up as a prescription for unilateral nuclear disarmament in the European theater. If the Alliance will not resort to nuclear weapons to avert conventional defeat, it will not even use the threat of going nuclear to deter a conventional attack—against its bases, stockpiles, and launch vehicles—let alone to repel such an attack with the aid of nuclear weapons. To propose such a policy is to issue the Soviets a standing invitation to turn a Western NFU pledge into a certainty by launching a preemptive conventional attack against NATO's nuclear assets in Europe. And if the Soviets are so tempted (as they should be, because they could not possibly want to fight in the presence of NATO nuclear weapons), the distinction between no-first-use and no-use-at-all simply vanishes along with the weapons held in reserve for second use. With Western nuclear assets either obliterated or captured through a reduced-risk conventional foray by the Soviets, there will be neither a first nor a second strike, nor any strike at all.

No-first-use—possession for the sake of retaliation, and retaliation only—is thus a principle that, in practice, threatens to collapse upon itself. NFU may well be meaningless in terms of its own purpose, which is to preclude first use but to allow for second use. It could not change a key Soviet goal, which is to remove Western weapons from the battlefield. Nor could NFU transform Soviet strategy, which is to accomplish that goal, if possible, with conventional means alone. To offer one's weapons for conventional preemption, by renouncing the threat of escalation, cannot strengthen deterrence in Europe.

Indeed, the NFU proposal of the American *Foreign Affairs* authors makes little sense unless it is seen for what it really is: a halfway measure toward a strictly conventional posture. Hence the apocalyptic language of statements such as "Any use of nuclear weapons in Europe, by the Alliance or against it, carries with it a high and inescapable risk of escalation into a general nuclear war which would bring ruin to all and victory to none."[9] Hence, also, the "Son of No-First-Use" sequel one year later by the former secretary of defense, Robert S. McNamara, which makes that point in all its baldness: "Nuclear weapons serve no military purpose whatsoever. They are totally useless—except only to deter one's own opponent from using them."[10]

Conventional Versus Nuclear Deterrence

To be meaningful, the NFU principle must transcend itself; to change reality, the principle must be taken to its ultimate conclusion, which is what could be called NUN: "No Use—Never!" To do so requires taking concrete, visible, and credible steps beyond mere declarations. Most of NATO's battlefield weapons are concentrated in about twenty depots close to the inter-German border. Since the Soviets cannot dismiss them as long as they are in place, these weapons would have to be pulled back or pulled out.[11] A clear instance of the pull-back idea is contained in the Palme Commission Report.[12] The commission proposes the establishment of a nuclear-free zone (NFZ) in Central Europe—that is, an area void of nuclear munitions and storage sites extending 150 kilometers in either direction from the inter-German border. (A complete ban is, again, quite meaningless because that would force the British and the French to dismantle their independent deterrents.)

Nuclear-free-zones combined with NFU would evidently demonstrate to the Soviets that the West planned to practice what it preached. Yet would such a move really contribute to the stability of the European order? Stability is often confused with one of its conditions, namely, the rough equality of power between contenders. But there must in fact be more than that. Even ultimate defensive superiority does not necessarily discourage aggression. If it did, Egypt would not have attacked Israel in 1973. Nor would Hitler and Hirohito have launched a war against the Soviet Union and the United States, respectively, in 1941. Especially where the safety of allies is at stake, at least two additional conditions must obtain: the *clarity* and the *certainty* of commitments. If guarantees are ambiguous and riddled with qualifications, would-be aggressors will be tempted to test or ignore them—as did Austria when it moved against Russian-sheltered Serbia in 1914. Yet even the clearest of commitments may fall short of deterrence, as the German attack against Poland in 1939 demonstrated. Hitler moved in spite of formal obligations which bound Britain and France to treat aggression against Poland as casus belli. Hence the crucial requirement of certainty, which enjoins patron powers to limit their freedom of choice—including the freedom to abandon an ally at the moment of truth.

A classic implementation of the certainty principle is to take a hostage posture. The United States has tied its hands in Europe by inserting some 200,000 troops and several thousand nuclear weapons close to the potential locus of confrontation, the inter-German border. These dispositions embody a three-part message. First, the United States will be embroiled from the start. Second, nuclear weapons may be launched as soon as the conventional tide turns against the West. These two messages add up to the third: the threat of rapid escalation and damage vast enough to exceed the value of the aggressor's objectives.

Now assume that one element of this equation is physically removed —withdraw the nuclear weapons to a more distant periphery. At first sight, this is an attractive notion. Would it not help the cause of peace if adversaries put some distance between themselves and the brink of conflagration? The perverse logic of nuclear deterrence yields a different answer. Because nuclear weapons wreak swift and massive devastation, thereby favoring the offense over the defense, they deliver a crucial advantage to the side that moves first. Because this is so, both sides labor under the burden of pernicious expectations. In a time of crisis, each side would fear that the other side was about to move into the vacuum, tempting both to rush off first. Yet mere physical movement, though intended to deter, could signal the intent to use—building up pressures for preemption and war.

Alternatively, the Soviets might actually believe in a NFU pledge once the commitment was matched with a nuclear-free zone. That faith would surely change their cost calculations as they contemplate conventional aggression. As shown by the Egyptian thrust across the Suez Canal in 1973, nations do not necessarily go to war to defeat or occupy an enemy. They may aim for minor military gains in order to score a major political victory. They may want to dislodge an opponent or transform the political constellation so as to acquire a commanding position in future negotiations. In Sadat's case, gaining only six kilometers beyond the Suez

Canal sufficed to overturn a Middle East status quo that seemed to have been frozen in perpetuity.

Now assume, as the Palme Commission suggested, a nuclear-free zone stretching westward from the Elbe River for 150 kilometers. At its narrowest, the Federal Republic is only 225 kilometers wide. One-third of West Germany's population and one-quarter of its industrial potential are located within a 100-kilometer strip west of the inter-German border. Hamburg is but one tank hour (40 kilometers) from the Lauenburg checkpoint, and the Federal Republic's industrial heartland in the Rhine–Ruhr area begins about 150 kilometers from the line of demarcation. With nuclear weapons withdrawn, and the risk of immediate escalation palpably diminished, a conventional lunge—stopping well short of the new nuclear perimeter in the West—would look considerably less irrational than under current circumstances. If victorious, the Soviets would pocket a momentous political and strategic asset while shifting the onus of escalation (for the purpose of dislodging them) onto the West.

The point here is not to invoke scenarios of doom and to elevate worst case analyses into a theory, but to dissect some paradoxes of nuclear deterrence. It is not likely that an NFU commitment would indeed dispel suspicions and reduce "possibilities for miscalculation," as General Milshtein has claimed.[13] In a deterrence setting, forces-in-being and in place are better than the threat of Armageddon one or several steps removed. It is better to be safely ensconced at the brink than to rush back to it in a moment of crisis, thereby provoking the degeneration of the crisis into an actual conflict. A low nuclear threshold, embodied in the sheer physical presence of nuclear weapons, is better than a high nuclear threshold, or none at all. If the former inhibits adventurism by imposing an exorbitant price on miscalculation, the latter may virtually invite such folly, leaving us with the worst of all possible worlds: "a failure of conventional deterrence *and* nuclear war,"[14] because we might rebel at the verdict of conventional defeat and go nuclear to reverse it. In short, if nuclear weapons are the queens of deterrence, then their removal from the board will liberate the conventional pawns from the restraints of the game.[15]

The problem is not that the Warsaw Pact may have more pawns (which it does). Nor does the problem merely grow out of the very practical consideration that the threat of first use imposes a healthy dose of caution on the Soviets; since their planners cannot totally dismiss the prospect of massive and early punishment, they must refrain from concentrating their conventional forces for a rapid breakthrough. The most fundamental problem flows from the notion of "conventional deterrence" that has come to fascinate those who believe that nuclear weapons are not only dangerous but also unnecessary. The critical assumption behind that concept is that the West could muster enough conventional power to deny victory to the aggressor, thus deterring him from ever launching a war. The practical difficulties of accumulating overwhelming defensive strength are legion. (NATO has tried and failed routinely since 1952.) Yet the real flaw rests in the concept itself because it ignores the most important element of deterrence: the threat of unacceptable punishment.

Deterrence through defense sends the message, "You will not get what you want because I shall repulse you." Deterrence through punishment signals, "If you try, you (and your society) might be destroyed." To which a conventionalist might reply: "It is true that the second threat is more effective, but the first is surely more credible. You will not impress your opponent if you threaten mutual suicide, especially since the United States would have to threaten suicide on behalf of nations other than itself."

This argument is persuasive as far as it goes. For there is more to deterrence than credibility. Deterrence flows from both the size of the threat, and the probability of its execution. (Deterrence, in other words, is the mathematical product of both factors.) A very low probability multiplied by potentially infinite damage still yields a deterrence product of potentially infinite value. While it is plausible that the West might be self-deterred from launching nuclear strikes, which is the more effective threat: denial through conventional defense, or incalculable punishment through nuclear retaliation? Even the small probabiity of losing one's head (nuclear war) seems more paralyzing than the more certain prospect of losing a hand (conventional defeat). It is the difference between mutilation and death. And so the gains of aggression must inevitably pale in the face of the existential costs that lurk further down the road. The West will not be better off if it merely keeps the conventional stumbling blocks in place, while renouncing the threat to trigger the nuclear avalanche when the situation so demands.

Finally, nuclear deterrence has a good track record; at best, conventional deterrence has only a very dubious one. After surveying twelve instances of conventional deterrence between 1938 and 1979, John J. Mearsheimer concluded that it worked in two cases and failed in ten.[16] "This 83.3 percent failure rate for deterrence by conventional defense after 1938," notes Samuel Huntington, "contrasts rather markedly with the zero failure rate for deterrence by nuclear retaliation for a quarter century after 1945."[17]

NFU and the Soviet Union: Some Practical Problems

Above and beyond these conceptual flaws, there are some practical problems with a meaningful NFU posture. With nuclear weapons no longer carrying the weight they presently do, NFU would require some compensation in the form of conventional improvements. According to one who understands these matters,

[a no-first-use] commitment makes rigid demands on further enhancing the combat readiness of our armies, their technical equipment, perfection of control and communication . . . and strengthening the moral and political conditioning of our troops. It is necessary that the influence of the factor of surprise be reduced to a minimum, so that the aggressor would not be tempted to use with impunity his nuclear weapons.[18]

These words were written by the Soviet defense minister, Dimitri Ustinov, but they might have been uttered by any of his Western counterparts. Indeed, such a prescription would put it too mildly from a Western perspective. For NATO the problem has always been the asymmetry of Eastern and Western capabilities, which required an asymmetrical Westtern response. From the early days of the Alliance, nuclear weapons were to compensate for some obvious geostrategic advantages of the Warsaw Pact. The pact has more forces and more equipment in Central Europe (most notably tanks, but also antitank weapons and artillery). The Soviet Union can also use that advantage more rapidly because its reserves are massed close to the heart of Europe, whereas the United States must ferry its reinforcements across some 3,000 miles of ocean. That asymmetry presumably prompted the *Foreign Affairs* authors to note that it "is obvious that any such NFU policy would require a strengthened confidence in the adequacy of conventional forces of the Alliance, above all the forces in place on the central front and those available for prompt reinforcement."[19]

There are three theoretical solutions to the problem of asymmetry. As one possibility, the Soviet Union would honor a meaningful Western NFU posture with a substantial reduction of its forward forces, most importantly by diminishing the 2.5 : 1 tank superiority the Warsaw Pact enjoys in Central Europe. A second solution would be a compensatory build-up by the West: a substantial increase in manpower and equipment, especially in tanks, self-propelled artillery, and precision-guided munitions that could strike beyond the line of battle. The third possible solution is a change in Western doctrine. In order to threaten unacceptable punishment without the use of nuclear weapons, the Alliance would abandon its strictly defensive posture, as laid down in the forward defense strategy, and adopt a conventional retaliation doctrine, as suggested by Samuel Huntington in his 1984 *International Security* article.

None of these solutions, however, stands a realistic chance of implementation. Solution Three — a deep, Israeli-like thrust into WTO territory as soon as hostilities had commenced — would force NATO to overturn an unwritten article of the Alliance constitution. While such a forward lunge would threaten a most precious Soviet asset — its political and pontifical glacis in Eastern Europe — and perhaps would buttress deterrence, it would also threaten what all of Western Europe tacitly regards as a vital reinsurance policy toward Moscow: the stance of nonprovocation and cooperation that goes by the names of Ostpolitik and détente. None of the European members will accept a new alliance agreement that purports to buy an uncertain increase in deterrence at the price of an immediate and frightening loss in détente, a point that will be elaborated later in this chapter.

Solutions One and Two, on the other hand, are both predicated on a fundamental change in the balance of conventional power in favor of the West. Yet the logic of international politics, based on the principle of reciprocity, does not countenance free gifts — and neither do the Soviets. While the Soviet Union would claim for itself the right to enhance its own conventional might in parallel with an NFU posture (as elucidated by Marshall Ustinov in the pages of *Pravda*), it would deny such compensation to the West. As a Hungarian official familiar with these matters has noted:

A no first use policy, even if jointly adhered to, would not be of much help in alleviating the risks and burdens of military confrontation in Europe if it leads NATO to such a heavy investment in conventional arms that the balance, as perceived by the East, is upset. The Western claim for an improved balance can hardly be endorsed. . . . The crucial issue . . . is that an increase in NATO's conventional offensive capabilities as planned in Airland Battle 2000 [sic] will clearly be seen as provocative and part of the broader U.S. effort to attain military superiority.[20]

In other words, there is no squaring of the circle. To close the deterrence gap opened by the removal or the devaluation of the nuclear threat, a Western NFU posture would have to make up the difference by adding to NATO's conventional wherewithals. Yet to do so, as even the détente-minded proponents of NFU demand, will not pacify, but provoke, the East. Given the logic just outlined, NFU plus the requisite conventional increases by the West would be met by countercompensation on the part of the Warsaw Pact. The result would be a net loss in security for the West. In exchange for renouncing the first-use threat, NATO would gain nothing but the reaffirmation at a higher level of the present conventional asymmetry, yet without the nuclear reinsurance that has always functioned to render an age-old imbalance tolerable. Such an outcome would not enhance military stability in Europe.

Allies, Angst, and No-First-Use

When McGeorge Bundy and his colleagues published their NFU proposal, the swiftest and most massive counterattack came from the Federal Republic, and predictably so.[21] Among all the European allies, West Germany stands to lose the most from any doctrinal shift that would loosen the link between conventional aggression and the threat of general war. The German *Foreign Affairs* foursome devoted painstaking efforts to reading between the lines of the American NFU proposal, and the exercise left them predictably rattled. As could be expected, they fastened on the American authors' "redefinition" of America's "extraordinary [security] guarantee" and read it as an implied "withdrawal from present commitments of the United States." Moreover, "if the ideas of the authors were to be followed, conventional conflicts in Europe would no longer involve any existential risks for the territory of the Soviet Union and . . . *would be without risk for the territory of the United States as well.*"[22] No wonder, then, that the NFU proposal fueled the worst of German anxieties by evoking the specter of abandonment. It was immediately interpreted as a prod to greater conventional efforts that would at last permit the United States to retract safely behind its nuclear umbrella on the opposite shore of the Atlantic.[23]

These fears were not blunted one year later by Robert McNamara's one-man sequel, in which he admitted to having counseled Presidents Kennedy and Johnson to "never initiate, under any circumstances, the use of nuclear weapons."[24] Whatever the reality of these fears, one political lesson stands out in dramatic detail. In their NFU plea, Bundy and his cohorts were inspired by NATO's "disarray" and its "divisive debates" on matters nuclear. To address oneself to the "internal health of the Western alliance" (meaning, to the domestic revulsion against nuclear weapons), was an appropriate and timely effort. Yet what use is an idea like no-first-use if it cannot really pacify the militant pacifists (who resent the very existence of nuclear weapons on their soil), while profoundly unnerving those who are strongly opposed to NFU and who represent the political establishment of Western Europe? If the issue is reassurance and the reinvigoration of public support for defense, then the real question in a divided society is, Reassurance for *whom*?

The Federal Republic's established political elites have never been reassured by American attempts to marginalize nuclear weapons, and hence the NFU idea struck the rawest of nerves. According to the four German critics, the NFU plea "makes it completely clear that a withdrawal of the United States from its previous guarantee is at stake. . . . The proposed no-first-use policy would destroy the confidence of the Europeans and especially of Germans in the European-American Alliance as a community of risk."[25]

Why would an idea like the NFU trigger such an obsessive reaction? It did so because it went squarely against the First Commandment of Extended Deterrence Under Conditions of Parity—there shall be no sanctuaries. Non-nuclear allies feel safe when their protector is not, when he is just as likely to be the target of attack as they are. Helmut Schmidt used precisely this rationale in favor of the INF deployment; moving against Western Europe, "the Soviet Union will always have to take into account that its threats will necessarily be targeted on American [INF] systems, too—hence that the U.S. will be inexorably involved."[26] Conversely, Western Europeans are oppressed by the nightmare of an aggression that would begin and end in Europe, a battle that would sacrifice Europe on the altar of limited war while sparing the United States. Hence the eternal European quest for coupling, which has always had the same motive in all its myriad variations: to tie America's hands by rendering it just as vulnerable to Soviet aggression as Western Europe is by dint of its weakness and geography.

Nor is it so strange that the weak should draw solace from the vulnerability of the strong. Unable to defend themselves, yet wary about the solidity of guarantees in the moment of truth, they want to make sure that an attack on them is an attack on their patron. Only if both are chained together in a community of risk will there be safety for dependents who might otherwise appear to be easy prey. This is why the Strategic Defense Initiative (SDI)—launched by President Reagan in 1983 and promoted in earnest in 1985—was bound to profoundly unnerve the Western Europeans. In theory, of course, SDI should have achieved the very opposite; it should have reassured the Allies. For if technically feasible, SDI promises a return to those halcyon days of extended deterrence in the 1950s, when the United States could safely threaten nuclear devastation on behalf of its allies without fear of Soviet retribution.

Yet for most Europeans, SDI is no source of comfort. It evokes a world of sheltered superpowers, safely ensconced behind Maginot Lines in the sky and tempted to act out their military rivalry in the unprotected arena of Europe. "One . . . great concern of France," said Defense Minister Paul

Quilès, "is the emergence of zones of unequal security within the Alliance. The space-based system . . . could not cope with intermediate or short-range ballistic missiles which threaten Europe."[27] In addition, SDI conjures up yet another array of weapons that threaten, because of astronomical cost and technological sophistication, to elude the control of the Europeans and to sharpen their existential dependence on a remote superpower. Rightly or not, the Europeans seek deterrence not in an invulnerable patron but in one who is as exposed as they are. Only a United States unable to stay aloof from Europe's conflicts with the Soviet Union is likely to give pause to the would-be aggressor. Only a United States destined to be dragged into all of Europe's quarrels could inflict existential costs on the Soviet Union that exceed by far the value of any conceivable objective it might covet in Europe.

Nuclear weapons in a forward position offer a perfect coupling device. As long as they are in place, they might be used; once even the smallest weapon explodes, there may be no firebreak short of Armageddon (total vertical escalation) and Moscow (total horizontal escalation). The ultimate logic of nuclear weapons being placed in close proximity to the potential battlefield is the destruction of sanctuaries. If the great are as vulnerable as the small, dependents will enjoy as much security as those who can fend for themselves. If a war in Europe threatens to engulf the United States, the Soviet Union will be less tempted to start one. In short, nuclear weapons in Europe promise to eradicate the distinction between limited and global war, and that is precisely the soil on which extended deterrence flourishes.

The German critics reacted as harshly as they did to the NFU proposal because they read its implications correctly. A strategy that would deliberately accept conventional defeat in Europe is the very opposite of coupling. It would increase American options rather than compress them. It would sharpen, rather than eradicate, the distinction between regional and global war. It would deliver the United States from imprisonment as the hostage to Western Europe's security, and it would reaffirm Europe's role as the hostage to Soviet might. Hence the evident Soviet interest in NFU. In the absence of countervailing conventional measures (which, if implemented, the Russians would not leave unanswered), the Soviet Union would gain twice.

Militarily, the withdrawal or devaluation of the nuclear queen would strengthen the advantage of the more numerous Warsaw Pact pawns. Politically, an American no-first-use pledge would undoubtedly weaken European faith in the certainty of America's commitment, thereby weakening the bonds of the Euro-American alliance as well. Such a constellation—a Europe not strong enough to defend itself, yet dependent on a diminished American guarantee—spells a diplomatic advantage for the Soviet Union that need not be belabored. Nor can NFU restore the "health of the Western alliance" once it is seen for what it is: a strategy that would accept conventional defeat rather than resort to nuclear weapons. In short, an NFU posture would strike at the core of the transatlantic security bargain; while the compact might still hold, it would not be the kind of alliance that has underwritten Europe's stability for forty years.

The New Conventionalism: Defense in Depth

If it is hard to imagine the Alliance minus its nuclear girders, it is no less difficult to visualize how the West would ever make good on its threat to take the first step into the nuclear unknown. The historical conditions that spawned NATO's first-use strategy have long since evolved into a grimmer setting. The United States is no longer immune to Soviet counterstrikes and in Europe proper, the Soviets have matched, if not overmatched, the West's nuclear arsenal on every level. In a world of parity and Soviet theater superiority, how can the victims credibly threaten Armageddon?

That an escape from this dilemma does beckon is precisely the message of the New Conventionalists. On either side of the Atlantic, civilian and military strategists as disparate as NATO's supreme commander and the "counter-experts" sympathetic to the peace movement, have joined their voices in praise of the "third way." The chorus proclaims that NATO need not mortgage its security to a shaky nuclear response, because it can rely on a conventional alternative to the Hobson's choice of "preemptive surrender" or "Apocalypse Now."

The New Conventionalists assume that the Alliance must continue to live with its congenital defects. First, more than a generation after the aborted Lisbon force goals (ninety-two divisions) were set, there is little hope in harnessing enough troops for defensive superiority. Second, NATO will always be at a natural disadvantage because it relies for reinforcements on a faraway protector, whereas the Soviets can mass their reserves close to the focus of potential battle. Yet in spite of these social and geographic handicaps, the New Conventionalists believe that the nuclear moment of truth could be maximally postponed, if not avoided altogether. Buttressed by a steady 3 to 4 percent annual rise in real defense spending, the Alliance would only have to learn how to neutralize sheer mass by maneuver, interdiction, technological prowess, or some combination thereof.

The New Conventionalists can be roughly divided into two subgroups: the Forward and the Rearward Schools. Both proceed from the common premise that NATO's forward defense strategy—the thin "layercake" of national military contingents along the inter-German border—could hardly withstand a determined Soviet punch. Indeed, this Bar-Lev Line writ large all but invites a high-energy Warsaw Pact attack along multiple axes so as to conceal its true focus from the defenders.[28] After the initial breakthrough, momentum would be maintained by WTO reinforcement armies in tight echelons, swept to victory by thousands of tactical aircraft blazing an air superiority corridor across Germany and the Lowlands.

Given the assumption of a shallow "layercake" of Allied armies, the New Conventionalists logically propose to shift the focus of battle either forward or backward. The Rearward School would like to defend in depth, hoping to compensate for NATO's lack of manpower with fleet-footed maneuver through an extended defensive space. The Forward School would overcome the same handicap by carrying the war into WTO territory in one of several ways: by deep interdiction with a supersophisticated fire-and-forget technology (Deep Strike, or Follow-On Forces Attack); by "counteroffensive" as laid out in the U.S. Army's Airland Battle concept; or by a strategy of immediate conventional retaliation, as suggested by the former White House adviser, Samuel Huntington.

Both approaches are understandable responses to the conundrums of forward defense and extended deterrence in a postparity age. At first glance, they yield a good deal of psychological satisfaction when compared to the unease attending any defense based on a tightly compressed line-up like NATO's. If the line breaks, what is there to stop a Soviet lunge short of the Rhine? Alternatively, if war is not deterred, why not fight it on the enemy's territory rather than on densely populated home ground? Indeed, why not seize the initiative from the very beginning? Yet the pleasure of transcendence—especially when fortified by visions of low-cost solutions to NATO's eternal complaints—may well be the strongest appeal, for both schools.

Defense in Depth: The Territorial Approach

The defense in depth school encompasses a motley crowd. At one extreme of the spectrum are those German reformers who turn out high technology variations on territorial defense; on the other end are mainly American strategists who have become enamored of "maneuver" (as opposed to the "classic" American style of "attrition"). While the German reformers are largely associated with the cause of the peace movement or with the SPD left wing, their American counterparts hail mainly from conservative or neo-conservative quarters. (In both cases, the ideological label fits only loosely, yet as shall be seen, it may be no accident that two such disparate groups should be attracted to similar notions of strategic reform.) In both camps, the target of discontent is NATO's flexible response doctrine, which bids NATO to stop a Soviet assault as close to the inter-German border as possible and, if need be, with nuclear weapons.

The key premise of the German reformers was expressed by an elder statesman of the German peace movement, Carl-Friedrich von Weizsäcker: "More and more voices are being raised in the West in favor of a conventional defense, yet not all types of conventional arms preserve the peace. An arms race of tank armies is expensive and hence destabilizing. A conventional posture would have to be designed for defensive purposes only. Such a posture is feasible with modern precision weapons carried by infantry."[29]

His disciple, Horst Afheldt, would have the *Bundeswehr* (West Germany's federal forces) field only "military instruments which offer no targets, hence do not warrant the use of mass-destruction weapons on the part of the opponent. . . . Protection against area weapons is found only throughout an extended space [*Tiefe des Raumes*]. Whence it follows that we cannot establish any fronts, that we cannot defend any borders."[30] Specifically, he would rely on a countrywide network of motorized, self-sufficient twenty-man units, which are to take a heavy toll on enemy armor. "Technological progress . . . provides the means required for the 1990s: precision-guidance weapons of the third generation . . . which can be effectively deployed by small units [operating from] well-prepared hideouts—the techno-commandos, the techno-guerrilla."[31]

By the mid-1980s, key elements of this concept had filtered into the strategic thinking of the West Germany Social Democratic party. The most prominent instance was a proposal authored by the chairman of the SPD's Executive's Security Policy Commission, Andreas von Bülow.[32] Based on the withdrawal of all battlefield and medium-range nuclear weapons and the establishment of a 300-kilometer wide nuclear-free zone in Central Europe, the strategy would dispense with the bulk of the Bundeswehr's tanks and invest in "third-generation" antitank weapons instead. Attack aircraft would similarly be sacrificed in favor of an "area air defense" (presumably based on surface-to-air missiles) which would "trap and bleed the aggressor." The territorial and the regular army would be rolled into one. The strategy's backbone would be a far-flung and "close-knit anti-tank net [that] offers no worthwhile targets to enemy artillery and aircraft." In contrast to a pure area defense concept, however, this scheme would seek to stop an invader as close as possible to the inter-German border (within 70 kilometers). Yet the underlying aspiration of both area and antitank net defenders remains the same: to build a "structure incapable of attack."[33]

How do such reform proposals relate to NATO's prevailing doctrine? If flexible response threatens the enemy with the maximum price of invasion, territorial defense would obey latter-day partisan tactics and seek to extract the maximum price of occupation.[34] Essentially, the German reformers propose to marry the idea of *Heimatverteidigung* ("territorial defense") to highly mobile forces and precision-guided munitions (PGMs). In general, they envision a sophisticated guerrilla war in Central Europe, with light infantry units exploiting terrain for dispersal and concealment, and close-up PGMs for antitank warfare. Their dream is to break down the big battle into a multitude of little ones, and though they might lose every single one of them (by having to yield and withdraw), they would best Goliath in the end through a relentless campaign that would exhaust and demoralize him.

Victory by whittling down the enemy is a noble but naive dream. First of all, it endows infantry-operated PGMs with exaggerated powers. These munitions have not yet turned the tank into an evolutionary dud. From the Yom Kippur War in 1973 to the Lebanon War in 1982, it was mainly tanks that killed tanks, not smart munitions.[35] Nor do such PGMs (especially hand-held ones) stand up to well-led, well-deployed, and well-armored tanks, as the Israelis easily demonstrated in Lebanon in 1982— even though some of their axes of advance led through perfect (that is, mountainous and wooded) guerrilla territory. And the Israelis did so by changing their traditional blitzkrieg tactics; they enveloped their armor with infantry (forward) and artillery (in the rear), which shielded the tanks against PGM-equipped PLO forces. "Reactive armor," hung like chainmail from turrets and hulls, easily defeated those projectiles that did manage to engage their targets.

Secondly, while West Germany's forests afford ample opportunity for ambush and concealment, two-thids of the country is not so blessed. Against a mechanized enemy operating under an air superiority cover in open spaces, techno-commandos and militias are no match, just an easy prey. They might still be able to disperse (which is one injunction of the

German reformers), but they would not be able to move in order to be in the right place at the right time with the right mass and momentum (the reformers' second injunction). The antitank net defense along the East German border, as envisaged in SPD circles, would court failure even more quickly. Essentially stationary (being bereft of tanks and attack aircraft), such a defense would be overwhelmed the moment it was pierced, its lack of mobility precluding any second chances.

But thirdly, and decisively, there is the flaw of the false (political) analogy. The great historical model of all territorial defense schemes is Tito and his ultimately victorious struggle against the German and Italian invaders. Yet West Germany is not Yugoslavia, nor is Western Europe like the Balkans of World War II. The Federal Republic is not a second- or third-order concern of NATO as was Yugoslavia for Hitler, who had more important battles to fight as the fortunes of war turned against him. By 1943–1944, the Third Reich was no longer eager to crush Tito's partisans but rather to speedily extract its troops from Yugoslavia for deployment in more critical arenas. (In Afghanistan the Soviet Union is under no such pressure, and thus it shows no sign of demoralization even after a seven-year war of occupation, and in a locale that ideally favors the insurgents.)

West Germany, however, is not the periphery but the prize of the East–West contest, and the pillar of the Western alliance structure. With an area defense scheme, there is only a slender hope of dispatching the invaders. Yet maximizing the "rent" exacted from the occupation would mean little to the Soviets as compared to the ease of entry afforded (indeed, purposely accepted) by a territorial defense. Given Germany's critical position at the fulcrum of the East–West balance, entry itself is the most precious victory, against which the costs of occupation must pale beyond recognition.

In sum, area defense schemes as proposed by German reformers do not offer a military solution to NATO's quandaries. These schemes must be seen for what they are: expressions of political aspirations. Foreshadowed by Helmut Schmidt a quarter century ago, the underlying objective of such reforms is to build "an armaments structure clearly unsuited for the offensive role yet adequate beyond the shadow of a doubt to defend German territory."[36] Today, that idea has recaptured the SPD left and the Greens, and is now labeled *strukturelle Nichtangriffsfähigkeit*—an untranslatable shibboleth suggesting a posture inherently incapable of offensive operations. The basic purpose is not, of course, strategic but political; the key aspiration, though unstated, is to remove West Germany whence geographic destiny has placed it—away from the center stage of potential war. If the country could not attack, it might not provoke either and thus offer itself as the venue (and victim) of aggression. With nuclear weapons dispatched, West Germany would present neither legitimate nor lucrative targets for nuclear strikes. Finally, the strategy of stopping a superior enemy with inferior but agile forces would require a hefty measure of defensive and ultimately political autonomy—a heady vision for a country whose fate is uniquely beholden to the loyalty of foreign armies and subject to the vagaries of Alliance, and especially American, policies.

That underlying aspiration emerges most explicitly from the SPD draft cited above. It speaks of a drastic reduction of West Germany's forces-in-being, which "ought to enjoin the Soviet Union to do away with a substantial portion of its units in the GDR . . . and Eastern Europe." Thereafter, the "Europeans in the West and in the East ought to be able to defend themselves, at least conventionally." By the year 2000, Soviet troops would be gone, as would the American armies, "except for a symbolic remainder in West Berlin."[37] At heart, then, area defense schemes merely address German political dilemmas in the guise of military reform. Above all, they conjure up freedom from the excruciating dependence that informs German security policy, and ultimately an escape from the iron grip of bipolarity. The dream is not security but liberation from its imperative—and from the price it exacts: alliance, choice, and denial. The promise of area defense is not a better common defense, but sovereignty restored—all the way to a posture of optional neutrality.

Defense in Depth: The Maneuver Approach

Similar political considerations must surely inform the thinking of those American strategists who have come to plead for a "maneuver-oriented" or "mobile" defense in Central Europe.[38] Like an area approach, a mobile defense would not seek to stop an attacker at the inter-German border but would virtually usher him into an extended operational space. Having sidestepped the aggressor, the defender would first distinguish the true axis of advance from any feinting thrusts and then maneuver to strike at the aggressor's vulnerable flanks and lines of communication. Above and beyond the military virtues and flaws of such a doctrine (which are analyzed below), mobile defense would lead to one obvious political advantage for U.S. operations in Europe that hardly needs belaboring. First and foremost, such a strategy trades space for time. Unlike NATO's forward defense, which embroils American forces in an automatic as well as lasting manner, a maneuver approach yields both time and options through a choreography of fluid motion and deliberate withdrawal. Most importantly from an American vantage point, maneuver defense postpones the nuclear moment of truth—that fateful step into escalation that might not abate before the firestorm had engulfed the continental United States as well.

From a European perspective, however, such a decoupling option for the Americans is precisely the mortal political sin of a maneuver-oriented doctrine, and one that towers far above its numerous military flaws. To begin with, there is a conceptual problem. As even one of the leading advocates of maneuver defense concedes, the strategy is by no means "a fully analyzed idea, and it is, of course, at the extreme end of the risk/payoff spectrum."[39] Hence, the crucial variable frequently remains shrouded: how *deep* is the extended defensive space the maneuver proponents envisage? That is by no means a paltry question; it happens to be the fateful one for the one country—the Federal Republic—that would provide the main stage for maneuver-style warfare.

At its narrowest, the Federal Republic boasts a width of 225 kilometers. It makes an existential difference to the West Germans whether a mobile defense involves a set of Cannae-style operations to meet the attacker up front, deliberately open a "gate," and then slice into his vulnerable flanks at the "gateposts"—or whether the scheme would actually involve a series of strategic retreats, tempting the enemy into overextension while gaining time for reinforcement and counterattack. If it is the former, mobile defense is not so much a reform as a gloss on contemporary Bundeswehr tactics already employed by the forward defense orthodoxy.[40] If it is the latter, the Germans certainly will not be flattered. Situated where they are, they will not embrace a reform that promises to sacrifice their national space for the sake of an ultimate Allied victory.[41]

In his superb analysis of the traditional mobile defense concept, John J. Mearsheimer has amply highlighted the weaknesses of a rear-based maneuver strategy. In the first place, "there are no historical examples of a maneuver-oriented defense that has defeated an armored offensive."[47] Moreover, such a strategy is saddled with an excruciating risk as it literally invites the enemy to forge through a thinly manned screening line into the defender's hinterland. If the enemy's momentum is not enveloped and absorbed, there is no second chance. The strategy might hold promise for the Sinai or the vast expanses of Russia (even there, the Wehrmacht in the end mobile-defended all the way back to Berlin), but not in a country like West Germany where one-third of the population is concentrated in a 100-kilometer strip west of the East German border.

Nor does the Central Front lend itself very well to maneuver of any kind. Contrary to popular conceptions, West Germany is actually a highly wooded country, with forests covering almost one-third of the terrain. Woods do not offer a first-rate arena for mechanized combat, and neither do the Federal Republic's conurbations, mountains, rivers, marshes, and canals. On the other hand, the forests and mountains along the Czech and East German borders, stretching all the way from Bavaria in the south to Braunschweig in the north, clearly favor defense up front. By resorting to fluid, fleet-footed maneuver, the defender sacrifices his most important natural advantage: fighting from prepared positions. That handicap of a mobile defense could perhaps be overcome by studding the country with prepared sites à la Suisse, but at social and political costs that no Western government would avidly contemplate.

Finally, there are the psychological and organizational costs of a rear-based maneuver defense. NATO's commanders would have to possess more sangfroid than Schlieffen's disciples during World War I—and even they lost their nerve as they watched the Russian mobilization steamroller gather speed in 1914. As a result, the Reich's military leaders started shifting troops to shield Germany's eastern front even before France was crushed—rather than accept short-term losses for the sake of ultimate victory (as the Schlieffen Plan had dictated). Would their successors react with any greater equanimity as Warsaw Pact forces surged forward into the NATO heartland?

Even worse, once they were inside Germany, the attackers would confront the defenders with a hoary asymmetry. The aggressors would exploit West Germany's sprawling road network for mobility, and its myriad villages and towns for ready-made protection. The defenders, however, would be boxed in both morally and physically. They would have to struggle against the westward stream of refugees clogging roads and towns. And then they would have to target their own settlements for destruction by friendly fire.

In the end, mobile defense falls apart precisely where its nonarmored cousin, area defense, is bound to fail most grievously, too. Given the precarious nature of a coalition whose linchpin—West Germany—is also its most exposed member, any Soviet advance at all into the Federal Republic guarantees a virtually irreversible political victory of historic proportions. The country at the fulcrum of the East–West balance in Europe cannot serve as a glacis—because to lose the glacis is to lose the game.

The New Conventionalism: Offense in Depth

Offense in Depth: Deep Strike

If the rear is studded with pitfalls for the defender, why not take the battle into the enemy's hinterland instead? Variously celebrated as "Deep Strike," "Follow-On Forces Attack" (FOFA) or the "Rogers Plan,"[43] the idea of deep interdiction echoes Liddel Hart's concept of the "bloodless victory," and at a safe stand-off distance to boot. Aircraft- or missile-borne supersmart munitions would crater runways deep in the Warsaw Pact's hinterland, destroy bridges, stop second-echelon tank units, disrupt command and communications (C^3I) networks, and generally wreak havoc on the enemy's battle formation.

Given the West's resurgent nuclear anxieties and domestic cost-cutting pressures, it is no surprise that Deep Strike should have captured so many imaginations so swiftly. To rattled political leaders (on either end of the ideological spectrum), the fabled revolution in guidance precision conjures up a wondrous arsenal of conventional deterrence that promises relief from their antinuclear tormentors. To their finance ministers, this shiny new technology promises to finally stop, if not reverse, exponential growth in the costs of tactical airpower. And to many strategists, Deep Strike and emerging technology (ET) proffer an elegant antidote to the nightmare of Soviet mass and momentum. If long-range interdiction will stave off the Warsaw Pact's second and third echelon, if it unhinges the aggressor's delicate reinforcement schedule, then NATO's forward forces will be amply prepared to trap and destroy WTO breakthrough armies.

Such a vision is evidently more heartening than that of a murderous melee at the inter-German border. Would cutting off its tail really stop a Soviet advance—or do so more cost-effectively than blunting its bite? The most honest answer is that we do not know. Nor can we calculate the economic costs with any confidence so as to match them against former SACEUR General Bernard Rogers' enticing one percent price tag. (NATO's supreme commander believed that "only one percent more" than the three-percent annual increase in real defense spending, as agreed by NATO in 1977, would foot the bill.)[44]

We do know something, however, about the historical record, and that reveals two sobering facts. First, the price of sophisticated weapons—or more precisely, the difference between early contractors' estimates and realistic program costs—tends to soar by multiples rather than by mere percentages. Thus, the cost of the West's most recent miracle weapon—the ground-launched cruise missile deployed in Europe since 1984—rose by a factor of almost three, within five years.[45] Nor does ET offer an exception to this familiar pattern. An early star of FOFA, the Assault Breaker missile system, was put on hold in 1984, in a rare display of air force and army unanimity, because it had become too expensive even before the testing phase was completed. According to a study conducted by the U.S. Air Force, the cost of only *one week's* munitions requirement on *one corps front* would amount to $8 billion.[46]

The second sobering fact is seen in the history of previous interdiction efforts, which shows no grand prizes given to such campaigns. "One of the most important conclusions to be drawn from an examination of interdiction experience," notes a Rand Corporation study, "is that the outcomes seldom came close to the expectations of the interdiction planners. . . . Even if . . . interdiction is successful, the payoffs are often long deferred."[47] The last point is crucial precisely because Deep Strike/FOFA is not predicated on the kind of leisurely war fought in Italy, Korea, and Vietnam (from which the study's data on logistics interdiction were drawn), but on a tightly timed Soviet attack that would unfold in days rather than in months or years.

Beyond the historical record, we also know something about some classic fallacies of warfare that keep dramatizing the obvious: there is no quick technological fix for stubborn strategic problems. One is the "fallacy of the single instance." A conventionally armed, high-precision missile will do well against a single bridge, and we have the legendary Thanh Hoa Bridge in North Vietnam to prove the point. In the sixties, 873 American sorties ended up with eleven U.S. aircraft lost but the bridge still standing. In 1972, eight American planes armed with fairly simpleminded laser bombs felled the bridge without a single loss among them.

But the Deep Strike/FOFA strategy is more ambitious. According to one calculation, there are about 2,700 time-urgent, high-value targets in the Warsaw Pact's rear (up to 800 kilometers), only 425 of which are stationary (airfields, bridges, nuclear storage sites).[48] The rest are maneuver and artillery battalions as well as nuclear missile and support units. Yet these 2,200-odd mobile objectives would hardly present the final tally for NATO targeters, as these would realistically have to be broken down further into company-sized units, raising the mobile total to about 5,500. How many Assault Breaker missiles and MLRS (multi-launch rocket system) salvos might such a target list require? Perhaps ten or fifteen thousand? Given these enormous figures, it is not difficult to understand how the U.S. Air Force arrived at the gargantuan price tag for the Assault Breaker system cited above.[49]

Nor ought we to equate theoretical with effective kill capability, no matter how sophisticated a fire-and-forget technology ET weapons embody. "Just imagine," writes a protagonist of ET, "a mortar round destroying armor [and] two volleys of the multiple-launch rocket system destroying a tank company."[50] Such claims might be tested against actual combat experience with precision-guided munitions in the past. Before the Vietnam War, for instance, the AIM-7 radar-guided air-to-air missile was supposed to have a kill probability (P_K) of 0.5. In actual fighting in Vietnam, however, the effective P_K turned out to be 0.08.[51] (At that rate, about fifty missiles would be required to score a perfect kill.) One explanation for such a gap was offered by none other than Secretary of Defense Harold Brown, when speaking about the disappointing performance of new, more sophisticated fighter aircraft: "The higher effectiveness we had hoped for . . . has at least in part been compromised by lower reliability that higher complexity has brought with it."[52]

Brown was noticing, in other words, that reliability (crucial in actual combat) varies inversely with complexity, and hence it takes a long time and even more money for sophisticated weapons to live up to their laboratory promise. In the contemporary ET case, even the promise has so far appeared rather meager, all the more so since the tests designed to demonstrate the "single instance" were heavily skewed toward success. While JSTARS, one of the critical radar components in the Deep Strike system, managed to pick up a handful of moving target tanks, these happened to be located in a setting not exactly typical of Central Europe: a desert mercifully bereft of "ground clutter" and ambiguous contrasts. In another test, an Assault Breaker missile managed to engage a cluster of ten tanks, a task that was considerably lightened by a carefully planned target site (to remove "clutter"), clear skies, and the stationary setup of the targets. In addition, the air was cool while the tank engines were heated up and running; thus excellent thermal contrast was provided for the missile's heat-sensitive seekers.[53]

Over time, human ingenuity and financial plenty will overcome such failings. But there is a second fallacy of warfare that is more difficult to circumvent. Well known to economists, it might be called the "fallacy of continuous substitution." Trading raw explosive power for precision — which is the paramount promise of Deep Strike and other ET strategies — will inevitably lead into a zone of rapidly diminishing returns. Think of a well-aimed sniper's bullet. With a "circular-error probable" measured in centimeters, it will hit its target with breathtaking precision, yet it will not even dent a tank's steel turret. By the same token, area submunitions borne by Deep Strike systems must inevitably sacrifice lethality for the numbers that give them their aggregate hit probability, and area systems that must strike over great distances will inevitably sacrifice throw-weight in favor of range.

Tanks that are merely punctured, however, may still roll onward to victory—and especially those tanks far in the rear of Warsaw Pact territory that are transported westward on flatcars or trailers. To begin with, their silent engines do not provide hot spots for heat-seeking missiles. More importantly, such tanks are not combat-loaded; hence, a minor explosion inflicted on them by diminutive submunitions will not trigger the decisive secondary explosion of fuel and ammunition. Similarly, runway penetrators can work impressive damage on tarmacs; nonetheless, craters wrought by sophisticated weapons are more easily repaired than entire bases demolished by a nuclear blast.

It is true, of course, that Deep Strike/FOFA is precisely designed to circumvent the West's nuclear nightmare. Yet it might achieve such a feat only at the price of bringing on another, no less fearsome dilemma. If a conventional attack wreaks as much havoc on Warsaw Pact assets as its banished nuclear twin would inflict, what will keep the Soviets from going nuclear in retaliation—if not preemption? It is not self-evident that a high tech conventional deterrent will dispel the nuclear curse. If it works, or is merely believed to work, it might raise the nuclear threshold in the West, while lowering it, precisely for that reason, in the East. Feeling outclassed by Western technological prowess, the East might opt for massive nuclear blows from the very beginning. "The significance of conducting pre-emptive strikes against precision weapons has increased," writes Major-General I. Vorobyev. "It is important to provide reliable air cover of units, undertake defensive measures in a timely fashion, preempt the enemy's fire and quickly destroy his weapons."[54]

Third, there is the "frozen frame" fallacy, or the fallacy of the "last (technological) step," born out of the tendency to assume ironclad parameters where there are only fuzzy variables once time begins to have its leveling effects. The spear, the longbow, the machine gun—none of these have reduced the infantrist to an "obsolete weapons platform" just because it can be demonstrated that high-density projectiles turn humans into "soft targets." Soldiers have always just changed tactics and developed countermeasures—and have continued to fight all the way into the twentieth century.

The point is hackneyed, but it bears repetition because of the eternal Western temptation to view the latest technological breakthrough as its final liberation from history. Warfare, especially in times of exponential technological change, is among man's most highly evolved enterprises. "The most important shortcoming of [Deep Strike]," writes military historian, Colonel Trevor N. Dupuy, "is the basic assumption that our potential foes are a bit stupid"—that they will adhere rigidly to outmoded doctrines and tactics.[55] Like the prophets of all past "miracle weapons," many Deep Strike/ET enthusiasts seem to assume that the enemy is both "passive" and "predictable."[56] The point is not only that there are always countermeasures and countertactics, but also that they may be cheaper and simpler than the new queen on the battlefield.

For the "slingshot syndrome" often makes the best laid technological schemes go awry. It is worth recalling that David was facing a technologically superior enemy in Goliath; the Philistines had already mastered the art of iron-forging whereas the Israelites were still fighting with soft bronze swords. Yet David felled the giant with "tactical surprise" and a cheaper, more primitive counterweapon: the slingshot-launched pebble. Nor is there only Biblical legend to support the point. Two and a half millenia later, the British navy was extremely successful in foiling Exocet antiship missiles with a World War II defense: aluminum chaff.

Night-fighting, camouflage, infrared suppression paints and nets, smoke, aerosols, radar reflectors, flares, and decoys—all offer low-cost defenses against the accoutrements of Deep Strike. Already, the Soviets have reacted to Deep Strike/FOFA by openly discussing such measures in their military literature. They are talking about the hardening of combat equipment, about terrain exploitation for concealment, and about such primitive countermeasures as lighting old tires along their axes of advance to confuse and deflect infrared-seeking sensors.[57]

Moreover, tactics can be changed more swiftly than systems. The Israelis demonstrated this point a few days into the Yom Kippur War. They soon succeeded in neutralizing Egyptian PGMs with combined-arms operations that protected their tanks with agile infantry troops in front and mechanized artillery in the rear. Finally, to imitate is surely cheaper and faster than to invent. To overcome cost-effective countermeasures and the inevitable dispersion of technology, the West will have to race ever faster just to end up with ever more sophisticated munitions that become ever more expensive. This is, of course, true of all weapons; such a perverse dynamic can hardly serve as a general injunction against technological progress. The moral is rather that the West ought not to stake its security on weapons that might add to costs as well as to vulnerability.

"Complicated weapons systems tend to break down more frequently in operation; and when they do, they require high quality logistical support [which] puts increased demand on finding higher quality manpower."[58] In other words, high tech weapons may be triply expensive: in terms of sheer money when they are bought; in terms of reduced fighting power when they are out for repair; and in terms of soaring opportunity costs when they monopolize precisely those precious human resources they are supposed to set free. Worse, the instruments of Deep Strike may end up making their possessors more vulnerable than their intended victims. Deep Strike/FOFA is a highly centralized operation that rests on highly centralized and vulnerable command and communications systems: airborne radars near the frontline for acquisition and targeting in conjunction with ground-based "fusion" centers for data processing, command, and control. They make perfect targets for swift destruction, and without them, the strike weapons themselves are reduced to an array of expensive junk.

To be sure, NATO will have to complement its costly strike aircraft with missiles and standoff weapons just to compensate for the ever more lethal environment over the Warsaw Pact's territory. Given the pact's growing investment in frontal aviation, counter-air operations ideally must succeed even before the enemy's air armies have crossed the border. The second best (and politically more likely) choice is to destroy runways and depots after hostilities have commenced so that enemy aircraft have no place to return to for refueling and resupply. Yet the sheer quantity of WTO air defenses would force NATO to deploy planes sparingly and to fall back on missiles instead. So a sophisticated interdiction panoply is a bare bones necessity rather than a fancy luxury when it comes to the most urgent task, namely, counter-air operations.

Similarly, the Alliance must be able to execute precision strikes against stationary targets like logistics centers and traffic choke points (bridges and railroad facilities, for example) to slow down the enemy's movement. But as far as the larger vision is concerned—stopping Soviet land armies in their tracks via remote control, as it were—the obvious still needs to be stressed: technology may be endlessly alluring to the Western mind, but there is no end to the dialectic of warfare and no exit from painful financial and strategic choices.

And there is a deeper issue than the promise and pitfalls of advanced technology. Apart from counter-air and counter-mobility operations, Deep Strike may be tomorrow's solution to yesterday's problems. If Assault

Breaker and its successors actually live up to their as yet unproven talents, they may well target enemy echelons no longer in place and timetables no longer in operation. The Soviets are apparently quite aware of the lengthening shadow over their follow-on forces, mainly because more precise, longer range nuclear weapons threaten to take a heavy toll on massed formations and tightly echeloned axes of advance. Hence their own reforms, launched in the 1970s, have aimed at a dual objective: to execute an unreinforced attack (which puts a premium on preemption), and to deny lucrative targets to NATO's nuclear weapons (which puts a premium on multiple axes of advance, lateral movement, and dispersal).

A look at the Warsaw Pact's deployment pattern serves as a dramatic reminder of NATO's real problem, which lies in the first echelon rather than farther to the rear. Within the area encompassing East Germany, Czechoslovakia, and Poland, one authoritative tally has located 75 percent of Soviet ground assets in East Germany alone—with 18 percent based in Czechoslovakia and 7 percent in Poland.[59] Measured very roughly, armored power is distributed in the ratio of 4 : 2 : 1 as one moves eastward from the first strategic echelon via the second to the strategic reserve inside the Soviet Union. And the "problem of the Warsaw Pact," notes Phillip Karber, "is less one of *creating* gaps in the front via the massed breakthrough then of *exploiting* gaps where a continuous front does not exist due to the conditions of a short-warning attack."[60] If the Soviets have been looking for new solutions, they are evidently more impressed by NATO's forward defense than its Western critics are. Presumably, then, the Soviets have been rewriting their long-standing echelon choreography (of World War II vintage) in favor of surprise, unreinforced attacks, more "disorderly" timetables, and opportunistic probing/breakthrough operations along a fluid, indeterminate front.[61]

Such reform would turn Deep Strike into a revolution without a cause; to blunt the WTO's bite, the West would be investing in a costly interdiction technology that could only crush a tail no longer waiting to be hit. Gearing up for Deep Strike would once more put the horse before the cart. Politics and geography bid NATO to deny territory, not to liberate it after the Warsaw Pact's supply train has been chewed up. The Alliance's most urgent problem is the glaring lack of reserves strong enough to counter a rapid Soviet breakthrough. It is this deficit—not the dearth of sophisticated long-range weaponry—that informs NATO's murderous nuclear dilemma: having to use nuclear weapons as the ultima ratio, but not being able to launch them because they would devastate Alliance territory first and foremost.

If NATO cannot stave off the first echelon, the second and third cease to matter. Logically, then, the emphasis ought to be on buttressing the forward defense line—which means, above all, massive investments in readiness plus a highly mobile reserve as insurance: tanks, helicopters, and self-propelled artillery. Only then will Deep Strike make sense as a reinsurance policy—against WTO armies once more forced into vulnerable concentration and reinforcement posture because opportunities for preemption and speedy breakthroughs no longer beckon.

Offense in Depth: Conventional Retaliation

The most ambitious proposal of the Forward School is Samuel Huntington's strategy of "conventional retaliation."[62] Inviting NATO to break out of its strictly defensive mold, the concept goes beyond the idea of a mere counteroffensive—because a conventional offense would *immediately* be launched into the pact's hinterland "whether or not the Soviet conventional offensive had been stopped."[63] For that purpose, Huntington suggests a northward and eastward thrust from Bavaria into East Germany and Czechoslovakia.

It is intellectually the most elegant, but politically the most dubious variant of Forwardism. Its attraction is fourfold. The strategy would liberate the Alliance from the debilitating constraints of passivity that allow the Soviets to choose the place of engagement. Second, it would shift at least one focus of battle into the enemy's territory. Third, by drastically increasing the price of war to the Eastern Europeans, conventional retaliation would correspondingly reduce the enthusiasm of their support for Soviet aggression. Fourth, and perhaps most importantly, such a deep-thrust strategy would return the logically indispensable element of punishment to the idea of conventional deterrence by threatening an asset the Soviets presumably value even more dearly than the resources of Western Europe: their political and pontifical empire in Eastern Europe.

The logic is sound, especially where it highlights what is so often overlooked by many enthusiasts of conventional deterrence—that deterrence must threaten unacceptable costs (retaliation) and not just denial of the aggressor's objective (defense). Yet the operational side of the scheme leaves open one awesome question. Moreover, the politics are no less than disastrous. What will the Alliance do if deterrence fails?

Indeed, where will the Alliance be once the Warsaw Pact's armies take the plunge into West Germany, and American troops in Bavaria do not rush off to attack the aggressor's flanks but instead drive toward the northeast? Such a revolving door maneuver might perhaps trigger the collapse of the Soviet empire in Eastern Europe, but even that outcome is not certain. Ultimately beholden to Soviet power, the East European regimes would be spurred by the best of all possible incentives to fight alongside their Soviet protector-ally: to ensure their own survival. Yet whatever the effect in the Soviet glacis, it could hardly add to NATO's health to have Warsaw Pact armies slicing through a weakened Western front and gaining possession of the Federal Republic, the greatest prize of them all. Perhaps the U.S. Army could take Dresden—but at the price of the Red Army being ensconced in Frankfurt. Which side would be deterred more by which position in that revolving door? And whose alliance would collapse first?

As to the politics, it would not even have to come to such cataclysmic events to threaten the early demise of the Western alliance. Because any serious peacetime move toward a conventional retaliation posture might have already had the same effect. No West European government will associate itself with a strategy that poses an existential threat to Moscow's control over Eastern Europe. The Allies expect the United States to come to their rescue—and with nuclear weapons if need be—if the Soviets attack. Given the Soviet Union's oft-demonstrated stake in preserving its East European *cordon Stalinaire,* the West Europeans expect, and fear, no less from Moscow. They will not, therefore, countenance a conventional retaliation posture that might exponentially increase the risk of Soviet nuclear strikes.

Nor will they swallow the political implications of such a posture. The aftermath of Afghanistan—when the West Europeans resisted American sanctions against Moscow and especially against its East European satraps—highlights a subtle but lasting transformation in the pattern of intra-European relations. Toward the Soviets, détente as reinsurance provides the West Europeans with an extra margin of security, if not an extra margin of independence from the United States. Vis-à-vis Eastern Europe, the transformation is even more profound. Transcending the mainstays of classic bipolarity, there is now a shadowy parallel system extending across all of Europe. It is found not only in all kinds of economic and political ties but also in a West European *prise de conscience* that views the East Europeans not as enemies but as hapless victims and even tacit allies. As always, the most telling instance of that shift is the relationship between the two Germanies. With the Federal Republic in the vanguard, the West Europeans will fight tooth and nail against a doctrine that would seek to deter the Soviets by threatening the East Europeans, and thus the very fabric of Ostpolitik and détente.

Strategic Reform: Concluding Observations

In the end the three conventional alternatives or complements to flexible response and forward defense—no-first-use, Forwardism, and Rearwardism—fall apart where the logic of politics meets the logic of strategy. There is a reason why the messy and uncertain tenets of flexible response have survived so many powerful challenges. With all its shaky compromises between manpower needs and manpower yields, between force goals and force budgets, between the conventional and the nuclear, flexible response is the fine line separating two logical alternatives that are even more unattractive.

Strategic logic would certainly demand that NATO transcend that line. Given the Central Front's nightmarish geographical constraints, either a "Prussian" or a "Russian" doctrine would seem to hold far greater promise than forward defense. To escape from the curse of geography—which did at least enable Prussia to be better at offense than at defense—the Hohenzollerns, from Frederick the Great to Wilhelm II, regularly sought salvation in lightning strikes to break the tightening ring of encirclement around their nation. The Israelis, cursed with an even worse geographical fate, have obeyed the same imperative—only more frequently and successfully. Conversely, the classic Russian strategy has been to exploit territory as a trap—trading space for time in an ultimately victorious war of attrition.

Today, West Germany's critical position in the European order precludes either choice. Its iron constraints are anchored in the unwritten constitution of the Alliance. On the one hand, the Federal Republic's total military integration into NATO was based on a Western pledge never to sacrifice the country's space and population for the safety of its neighbors in the West. There could never be a replay of the Thirty Year's War or World War II when Germany became the stage and stake of general mayhem. On the other hand, the condition of the Federal Republic's admission into the Western community was Bonn's pledge never to use force on behalf of its unresolved national aspirations. Three decades later, the West Germans have, ironically, raised that vow of self-denial to the level of their own *raison d'état:* to protect the Federal Republic's national interests vis-à-vis East Germany, Eastern Europe, and the Soviet Union, NATO must never budge from its strictly defensive posture.

Moreover, none of the European allies have an interest in developing a conventional capacity commensurate with Western Europe's economic and demographic potential—that would be the road to decoupling European-style. For a Europe truly strong enough to balance the Soviet Union all by itself would naturally allow the United States to extricate itself from the most entangling of its alliances. Hence the distinct lack of applause—at least on the part of Europe's governing elites—for American no-first-use proposals. The nuclear tie between the United States and Western Europe is the very core of Europe's American-guaranteed security, and thus a purely conventional stance (which no-first-use must be in practice) would merely undo a guarantee that has blessed the Continent with more stability than it has ever known.

Finally, the system has worked too well to be lightly abandoned in favor of reform-minded conventionalism. Nuclear deterrence in Europe has a record, conventional defense has not, and four decades of ultrastability is an impressive argument for the status quo. Nuclear weapons may not always reassure those whom they protect, yet we must not conclude too much from the drama of discontent played out on a populist stage in the early 1980s.[64]

The crucial point is that nuclear weapons deter precisely because they do not reassure completely. Deterrence works, paradoxically, because it might fail; it is the never quite tamed terror of nuclear weapons that makes their possessors vastly more cautious than great powers had been in the centuries before Hiroshima. Nor has the nuclear taboo declined during the last forty years. The most striking lesson of the post-Hiroshima age is that the taboo has inexorably spread so as to deter the use of *any* force between the great powers—whether conventional or nuclear, whether before parity or after. Why, then, seek reassurance in weapons and strategies that weaken the terror as well as the taboo?

Notes

1. McGeorge Bundy, George F. Kennan, Robert S. McNamara, and Gerard Smith, "Nuclear Weapons and the Atlantic Alliance," *Foreign Affairs* (Spring 1982). For an elaboration, see McGeorge Bundy, "No First Use Needs Careful Study," *Bulletin of the Atomic Scientists* (June/July 1982), and Robert S. McNamara, "The Military Role of Nuclear Weapons," *Foreign Affairs* (Fall 1983). For a similar position, see Kurt Gottfried, et al., "'No First Use' of Nuclear Weapons," *Scientific American* (March 1984). For a German critique, see Karl Kaiser,

Georg Leber, Alois Mertes and Franz-Josef Schulze, "Nuclear Weapons and the Preservation of Peace," *Foreign Affairs* (Summer 1982). For a British view, see Neville Brown and Anthony Farrar-Hockley, *Nuclear First Use* (London: Buchan and Enright, 1985). For general analyses, see John D. Steinbruner and Leon V. Sigal, eds., *Alliance Security: NATO and the No-First-Use Question* (Washington, D.C.: The Brookings Institution, 1983), and John J. Mearsheimer, "Nuclear Weapons and Deterrence in Europe," *International Security* (Winter 1984/1985). An agnostic analysis, which comes down in favor of the doctrinal status quo, is P.J. Liberman and N.R. Thomason, "No-First-Use Unknowables," *Foreign Policy* (Fall 1986). For a Soviet view, see Mikhail A. Milshtein, "On the Question of Non-Resort to the First Use of Nuclear Weapons," in Frank Blackaby, et al., eds., *No First Use* (London: Taylor and Francis, 1984).

2. Foreign Minister Andrei Gromyko before the Second Special Session of the UN General Assembly on Disarmament, UN Documents A/S-12/PV, 15 June 1982, pp. 28–30. See also John Goshko, "Soviet Chief Renounces First Use of A-Weapons," *Washington Post*, 16 June 1982.

3. Dimitri F. Ustinov, *Serving the Country and the Communist Cause* (Oxford: Pergamon Press, 1983), p. 61.

4. Dimitri F. Ustinov, "To Remove the Threat of Nuclear War," *Pravda*, 12 July 1982.

5. Milshtein, "Question of Non-Resort," p. 116. This quote is in direct response to Ustinov's *Pravda* article of 12 July 1982.

6. Benjamin F. Schemmer, "Three Threats NATO Is Not Addressing," *Armed Forces Journal International* (May 1984): p. 87 table.

7. These missiles play an ambiguous role, however, because they are thought to be triple-capable, i.e., usable in a high explosive, chemical, or nuclear mode.

8. Bundy et al., "Nuclear Weapons," p. 762.

9. Ibid., p. 757.

10. McNamara, "The Military Role," p. 79.

11. This logic is clearly recognized by those advocates of NFU who have thought about the practical implications of such a posture.

> [While] a policy of NFU does not imply a policy on nuclear disengagement from Europe, [NATO's classic] nuclear posture in Europe would have to be changed in order to lend credibility to the principle of NFU. Most of the nuclear munitions for short-range battlefield artillery could be withdrawn from Europe, as well as ADMs, demolition mines, and nuclear air defense munitions. . . . With respect to medium-range (150–1500 kms) nuclear systems, NFU could be strengthened by the abrogation of present arrangements for dual-capable systems, including aircraft.

> Johan J. Holst, "Moving Toward No First Use in Practice," in Steinbruner and Sigal, *Alliance Security*, p. 188.

12. The Independent Commission on Disarmament and Security Issues (Palme Commission), *Common Security: A Blueprint for Survival* (London: Pan Books, 1982).

13. Milshtein, "Question of Non-Resort," p. 115.

14. Henry A. Kissinger, "Arms Control and the Peace Movement," *Washington Quarterly* (Summer 1982): 35.

15. This simile was borrowed from R.A. Mason, "Military Strength," in E. Moreton and G. Segal, eds., *Soviet Strategy Toward Western Europe* (London: Allen & Unwin, 1984), p. 193.
16. John J. Mearsheimer, *Conventional Deterrence* (Ithaca, N.Y.: Cornell University Press, 1983), pp. 19–20. Mearsheimer's list of the twelve cases studied might be expanded by another six cases, which the author lists on p. 20 (e.g., the Iran–Iraq War beginning in 1980). If so, the failure rate for conventional deterrence increases to 88.8 percent.
17. Samuel Huntington, "Conventional Deterrence and Conventional Retaliation in Europe," *International Security* (Winter 1983/1984): 38.
18. Ustinov, "To Remove the Threat."
19. Bundy et al., "Nuclear Weapons," p. 759.
20. Istvan Frago (pseud.), *No-First-Use: A Window of Opportunity?* (New York: Institute for East–West Security Studies, 1985), pp. 25–26. Mr. Farago deals with arms control in the Hungarian Foreign Office.
21. Kaiser, et al., "Preservation of Peace." The authors represent a broad coalition from the German political spectrum. Karl Kaiser, a professor of political science, is an active SPD member. Georg Leber is a former SPD minister of defense. Alois Mertes, a Christian Democrat, was until his death in 1985 a state secretary (equivalent to an American under secretary) in the Foreign Office. General (ret.) Franz-Josef Schulze was Deputy Chief of Staff, Allied Command Europe, from 1973 to 1976.
22. Kaiser, et al., "Preservation of Peace," p. 1162 (emphasis added).
23. Unlike Messrs. Bundy et al., who remain attached to the purposes of the Alliance, radical isolationists like Earl Ravenal advocate NFU precisely in order to decouple the United States from its perilous commitment to Western Europe. For him,

    the critical question is: How can we continue to defend Europe in a way that is consistent with other, overriding values, such as avoiding our own physical destruction in a nuclear war? . . . No-First-Use must be seen its appropriately wide context. . . . *This larger scheme and purpose I would take to be the attainment of nuclear safety for ourselves and our country.* . . . In this regard, it appears that Bundy and his co-authors fail to recognize . . . the consequences of their own argument.

    Earl Ravenal, "No First Use: A View from the United States," *Bulletin of the Atomic Scientists* (April 1983): 11–13 (emphasis added).
24. McNamara, "The Military Role," p. 79.
25. Kaiser et al., "Preservation of Peace," p. 1162.
26. Helmut Schmidt, on November 20, 1983, before the Cologne Congress of the SPD—which almost unanimously rejected the deployment. For an excerpt from Schmidt's speech, see Helmut Schmidt, "Warum ich dabei bleibe," *Vorwärts*, 25 Nov. 1983.
27. Paul Quilès, "L'Avenir de notre concept de défense face aux progrès technologiques" (Address to the Institut des Hautes Etudes de Défense Nationale, November 12, 1985), reprinted in *Défense Nationale* (January 1986): 16.
28. It is worth emphasizing, however, that the breakdown of the Bar-Lev Line in an early stage of the Yom Kippur War should not be confused with its failure. While it neither stopped nor repulsed the Egyptians, it held long enough to

give the Israelis precious time for mobilization and counterattack. The line would have been even more effective had the Israelis been less contemptuous of the Egyptians and filled it out in time.

29. Carl-Friedrich von Weizsäcker, "Abschreckung – nur eine Atempause?" *Die Zeit*, 2 April 1982.

30. Horst Afheldt, *Verteidigung und Frieden* (Munich: Hanser, 1976), p. 225. This book is Afheldt's key work; its message has remained substantially unchanged in his subsequent publications throughout the eighties.

31. Horst Afheldt, "The End of the Tank Battle: Atomic War or Area Defense?" *Bulletin of Peace Proposals*, no. 4 (1977): 331.

32. Andreas von Bülow, "Entwurf eines Antrags zur Sicherheitspolitik für den Bundesparteitag 1986: Strategie vertrauensschaffender Sicherheitsstrukturen in Europa," Bonn, September 1985, reprinted in its entirety in *Frankfurter Rundschau*, 13 Sept. 1985.

33. von Bülow, "Entwurf eines Antrags...," proposition no. 18.

34. For other area defense schemes, see General Franz Uhle-Wettler, *Gefechtsfeld Mitteleuropa* (Koblenz: Bernard und Graefe, 1980), and "NATO Strategy Under Discussion," *International Defense Review* (September 1980), as well as General (ret.) Hans-Joachim Löser, "Vorneverteidigung in der Bundesrepublik Deutschland?" *Oesterreichische Militärzeitschrift*, no. 2 (1980), and "Überleben ohne Atomkrieg," *Allgemeine Schweizerische Militärzeitschrift*, no. 4 (1980). Löser, who became active on the fringes of the German peace movement in the 1980s, claims that modern antitank technology has given the advantage to the defense. He would dispense with heavy armor and shift the burden of homeland defense to small *Jäger* ("hunter") units (no larger than brigades), which would exploit terrain and artificial barriers for dispersal and concealment, while engaging the invader in continuous small-scale, guerrilla-like combat. Uhle-Wettler would also use partisan tactics and systematic dispersal but, in contrast to Löser, he would retain armored and mechanized units for battle in open terrain.

35. The "true lessons" of the Yom Kippur War "may be extracted from the knowledge that, of the approximately 3000 Arab and Israeli tanks destroyed or damaged... at least 80 percent were knocked out by other tanks." Kenneth Rush, Brent Scowcroft, and Joseph J. Wolf, eds., *Strengthening Deterrence: NATO and the Credibility of Western Defense in the 1980s* (Cambridge, Mass.: Ballinger, 1982), p. 129. In 1982, about 60 percent of Syrian tank losses were caused by Israeli tank fire, and a substantial portion of the rest by "dumb" air-to-surface missiles and artillery (author's interviews with Israeli officers and analysts in Israel in June of 1982).

36. Helmut Schmidt, *Defense or Retaliation?* (New York: Praeger, 1962), p. 102.

37. von Bülow, "Entwurf eines Antrags...," propositions no. 20 and 21.

38. See, for instance, Steven L. Canby, "Mutual Force Reductions: A Military Perspective," *International Security* (Winter 1978), and "Military Reform and the Art of War," *Survival* (May/June 1983); William S. Lind, "Some Doctrinal Questions for the United States Army," *Military Review* (March 1977), and "Military Doctrine, Force Structure, and the Defense Decision-Making Process," *Air University Review* (May/June 1979); and Edward N. Luttwak, "The Operational Level of War," *International Security* (Winter 1980/1981).

39. Edward N. Luttwak, "The American Style of Warfare and the Military Balance," *Survival* (March/April 1979): 87.

40. "A defense against a sophisticated and numerically superior opponent must be conducted in a mobile manner. On the field, the troops must be able to establish *Schwerpunkte* ("force concentrations") rapidly and to embark on counter-attacks. . . . . The tactical offensive is an integral part of a strategically defensive posture." Bundesminister der Verteidigung, *Weissbuch 1975/1976* (Bonn: Bundesministerium der Verteidigung, 1976), p. 85. See also *Weissbuch 1983*, pp. 147–148.

41. According to the German minister of defense, Georg Leber, "Forward defense means to defend the territory of the Federal Republic with all available forces . . . so effectively up front that the country will not be turned into the stage of war." Georg Leber, "Abrüstung: Ein Gebot der Vernunft," *Deutsches Allgemeines Sonntagsblatt,* 24 July 1977, p. 3.

42. John J. Mearsheimer, "Maneuver, Mobile Defense, and the NATO Central Front," *International Security* (Winter 1981/1982): 108.

43. See, for instance, SACEUR General Bernard W. Rogers, "The Atlantic Alliance: Prescriptions for a Difficult Decade," *Foreign Affairs* (Summer 1982); "Sword and Shield: ACE Attack of Warsaw Pact Follow-On Forces," *NATO's Sixteen Nations* (February/March 1983); and Rogers' congressional testimony, *Senate Committee on Armed Services Hearings on Department of Defense Authorization for Appropriations for Fiscal Year 1984,* part 5, March 15, 1983, pp. 2384–2414, especially p. 2405 ff. For some conceptual underpinnings, see *Strengthening Conventional Deterrence in Europe,* Report of the European Security Study (New York: St. Martin's Press, 1983), especially the contribution by Donald R. Cotter. For a useful survey of the many concepts and systems subsumed under the shorthand label *Deep Strike,* see a series of articles entitled, "Defend Forward, But Strike Deep," in *Armed Forces Journal International* (November 1982–April 1983). For a good analytic survey (and an extensive bibliography), see Daniel Gouré and Jeffrey R. Cooper, "Conventional Deep Strike: A Critical Look," *Comparative Strategy,* no. 3 (1984).

  FOFA is often confused with AirLand Battle and AirLand Battle 2000, as described in *Field Manual No. 100–5 Operations* (FM 100–5) (Washington, 1982), and *AirLand Battle 2000* (Washington, 1981), respectively. Both documents share with FOFA the concept of the "extended battlefield," where counterattack and maneuver would play a prominent role. Yet FM 100–5, which lays down the army's new tactical and operational doctrine, foresees strikes on the enemy's first echelon (corps level) only, i.e., at a maximum distance of 150 kilometers. *AirLand Battle 2000* speaks of attacking "the enemy deep in his rear," i.e., at a distance of 300 kilometers. It is important to note, however, that *AirLand Battle 2000* presents not a new doctrine but a speculative exercise in foreseeing the battlefield of the twenty-first century and its technological requirements. Both differ from FOFA in four respects: FOFA was developed by NATO planners independently of the U.S. Army; it is tailored specifically to the Alliance's needs in Europe (whereas the AirLand concept applies to U.S. Army operations around the world); it is to be executed at the highest (central) command levels and not on the brigade/division/corps level, which is where AirLand Battle would settle authority for extended strikes; finally, FOFA's envisioned battlefield would extend "well beyond the forward edge of battle" (Rogers, "Sword and Shield," p. 18). While numbers are kept deliberately vague, the plausible range for second- and third-echelon attack is between 300 and 800 kilometers.

FOFA's historical origins are found in the communique of the 1982 Bonn Summit, which stated that NATO would "explore ways to take full advantage . . . of emerging technologies." (*NATO Review*, no. 3 (1982): 27). FOFA acquired an official American cachet when Secretary of Defense Caspar Weinberger "presented the U.S. proposal for initiating this NATO-wide effort for improving conventional defense . . . against first-echelon attack, interdiction of Warsaw Pact follow-on forces . . . and disrupting Warsaw Pact [command and communications]," at NATO's December 1982 Ministerial Meeting. See Department of Defense, *Annual Report to the Congress, Fiscal Year 1984* (Washington, 1983), p. 275.

In November 1984, NATO's Defense Planning Committee approved SACEUR's "Planning Guidelines for Follow-On Forces Attack." Since then, various Alliance bodies have tried to flesh out the "operational subconcept" and to determine the capabilities required for its implementation. In some form, FOFA is expected to become a part of official NATO doctrine. For a brief overview, see Kenneth Watman, "Follow-on Forces Attack and Emerging Technologies," *Military Technology*, no. 2 (1986).

44. SACEUR General Bernard Rogers, "Prescriptions for a Difficult Decade," *Foreign Affairs* (Summer 1982): 1155.
45. From $2.2 million each in 1978 to $6.4 million in 1983. As reported by Walter Pincus, "Cost Jumps for Weapons in Europe," *Washington Post*, 14 June 1983, p. A4.
46. "Services Defer Assault Breaker Development," *Aviation Week & Space Technology*, 28 May 1984, p. 23. For a very pessimistic cost calculation of Deep Strike and a trenchant critique of the entire concept, see Steven L. Canby, "The Conventional Defense of Europe: The Operational Limits of Emerging Technology," Woodrow Wilson International Center for Scholars, Working Paper no. 55 (April 1984).
47. Edmund Dews and Felix Kozacza, *Air Interdiction: Lessons from Past Campaigns*, RAND N-1743-PA&E (Santa Monica, Calif.: Rand Corporation, 1981), pp. 15, 14. For a cautiously more sanguine assessment, see D.J. Alberts, "Deterrence in the 1980s: The Role of Conventional Air Power," Adelphi Papers, no. 193 (London: International Institute for Strategic Studies, 1984), pp. 33–39.
48. Benjamin F. Schemmer, "Higher Value, Time-Sensitive Targets in Warsaw Pact 2nd and 3rd Echelons: NATO's Central Region," *Armed Forces Journal International* (November 1982): 55.
49. For a very critical look at the cost side, see Canby, "The Conventional Defense," p. 23 ff.
50. Fred Wikner (formerly Director of Net Assessments in the U.S. Department of State), "NATO's Conventional Defense Myopia," Wall Street Journal, 24 July 1984.

51. Pierre M. Sprey, "The Century Series: F-100 to F-18" (Presentation to the American Management Science Conference, December 1978), p. 17. Mimeo.

52. Benjamin F. Schemmer, "SecDef Brown's Memo on Tac Air Readiness," *Armed Forces Journal International* (May 1980): 29.

53. For two devastating reports on test failures (under conditions heavily tilted toward success), see Michael R. Gordon, "Highly Touted Assault Breaker Weapons Caught Up in Internal Pentagon Debate," *National Journal,* 22 Oct. 1983, pp. 2152–2157, and Charles Mohr, "Antitank Testing Unrealistic, Some Officials Say," *New York Times,* 22 May 1984.

54. Major-General I. Vorobyev, "Contemporary Weapons and Tactics," *Krasnaya Zvesda,* 15 Sept. 1986, as cited in Sally Stoecker, "Soviets Plan Countermeasures to FOFA," *International Defense Review,* no. 11 (1986): 1608.

55. Colonel Trevor N. Dupuy, "Why Deep Strike Won't Work," *Armed Forces Journal International* (January 1983): 57.

56. Steven L. Canby, "Military Reform and the Art of War," *Survival* (May/June 1983): 121.

57. For a brief review of the recent literature, see Stoecker, "Soviets Plan Countermeasures," pp. 1607–1608.

58. Michael Handel, "Numbers Do Count: The Question of Quality Versus Quantity," *Journal of Strategic Studies* (September 1981): 242.

59. Phillip A. Karber, *An Alternative Approach to Military Stabilization Measures* (McLean, Va.: The BDM Corporation, 1986), p. 4. The Soviets alone have about 7,500 main battle tanks stationed in East Germany, which is about as many as the NATO *total* in the MBFR (Mutual and Balanced Force Reductions) area, i.e., the Federal Republic, Belgium, and the Netherlands.

60. Phillip A. Karber, "In Defense of Forward Defense," *Armed Forces Journal International* (May 1984): 41 (emphasis added).

61. On this point, see P.H. Vigor, "Soviet Army Wave Attack Philosophy: The Single-Echelon Option," *International Defense Review* (January 1979), and John G. Hines and Phillip A. Peterson, "The Soviet Conventional Offensive in Europe," *Military Review* (April 1984).

62. Samuel Huntington, "The Renewal of Strategy," in Samuel Huntington, ed., *The Strategic Imperative: New Policies for American Security* (Cambridge, Mass.: Ballinger, 1982) and "Conventional Deterrence and Conventional Retaliation in Europe," *International Security* (Winter 1983/1984).

63. Huntington, "The Renewal of Strategy," p. 23.

64. On this theme, see Howard, "Reassurance and Deterrence," *Foreign Affairs* (Winter 1982/1983).

CHAPTER 5

Conclusion

Alliance as Order

Cold War II, *circa* 1979–1986, was above all a Soviet–American contest in and over Europe. Like the original Cold War, it was triggered on the periphery but fought in the center. The invasion of Afghanistan was to the Second Cold War what Soviet probes into Greece and Turkey (the "periphery" of the 1940s and 1950s) had been to the First: the galvanizing event that rendered explicit a far larger conflict. Once the Truman Doctrine had been laid down in 1947, the main campaign shifted quickly from the Balkans to the heart of the Continent. The real issue was not Communist guerilla warfare in Greece but the balance of power in Europe: how to stop the westward expansion of the Soviet Union and deny it Germany, the key prize of the new conflict. Even the "hot war" in Korea did not shift the focus of the conflict to the Asian periphery. It merely intensified the struggle in Europe, which did not abate until the early 1960s when the Berlin Wall, sealing the status quo with concrete, finalized the partition of Central Europe.

Cold War II obeyed a similar pattern. The détente of the 1970s began to crumble in faraway Ethiopia and Angola; it collapsed entirely during the last days of the decade when Soviet troops marched into Afghanistan. But as in the forties and fifties, the central conflict unfolded once again in Europe. Though the Carter Doctrine—serving as the declaration of Cold War II—centered on the Persian Gulf, it was in Europe that the United States would marshall the forces of neo-containment and the Soviet Union would try to inflict a major political defeat on the United States. The battle was ostensibly over the arcana of the nuclear balance in Europe, over SS-20, Pershing II, and cruise missiles. In reality, the Soviet thrust was aimed at the Euro-American relationship, and hence at the very core of the global balance.

By deploying a new generation of continental-range missiles, the Soviet Union had begun to assemble a separate threat against Western Europe, which in itself was bound to tilt the balance against the West. Yet the challenge went deeper still. When the West began to sue for compensation, the Soviet Union not only denied the legitimacy of such a claim but also unleashed a massive four-year campaign against Western counterdeployments. Though outwardly a matter of missiles and warheads, the real contest was one of power and position. At issue was the Soviet claim to a veto right over NATO's nuclear choices, that is, over the terms of protection offered by the United States to its European allies. If successful, the Soviet Union would have won a historic victory; Moscow would have gained the power to act as arbiter of Europe's security.

The Isolationist Impulse

If one axis of the assault aimed at the strategic bond between the United States and Western Europe, the other blended pressures and blandishments to drive at the heart of the Euro-American political relationship. By extending the prize of a separate détente to Western Europe, the Soviet Union sought to divide the Alliance at the Atlantic's edge, thereby to rob its rival of coalition support in the Cold War II test of strength. Had the Soviets succeeded on both fronts, the Alliance could hardly have survived. Such a dual victory would have undone the tacit terms of the transatlantic bargain. Though nowhere formalized, these terms are transparent enough. For its part, the United States has undertaken to protect Western Europe with a nuclear guarantee that is anchored in a shared existential risk and strengthened by nuclear weapons that threaten to obliterate the distinction between regional and global war.[1] For their part, the Europeans are implicitly bound to "pay" for this guarantee by supporting Washington in its global rivalry with Moscow or, at the very least, denying such support—both economic and diplomatic—to the Soviet Union.

The Soviet double decoupling strategy came to naught in the end, and the bargain held. While the missiles were being installed on schedule, those domestic forces in Western Europe that would have staked their countries' future on "equidistance," if not on optional neutrality, failed in the voting booths. Still, the verdict of Cold War II was a narrow one, and the transatlantic crisis of the 1980s—the longest and deepest in the history of the Alliance—left scars that will not soon vanish. Though reasserted, the status quo has developed some nasty cracks.

It is instructive to compare the effects that both Cold Wars have had on the European–American relationship. Cold War I spawned and enlarged the Atlantic coalition; as discussed earlier, Cold War II strained it to the breaking point. Many Europeans – even conservatives who resisted the neutralist impulse traveling through their societies – were loath to accept America's quarrel with the Soviet Union as their own. Bound to a virtually permanent détente imperative, they regarded Cold War II as an imported conflict, and rightfully so in part. Where they did join America's call to arms, they paid their dues grudgingly – all the while keeping in mind the necessities of coexistence with the Soviet Union and the unpredictable dynamic of an American foreign policy that obeyed "world order" politics one day and militant neo-containment the next. If some West European leaders pursued Alliance loyalty to its outer limits, risking their political lives in the process, many Americans found the effort wanting – smacking of abandonment and betrayal.

The essence and the enduring legacy of the 1980s crisis is the resentment that interdependence has bred. In the United States the articulation of that resentment remains confined to a narrow but vocal neo-conservative fringe. In Europe the fringe is not so narrow, encompassing much of the democratic left and its allies in the peace and environmentalist movements. But Europe's fringe has also proved powerless for the time being, as most of Western Europe turned to the right in the first half of the 1980s – repudiating, if mainly on domestic grounds, those who would weaken the Atlantic tie in the name of nuclear and political abstentionism.

Yet the legacy of resentment remains imprinted on the Atlantic agenda. On the American side of the ocean, it now resides in the message of "nationalist unilateralism"; its West European counterpart is the ideology of "nationalist neutralism." Although these banners are unfurled at opposite ends of the ideological spectrum, the sentiments animating both camps spring from the same source. If the message of neutralism is "Leave us alone," the motto of unilateralism is "We shall go it alone." It does not matter that the neutralist impulse seeks safety in the escape from power, while unilateralism glories in its worldwide reassertion. In both cases the leitmotiv is retraction and insulation – from the grating demands of dependence, from the troubles of a strained partnership, and from commitment to uncertain allies who ruthlessly demand loyalty but yield little of their jealously guarded freedom of action.

On the American side, frustration with the vagaries of coalition politics, fed by a sense of betrayal, has jelled into the urge to loosen, if not cut altogether, the tie that binds the United States to its most entangling alliance. As one catechism of the new faith has it,

Abroad, an assertive American foreign policy meets with great resistance from our allies, most of whom are utterly risk-averse, and some of whom believe that a grudging appeasement of Soviet power will mollify its messianic appetite. This is especially evident in Western Europe, where, under the American nuclear umbrella, national pride has softened into something that resembles national pique. But that umbrella has become moth-eaten with time. It functioned when the United States had a clear superiority in nuclear weapons over the Soviet Union. Today, the umbrella is more myth than reality. There are few Americans, however much they cherish Western Europe, who are actually willing to engage in mutual nuclear annihilation with the Soviet Union in retaliation for non-nuclear Soviet aggression against Western Europe. This means that NATO, as currently structured is an archaic institution, that the defense of Western Europe will become primarily a West European responsibility, that Western Europe will have to gird itself to fight and (hopefully) win a conventional war against the Soviet Union —with American help if needed, but not with a recourse to nuclear weapons."²

That vision, an America free from the bondage of alliance and the existential threat it has come to carry, dovetails nicely with the European dream of nationalist neutralism. "What has come to be known as the peace movement today," proclaimed one of its ideologues, "is also part and parcel of the nation's will to self-assertion."³ The dream feeds on the nightmare of Europe's victimization at the hands of the superpowers. Accordingly, it is the United States and the Soviet Union that have taken possession of the Continent. They have sliced Europe in two, imposing their alien systems and ideologies on an ancient civilization. Without them, Europe would be whole again; without them, Europe would not serve as the "shooting gallery of the superpowers"⁴ but would live in harmony ever after.

It is an ancient dream, and echoes what George F. Kennan, an American sympathetic to the European critics, limned in his memoirs many years ago. "Some day, it appeared to me, this divided Europe, dominated by the military presence of ourselves and the Russians, would have to yield to something more natural—something that did more justice to the true strength and interests of the intermediate European peoples themselves." From this point of view, the United States and the Soviet Union have embroiled the Europeans in conflicts that are not their own. If one were to relinquish its grip on the European vassals, perhaps the other would follow suit, and thus, the "true strengths and interests of the intermediate peoples" would make for an order more just, natural, and certainly more tranquil than domination à deux.⁵

Alliance and Order

Dedicated to the proposition that Europe must take care of itself, such visions pose two questions. One relates to policy: can the Europeans in fact achieve what the critics of the Alliance, on both the Left and the Right, bid them to do? The other question raises a normative issue. If the contemporary order is either parasitical (and a threat to American security to boot) or oppressive (the bane of Europe's "true interests and strengths"), what are its remaining virtues, if any, and what are the alternatives?

This question directs attention to the nature of the contemporary order. How must an international order function so as to acquire a normative claim on men and nations? Western Europe's postwar order may be neither just nor cost-free. By enduring for more than four decades, however, it has already demonstrated an impressive ability to discharge the three key tasks of any international order worthy of the name. It has preserved the security and independence of its members. It has been stable. And it has muted—indeed, inhibited—the use of force.[6]

In short, there may be a dearth of justice in postwar Europe, but there is certainly a surfeit of stability—which stands in stark contrast to Europe's past. In the first half of the twentieth century, the West European state system had failed miserably on all three counts. By 1940, when Hitler's war of conquest had already begun in earnest, it was amply evident that the system could protect neither the security nor the independence of its members. Second, in terms of stability, the system could neither accommodate or suppress the hegemonic ambitions of Germany. Nor was it—finally—capable of inhibiting or muting the use of force, a failure dramatized by the Second Thirty Years' War that engulfed Europe from 1914 to 1945. Indeed, that war was ended only through the intervention of Europe's once remote flanking powers, the United States and the Soviet Union. Nothing could have symbolized the demise of the ancien système more vividly than the meeting of Soviet and American troops on the Elbe River at the close of World War II.

By contrast, the postwar West European system has been not only stable, but ultrastable. While wars and civil wars multiplied around the world, Western Europe remained a solitary island of peace.[7] No army has marched against another; not a single border has been changed by force. The independence of tiny Luxembourg has been preserved just as diligently as the independence of France, Great Britain, or Italy. Western Europe has become a "security community" in Karl W. Deutsch's sense of the term: where interstate rivalry and the competition for advantage persist, but where force is no longer the natural adjunct of policy that it once was.[8]

So benign a course of events was by no means a foregone conclusion in 1945. Given the precedent of the Versailles Treaty, one might have expected the implementation of a punitive policy toward Germany far more severe than the terms meted out to the Weimar Republic in 1919. Yet instead of dismemberment and a poisonous exercise in vengeance, there was the quick rehabilitation of one part of the German Reich. In 1923 France had still occupied the Rhineland; in 1957 it had already returned the Saarland to the Federal Republic. Instead of the perpetuation of the ancient arch rivalry between Gauls and Germans, the world witnessed the growth of Franco-German friendship and the grand experiment of European integration.

The nascent West European order endured beyond expectation because it succeeded in solving two existential problems at once. It managed to envelop the potential of Germany, Europe's most recent claimant to hegemony, and it succeeded in containing the might of the new contender, the Soviet Union. These historic achievements were not Europe's alone. They were made possible by America's lasting entanglement in the affairs of Europe. (Conversely, it might be reasonably argued that the precipitous U.S. withdrawal after 1919 delivered the permissive conditions for World War II.)

The U.S. protector role in the containment of the Soviet Union is familiar enough to require no elaboration. What is widely neglected, however, is the American role as the pacifier[9]—the *agens movens* in the construction of a Western European interstate order that not only muted but even removed ancient conflicts and shaped the indispensable conditions for cooperation. The most important condition was the extension of a unilateral American security guarantee to Western Europe. That guarantee is normally seen only as the cornerstone of the global Soviet–American balance, with the United States contributing a counterweight to Soviet power that the West European nations were unable to provide for themselves. Yet by extending its guarantee, the United States embedded still another girder into the postwar order. The lasting integration of the United States into Europe's state system dispatched the prime *structural* cause of conflict among its nations—the search for an autonomous defense policy.

States go to war for many reasons: greed for resources, dynastic or ideological ambitions, the sheer lust for domination. But an irreducible reason is built into the very nature of a sovereign state system whose members must ultimately rely on themselves to protect their security and independence. In an anarchic self-help system, the very search for security turns into the root cause of insecurity, since each nation's quest poses a threat to the others. Where there is neither a court of the last resort nor an ultimate guardian, states must assume the worst. Because their actions reflect their worst assumptions, they excite the worse suspicions of their neighbors and rivals. And the countervailing responses of the latter merely serve to reinforce the initial anxieties of the former. What John Herz has called the "security dilemma" and Herbert Butterfield labeled "Hobbesian fear" does not necessarily and always lead to war. But the perverse dynamic of self-reliance explains why wars break out even in the absence of pernicious motives such as greed, ambition, and aggrandizement.[10]

Europe, a fount of international conflict for centuries, has never suffered from a dearth of these motives. Yet by underwriting the security of the West European nation states, by sparing them the necessity of self-reliant choice in matters of defense, the United States banished the *systemic* cause of conflict at the root of so many of Europe's past wars—World War I being perhaps the best example. By protecting Western Europe from others, the United States also protected the half-continent from itself. America's very presence rendered obsolete the rules of the self-help system, wherein fear breeds conflict and conflict breeds fear. Since there was now a powerful arbiter in the system providing security to each and all, ancient and persisting rivalries lost their existential sting. By dint of America's intrusion, there was a base of mutual trust that would hold the edifice of cooperation erect in the 1950s. Without the passage from the grim arena of international anarchy to the happier ground of a "security community," the success story of European integration might never have been written.

Nor might Western Europe have turned into the world's largest bastion of democracy. From the Enlightenment onward, liberal theory—from Condorcet to Comte—has routinely claimed that war is the "game of princes," that republics would sooner heed the call of the commercial spirit than the heady call to arms and aggrandizement. This may or may not be true. The history of democracies—much less peaceful intercourse among them—is still too short to vindicate the Enlightenment's historical optimism. In the postwar West European case, however, the causal relationship between democracy and peace might well have operated in reverse fashion: democracy could flourish precisely because the peace was assured. With their security guaranteed by a powerful outsider, the nation-states of Western Europe did not face the kind of existential peril abroad that, for instance, had turned bourgeois revolutions after 1789 into Bonapartist empires. The "primacy of foreign policy"—the nineteenth century ideology that set the imperative of national strength against the demands of mass-based democracy—could no longer be wielded on behalf of authoritarian rule. Without a sense of impending victimization, ultranationalism and the garrison-state mentality could not prevail over democratic experiments. If insecurity, real or pretended, helped to legitimize the politics of totalitarian mobilization in the first half of the twentieth century, Europe's guaranteed security during the second half cleared the ground so that the habits of pluralism could thrive; antidemocratic forces withered, because there was no Hobbesian threat that could be manipulated to serve the behemoth state. Germany and Italy in the 1950s, Portugal and Spain in the 1970s—would they have overcome their antidemocratic traditions as smoothly as they did without so benign a setting?

Harmony Versus History: The Lesson of Failures Past

That the United States pacified Western Europe can evidently be challenged by pointing to Joseph Stalin as the true "federator" of the half-continent. Accordingly, it was the foe, not the friend, who changed the rules of the European game from internecine rivalry to friendly cooperation. Great Britain and France, Germany and Italy, Belgium and Holland—if left to their own devices, would these nations have pooled their resources against the looming Soviet threat? Such tricky "what if" questions are the most unreliable guides to history, and they cannot yield conclusive answers. Yet we do know something about the historical record of alliance building and about postwar European integration, and that epic does not appear to bear out the contention that the Soviet dictator was more important than Messrs. Truman, Dulles, and Eisenhower.

Indeed, the real or presumed threat from the East never proved strong enough to suppress either memories of the past or apprehensions about the future among those key West European states that were intent on transcending both considerations for the sake of collective defense. As late as March 1948—when the Cold War was already in full swing—Great Britain, France, and the Benelux countries signed the fifty-year Brussels Pact, the preamble of which explicitly identified Germany as the potential aggressor. But most instructive was the behavior of France, the country that was consistently more concerned about its security and status vis-à-vis a resurgent half-Germany than about the hegemonic pressures of the Soviet Union.

Although ancient history by now, the crucial years of this story were between 1950 and 1955—when the United States came down in favor of West German rearmament and the Federal Republic was at last integrated into the North Atlantic Treaty Organization. Initially dead set against the rearmament of a nation that had thrice invaded their country in the space of three generations, the French shifted under American pressure toward an outwardly cooperative strategy that was in fact designed to postpone the dread event indefinitely.[11] The chosen instrument was the so-called Pleven Plan presented on October 26, 1950. It all but mandated a West European confederation in matters of defense: a West European force beholden to a West European minister of defense and a West European assembly, with West German participation yet without either a German national army or a German general staff. Moreover, the West German contingent could not comprise more than one-fifth of the entire European army. As a French bon mot of the time had it, the envisaged West Germany contribution had to be strong enough to impress the Soviet Union and weak enough not to threaten Luxembourg.

The French calculated that so ambitious an integrationist venture would take years, if not forever, to reach the light of day. Thanks to mounting American pressure, however, the draft agreement for a modified Pleven Plan, rechristened the European Defense Community (EDC), was ready in May of 1952. Undaunted, the French quickly begain to raise the price for their consent. After signing the EDC treaty on May 27, the French unrelentingly insisted on tangible Anglo-American guarantees directed not against the Soviets but against their future comrades-in-arms, the West Germans. Above all, France demanded a permanent Anglo-American military presence on the Continent and a pledge to intervene against any EDC member (namely, the Federal Republic) who violated the treaty. Though London and Washington went a long way toward meeting French concerns, the hold of history proved too strong. In the end neither written guarantees nor John Foster Dulles' fabled threat of an "agonizing reappraisal" could save the EDC from a veto of the French National Assembly on August 30, 1954.[12]

Why then was West Germany admitted to the Western coalition after all? Even more instructive than the EDC's demise was the aftermath, in which France consented not only to German rearmament within the space of a few weeks but also to the Federal Republic's accession to sovereignty and NATO. France accepted community with its ancient rival and nemesis precisely because the United States and Great Britain stood ready at last to extend tangible assurances against the dread consequences of an unshackled and rearmed West Germany.

The British foreign secretary, Anthony Eden, had found the solution "in the bath on Sunday morning [September 5, 1954]. . . . I preferred to bring Germany into NATO, under the various safeguards which had been devised for her entry into EDC. . . . We would have to devise safeguards which were effective but not too blatant."[13] The Federal Republic would join both NATO and the West European Union (WEU), which offered a crucial advantage over the defunct EDC. A purely continental venture (of France, Italy, West Germany, and the three Benelux countries), the EDC included neither the United States nor Great Britain. In that framework, France would essentially have been left alone with its former archenemy. Enveloping the Federal Republic in the WEU would yield a double layer of additional guarantees. Great Britain was a member of the WEU system; and the WEU's terms, unlike NATO discretionary obliations, bound every member to automatic intervention against aggression from any quarter whatsoever – even from a co-signatory, like Germany.

The crucial prize was delivered during the London Conference in the fall of 1954, when Britain extended to France and the smaller Alliance members those critical assurances that Paris had earlier demanded in vain. Eden promised that the United Kingdom would maintain four divisions on the mainland and would not "withdraw those forces against the wishes of the majority."[14] The French obsession with British guarantees may seem puzzling today, but at the time those guarantees appeared to be the appropriate antidote for the fears of the Fourth Republic. In the 1950s Britain was not a former imperial power in economic decline but rather one of the true victors of World War II. To the French, who had twice relied on British arms to best the German invaders, Albion was America writ small – the indispensable continental balancer as a check on German might.

With Great Britain – America's continental sword – in the European system, Dulles' renewed assurances acquired the weight they had lacked before. He vowed that "the United States will continue to maintain in Europe, including Germany, such units of its armed forces as may be necessary and appropriate to contribute its fair share of the forces needed for the joint defense of the North Atlantic area . . . and will continue to deploy such forces in accordance with agreed North Atlantic strategy."[15] Together with France and Great Britain, the United States then delivered a contractual pledge that was certainly directed against West

Germany, the former foe but ally-to-be. "They will regard as a threat to their own peace and safety any recourse to force which . . . threatens the integrity and unity of the Atlantic alliance or its defensive purposes. In the event of any such action, the three Governments . . . will consider the offending government as having forfeited its rights to any guarantee and any military assistance provided for in the North Atlantic Treaty. . . . They will act . . . with a view to taking other measures which may be appropriate."[16] For its part, the Federal Republic accepted a host of unprecedented constraints on its policy and power—notably, the renunciation of nuclear weapons, the complete integration of its armed forces into NATO, and the solemn pledge never to use force in the quest for German reunification.

The point of this excursion into the dusty annals of the Alliance is to show that, even at a time of excruciating weakness, neither the Soviet challenge nor the destruction of the European balance during World War II were powerful enough to prompt the West Europeans to transcend their history. It was only the virtually permanent intrusion of the United States that changed the terms of state interaction to the point where the Europeans no longer had to conduct their business in the brooding shadow of violence. This development was a far more momentous event than just the birth of a new coalition. By committing its power to the protection of Western Europe as well as itself against the Soviets, the United States swept aside the rules of the self-help game that had governed and regularly brought grief to Europe in centuries past.

To elucidate the transformation, the Europe of the Pax Americana ought to be contrasted with the traditional ways of international politics.

In a self-help system each of the units spends a portion of its effort, not in forwarding its own good, but in providing the means of protecting itself against others. . . . . When faced with the possibility of cooperating for mutual gain, states that feel insecure must ask how the gain will be divided. They are compelled to ask not "Will both of us gain?" but "Who will gain more?" If an expected gain is to be divided, say, in the ratio of two to one, one state may use its disporportionate gain to implement a policy intended to damage or destroy the other. Even the prospect of large absolute gain for both parties does not elicit their cooperation so long as each fears how the other will use its increased capabilities. Notice that the impediments to collaboration may not lie in the character and the immediate intention of either party. Instead, the condition of insecurity . . . works against their cooperation.[17]

It is this perverse logic—the age-old logic of international politics— that collapsed in favor of West European cooperation once the Pax Americana was in place. Henceforth, the international relations of Western

Europe came to resemble domestic politics in one crucial respect: insecurity, the underlying condition of statecraft, and force, its ultima ratio, were banished from the system. Once the problem of security was dispatched, collective gain could overwhelm the zero-sum logic of rivalry and relative gain. In contrast to the interwar period, when the fears of the victors and the resentments of the vanquished made for a vicious cycle of repression and revanchism, France and Germany could join hands in the Alliance and the European Community because a nation more powerful than either would insure them both against the perilous consequences of their credulity. The smaller nations of Western Europe, especially the wary Dutch, could swallow integration with the large because they did not need to fear domination. Even Great Britain ultimately joined the continental venture because America's presence blunted the hard edge of its traditional rivalry with France and Germany.

International Politics Versus the Politics of Transcendence

Long forgotten, the London Conference of 1954 – the closest equivalent to a postwar settlement in Europe – provided the capstone for a West European order that has endured until this day. Equally durable has been America's political and military presence, which Franklin D. Roosevelt, meeting with Churchill and Stalin in Yalta in 1945, had foreseen as a fleeting episode only – intended to last no longer than two years after the end of World War II.[18] Today, the once obsessive preoccupation with Germany's power, both past and potential, has also yielded to a more sober and benign assessment. The West German successor to the Third Reich has proven a model ally and a model European precisely because it was not pushed into the poisoned atmosphere of the post-Versailles period. Cooperation between ancient enemies has been routinized within the expanding framework of the European Community, which jumped from ten to twelve members when Spain and Portugal joined in 1986.

It is tempting to conclude that so stable an order could stand on its own and dispense with the foundation laid by the United States in the early fifties. Could not Western Europe – pacified, prosperous, and with an economic and demographic base larger than that of either superpower – do without its patron power from across the sea? Could not Western Europe solve on its own the problems of protection and pacification? The critics of America's presence in Europe would not hesitate to answer that question in the affirmative. Their answer would echo the classic conviction of the Europeanist faith. Since the West Europeans have learned to cooperate on all other matters, they should be able to repeat such a feat in the realm of the common defense.

To argue thus is to base a tenuous conclusion on a shaky premise. The record of European integration since the birth of the European Coal and Steel Community in 1951 does not show that the West Europeans have learned to cooperate on all matters save defense. Not even a common market, Western Europe's least ambitious aspiration, is a reality. Though the EEC was founded in 1957, its members must continue to dismantle a myriad of barriers—kept in place by national tax, custom, immigration, health, corporation, and banking laws—to arrive at a unified internal market. (The current target date, which keeps moving forward, is 1992.)

Nor does this failure reflect only bureaucratic inertia or technical complexities, either of which could be overcome by political will and diligent effort. The root problem is that falling tariff barriers do not a common market make, let alone a political e pluribus unum. Even after these barriers crumble, all other obstacles would also have to disappear. If goods are to travel freely, so must labor, services, and capital. If all these are to move untrammeled from Athens to Lisbon and from Cork to Calabria, there must be a single market legally—that is, a unified system of laws to break down the walls that nation-states have erected around themselves over the centuries. But at that stage, integration's progress grinds to a halt before the ramparts of national sovereignty. For laws are not born from functional necessity; they are the codified will of the sovereign. In Europe there is not one sovereign; there are twelve. These sovereigns do not obey the call of "Europe" but listen to the voice of the national interest as articulated by the chorus of their domestic politics. And this is why the nation-state is still alive and well in Western Europe—ready to yield some prerogatives to a supranational bureaucracy in Brussels and the European Parliament in Strasbourg, but loath to relinquish control over either institution.

There is nothing—certainly no hegemonic unifier—to force the West European nation-state into liquidation. Nor is there any incentive potent enough to lure the states into self-abandonment. Decades ago, the European Community's founding fathers thought that they had found the right combination of pull and push. "Functionalism," their *idée clef*, had posited the steady subversion of sovereignty—"unification on the sly," as it were. The process would begin with the merger of certain sectors such as coal, steel, and agriculture.[19] As it unfolded, it would generate irresistible pressures for the integration of more and more sectors. That spill-over effect would set in motion a self-perpetuating, unstoppable march toward the unification of economies, polities, and armies. In reality that march was never more than a series of straggly forays. And the utopia of the Functionalists was soon exposed as an empty dream, when the waves of that ostensibly apolitical process began to lap ever more closely against the core of national sovereignty.

The counteroffensive against Brussels was prepared as early as 1960, only three years after the Treaty of Rome had established the EEC. In a September 30, 1960 directive to his prime minister, Michel Debré, Charles de Gaulle wrote: "The Europe of [state-to-state] cooperation will be launched as of now. The Europe of [supranational] integration cannot but yield forthwith. . . . If we succeed in giving birth to the Europe of cooperation, the communities will be put in their place ipso facto."[20] In 1965 the campaign was unleashed in earnest. By 1966 the Community of Six was to submit to a veritable constitutional revolution, as laid down in the Treaty of Rome, and to pass from unanimity to qualified majority voting. Thanks to unrelenting French pressure, that step into the realm of the supranational was never taken. To propitiate de Gaulle, the Six formulated a gentlemen's agreement in 1966, by which no member state could be overruled when its national interest was at stake. Since then, Western Europe has charted its course as nations have always done: in the shadow of each member's veto. By 1985 even the Federal Republic—heretofore the most European-minded of them all—resorted to the veto to block a minuscule fall in the European Community's official grain price, in order to protect the incomes of (relatively inefficient) West German cereal producers.

Such spill-back should not make for puzzlement. If nations integrate because they are no longer masters of their economic fates—as functionalist theory rightly proclaims—why should they compound the problem by offering up their autonomy to a supranational body that might trample it even more thoroughly in the process of executing majority rule? Precisely because the national *sacro egoismo* has been battered by transnational forces beyond its reach, nation-states strain to recapture control, not to yield it. To have a truly common market, the Twelve would need a truly common monetary and fiscal policy. Yet a nation's fiscal-monetary mix determines the pace of unemployment and inflation at home—the two factors that, in turn, largely determine the outcome of elections and the fate of governments. And thus Western Europe will enjoy neither a common market nor a common monetary and fiscal policy unless it has a common government.

The history of European integration has rarely failed to illustrate that moral. The process lumbers on, and after each failure there is a fabled *relance:* In Messina, the Treaty of Rome followed the debacle of the EDC in 1957. In The Hague in 1969, the Six celebrated their newfound *élan* in the aftermath of de Gaulle. The 1970s witnessed the birth of the European Monetary System (EMS) and popular elections to the European Parliament. In Luxembourg in December 1985, the Twelve compensated for the empty-handed return six months earlier from the Milan Summit with amendments to the Treaty of Rome that, if ratified by all the national legislatures, will expand the powers of the European Parliament. Yet none of these steps can disguise the fact that power over the core issues continues to rest in the hands of national governments.

If functional necessity does not make for union in the realm of "low" politics (that is, where a single internal market awaits completion), why should it do so in the realm of "high" politics—in defense and foreign policy, the most jealously guarded bastion of *raison d'état*? Necessity surely demands, and Western Europe's staggering resources surely permit, the birth of a common defense identity distinct from the United States. Resources, of course, have never amounted to a solution. As Dean Acheson pointed out almost a generation ago, "Prosperity is not power; nor a guarantee of peace. Power is a combination of population, resources, technology, and will. Will is the lacking element in Western Europe as a whole, the will to use the other elements for agreed ends."[21]

The absence of will—or more precisely, the presence of too many separate wills—prompted the demise of the EDC, Europe's first and last try at a common defense. At that time the problem of too many wills was overcome by the intrusion of one very large will—that of the United States, which thereafter acted in the double role of protector and pacifier. That historical fact suggests a curious twist on alliance theory. Conventional theory holds that states coalesce *in order* to assure their security. In the case of post-EDC Western Europe, however, states coalesced *because* their security was already assured—by a powerful outsider who had delivered an external shield as well as an internal order to Western Europe. America's benign empire was the precondition of alliance and integration, and thus, security came first and cooperation second. (NATO was founded in 1949, the European Steel and Coal Community in 1951.) If that logic still holds today, almost forty years later, Western Europe minus its protector-pacifier faces not just the familiar gulf between the dream and the power but also a vicious cycle. Without a quantum jump in cooperation that would subsume the half-continent's riches

under a general will, Western Europe could not generate sufficient security to hold its own against the Soviet Union. Yet will the West Europeans take that leap if their security is no longer guaranteed?

Which legacy of the past matters more to Europeans: centuries of
separate statehood in the shadow of war, or the few decades of partial
cooperation under the umbrella of the Pax Americana? In spite of its impressive record of functional integration, Western Europe remains, to recall Stanley Hoffman's verdict, "a collection of largely self-encased nation-states. . . . If the hostilities entailed by separate pasts appear to have
evaporated, [Western Europe's] separate pasts have not."[22] Whence it
would follow that Europe's separate pasts—its separate identities, interests, and involvements—will claim even larger dues from a system in
which security once more flows from self-help (as it did for centuries)
rather than from the munificence of the United States.

The habits of cooperation would not be unlearned, but its practice
would once again be soured by the logic of relative gain, which compels
each state to worry about the uses to which other states' shares in the
collective enterprise might be put. Pressures for self-sufficiency would
mount, inevitably leading nations to contribute less to the "collective
good" of security rather than more. Without the United States, Western
Europe not only might not rush forward into true integration but might
even fall back into a pattern of interaction resembling that of the pre-
war period. The weak would once more worry about the strong, and the
strong—such as Great Britain, France, and West Germany—would once
more worry about each other. Facing a new demand curve for security,
individual West European states would not necessarily engage in communal production but might scour the market for substitutes. These might
range from a limited defense cartel (e.g., a formalized Anglo-American
"special relationship") to a limited détente cartel whereby the weak would
seek to reduce their demand for security by appeasing the dominant
power on the Continent. In the absence of the United States, that mantle
would fall on the Soviet Union.

In such a system, the Soviet Union would not necessarily be the great
federator but would loom as the paramount power—with the chance to
use its overweening srength to play one West European state against another and to dictate the terms of its relationship to them all. History, at
any rate, does not assure us that the weak will always band together
against the strong. Nations facing a diminished supply of security might
try to produce more of it. But they can also try to reestablish equilibrium
by reducing their *demand* for security, by conciliating their adversary with

a policy of reinsurance, neutrality, or subordination. Although largely driven by the quest for reconciliation with the East and the overdue acceptance of Europe's postwar realities, the New Ostpolitik of Willy Brandt was also—and not surprisingly—inspired by "Mansfieldism."[23] Since a "substantial" cut in American forces (the leitmotiv of recurrent Senate resolutions) meant less reliable protection, a cooperative tie to the Soviet Union might add a measure of reinsurance to West Germany security. "My thinking," Brandt told French President Georges Pompidou in 1971, "proceeded on the . . . assumption that only a part of the American forces would remain in Europe at the end of the 1970s."[24] Thus, it is hardly self-evident that the West Europeans would necessarily convert their new-found autonomy into integrationist *élan*. More likely, they would find that they had only traded one dependence for another.

Nation-States, Nuclear Weapons, and the New Europe

Such speculations about the future of Europe minus the United States invite charges of historicism and faint-heartedness. After a murderous thirty years' war followed by a benign forty years' peace, might not Western Europe have finally transcended history? Perhaps the habits of cooperation are now so deeply etched in the collective West European unconscious that they will endure even in the absence of a powerful American guardian.

History never repeats itself, but its continuities have a crafty way of reasserting themselves in ever changing guises. And whatever the postwar experience might have taught the West Europeans, it has unhinged neither geography nor the nation-state. France, as usual, provides the most instructive case in point. In 1954 the Radical Socialist Edouard Herriot, decried the EDC as "the end of France . . . a step forward for Germany [and] and a step back for France."[25] Some twenty years later, President Giscard d'Estaing told his parliament: "I consider that it is important for the military balance of our continent that the French forces should be of the same dimension as those of the other continental military power, namely Germany."[26] These words were uttered by the least Gaullist leader of the Fifth Republic, and by a man who would always celebrate his spiritual and political friendship with the then German chancellor, Helmut Schmidt.

If France worried about German strength in the 1950s, it worried about German weakness in the 1980s—in both cases, ironically, as a threat to French security. And thus Europe was treated to a double twist of French policy in the early 1980s when French *raison d'état* (another term for "history") predictably triumphed over both Gaullist orthodoxy and socialist sentiment. First, the French warmly embraced the deployment of American Pershing II and cruise missiles on the Continent — as a counter not only to Soviet SS-20 missiles but also to German pacifist nationalism. Thereafter, François Mitterrand, a Socialist, demonstratively supported Conservative Helmut Kohl's 1983 bid for reelection, because the French president no longer trusted his Social Democratic confreres' devotion to the Atlanticist cause. The underlying logic of that irony is transparent. Both France's security and its policy of splendid aggravation rest on the twin pillars of a credible American nuclear guarantee and a well-defended glacis to the East — meaning, a Federal Republic reliably bound to the Atlantic Alliance.

It should not be surprising that security concerns lurk so close beneath the surface of stable, long-term cooperation. Even after several decades of integration, which have seen the European Community expand from six to twelve members, such arrière-pensée merely echoes an older insight of international politics: that even nations sheltered by a mighty superpower worry above all about survival, security, and status. How would the West Europeans assure their independence outside the American-built shelter? At the core of that question is the problem of the atom. In its shadow, the ultimate guarantee of a nation's existence is a credible deterrent. Western Europe could only dispense with the United States if it could field such a deterrent against the Soviet Union. Yet how could the Europeans accomplish that task in the absence of true unification?

The problem cannot be solved by postulating — as the American critics of the Alliance do — that demand will create its own supply, that a dramatically increased need for self-sufficiency in matters nuclear would finally push the West Europeans into political community. If anything, the opposite should be true. For nuclear weapons are inherently divisive, not integrationist. On the level of day-to-day politics, that tendency has been exemplified by the Alliance's endless strife over nuclear strategy since the mid-1950s. Yet the problem runs far deeper.

In theory there are three alternatives to the American umbrella. One is a European superstate with its own nuclear deterrent. The second is a European deterrent "on loan," so to speak, whereby either or both of the two existing nuclear powers — France and England — would commit its nuclear arsenal to the protection of the nuclear have-nots. The final alternative is a Western Europe of nuclearized nation-states. Yet on closer inspection, each of these three escape routes turns into a dead-end street.

One Europe, One Bomb

The first alternative—a nuclear-armed European superstate—presupposes a European sovereign; it cannot create one. As a purely theoretical exercise, one might take a page from Hobbes' *Leviathan* and construe a state of general nuclear insecurity so oppressive that each state, feeling equally threatened, would be eager to yield its powers to a European nuclear sovereign. Yet the states of Western Europe do not live in a Hobbesian state of war, nor are all of them equally vulnerable. France and Britain already have their independent deterrents; for them, there is absolutely no incentive to yield what has become theirs by dint of painful national effort—and sacrifice their sovereignty to boot. For those who have them, nuclear weapons are the ultima ratio, the very essence of sovereignty in the post-Hiroshima age. Britain and France built their national forces to preserve their status and independence; they could not possibly wish to relinquish the former to a European behemoth state that would destroy the latter.

One Europe, Two Bombs

The second dream—a nuclear umbrella of French and/or British manufacture—is only superficially more plausible. The reason that it is not realistic has been reiterated ad infinitum by French leaders, strategists, and ideologists; the more discreet British would concur, if they were pressed. *Le nucléaire ne se partage pas*—nuclear weapons protect only their possessors. Hence, "deterrence is exclusively national" and, "the nuclear risk cannot be shared."[27] Nor "can the decision [to launch] be shared."[28] To put it baldly, as the French have done endlessly: no nation will commit suicide on behalf of another. Such epigrams do not bode well for cordial ententes. Since nuclear weapons, if ever launched, threaten swift, complete, and mutual destruction, they render all vows and pledges null and void when the existential crunch arrives. Non-nuclear nations therefore could not rely on the nuclear shield of their allies; nations cannot share control over the ultimate weapon. Yet mutual control and mutual succor are the very stuff of alliance—whence it must follow that nuclear alliances are impossible. If ever uttered, any French guarantee must perforce be a hollow one. Or as French Prime Minister Pierre Mauroy put it in words evoking the very essence of his country's defense policy: "Autonomous in the commitment of its forces, France does not intend the suffer the consequences of conflicts that are not its own."[29]

To accept that logic is also, of course, to reduce to pure pretense the American deterrent threat that is supposedly the linchpin of the Atlantic Alliance. Surely the golden age of extended deterrence came to an end in 1957 when the Soviets acquired a rudimentary bomber force capable of striking the American heartland. Assured destruction, previously just a one-way threat, began to give way to peril parity; simultaneously, America's pledge to launch nuclear weapons on behalf of its allies was bound to become brittle. Once the United States was laid open to nuclear strikes, it *did* run the mortal risk of sacrificing its own cities for the sake of Bonn, Rome, Brussels, et al.

Nor have American officials been oblivious to the perils of parity. As early as 1959, Christian Herter, later to become secretary of state, conceded that the nuclear threat on behalf of allies might be no more than an empty bluff. "I cannot conceive of the President involving us in all-out nuclear war unless the facts showed clearly that we are in danger of devastation ourselves, or that actual moves have been made toward devastating ourselves."[30] That message was confirmed a quarter century later by former Secretary of Defense Robert S. McNamara when he admitted having counseled two presidents (Kennedy and Johnson) "never [to] initiate, under any circumstances, the use of nuclear weapons."[31]

Is the American nuclear guarantee then nothing but a historic hoax? If so, why has the Euro-American alliance endured in the face of drastic changes in the nuclear balance, which are said to pose unbearable risks for protectors and clients alike? The answer is surely that superpowers can more easily fudge the irreducible dilemmas of extended deterrence than can middle powers like France and Great Britain. Superpowers are in a different class of guarantors for at least three reasons.

The Factor of Quality

Threatening nuclear strikes on behalf of allies requires, at a minimum, a counterforce potential. To maneuver between the shoals of suicide and surrender, great powers must have weapons that are accurate enough to threaten the common enemy's forces. Only weapons capable of hitting their targets with high precision and low collateral damage ("selective strikes") can demonstrate commitment to allies or weaken the aggressor's warmaking potential without provoking an apocalyptic counterblow. The French and the British do not now possess such weapons; their arsenals are structured essentially to serve a countervalue strategy. Or as Prime Minister Mauroy outlined France's nuclear program for the

1980s and 1990s: "This modernization and enhancement of our potential does not at all imply a transformation of [our] anti-cities strategy. It remains the implacable but indisputable foundation of deterrence by the weak against the strong."[32] Such principles accurately reflect the facts of present and future possession. Apart from eighteen French land-based missiles on the Plateau d'Albion, the Franco-British forces are concentrated at sea. The British Polaris (sixty-four missiles with three warheads each) and the French MSBS M-20 (eighty missiles with a one-megaton warhead each) are neither accurate nor "small" enough to serve in a selective counterforce mode. "For technical reasons alone," declared French Defense Minister Charles Hernu, "our deterrent cannot serve to cover Europe or even France and the Federal Republic."[33]

The Factor of Quantity

For a superpower like the United States, equipped with thousands of strategic weapons, great numbers confer options short of Armageddon. A first volley would not be the last; nor would an initial breach of deterrence signify its complete collapse. A counterforce blow would not necessarily bring on an apocalyptic riposte, because large nuclear reserves should still make for "intrawar deterrence." It is the possession of abundant assets that raises the probability of an American first use above zero—which may well be enough. And it is the prospect of unlimited damage at the end of the day—no matter how limited the probability of a strike—that instills caution in those who contemplate aggression against American allies.

Having fewer weapons denies such extended deterrence options to small nuclear powers like France. Here, too, official doxology pays due respect to the limits of French power. Though fine-tuned over the years, France's deterrent doctrine remains based on the Gaullist premises laid down in the mid-1960s, when the deployment of Mirage IV A bombers gave the French a nuclear capability of sorts.[34] The key premise is proportional deterrence, or *la dissuasion du faible au fort*—the deterrence of the strong by the weak. Since France could not possibly hope to match the Soviet panoply, meeting the criterion of sufficiency means endowing its small nuclear force with a great deterrent effect. Accordingly, it is enough to "tear off an arm"—to inflict a level of damage on the Soviet Union that would exceed the value of a conquered or annihilated France.

The ability to mutilate a superpower, however, does not suffice for the protection of allies. For that purpose, there is too deep a gulf between inherently limited means and potentially unlimited penalties. "Tearing an arm" off the Soviet body politic would result in the death of the French one. Hence, it is only the impending destruction of France that lends weight to the threat of a second, and suicidal, strike. Moreover, the French force represents a one-shot potential only. If credible at all, it can be wielded only in defense of the supreme national interest, that is, the very existence of the nation. France's first strike will also be its last. It follows that threatening such action on behalf of any other nation would be no more than an empty bluff. The French have long recognized the vacuity of such a pledge by asserting, as an article of faith: no nation will commit suicide for the sake of another.

France's future options, it might be argued, will no longer be chained to the thirty-six Mirage IV A bombers it had to rely on in the sixties. By the mid-1990s, France should be in possession of seven missile-carrying submarines capable of hurling 592 warheads into Soviet territory.[35] (It has six at present; the 1986 budget provided for a seventh submarine to enter service in the mid-1990s.)[36] Similarly, if the British Trident program survives as planned, Great Britain nuclear capability might vault to anywhere from 512 to 1,088 sea-launched warheads in the 1990s, because the Trident II missiles scheduled to replace sixty-four Polaris missiles can carry between eight and seventeen warheads each. It is not self-evident, however, that such auspicious arithmetic would change the fundamentals of the current imbalance between the weak and the strong or enhance the ability of the weak to protect those who are even weaker.

The British will have many warheads, but still only four missile-bearing submarines. Since two of them are likely to be in port for overhaul or resupply at any given time—while the others might be easily shadowed by Soviet hunter-killer submarines—a preemptive first strike against the British deterrent would not be significantly more difficult than it is today. The same logic would militate in the 1990s against the seven French boats and their multiple-warhead loads, although France might by then have acquired some additional insurance in the form of the land-mobile SX missile. Moreover, all bets will be off if the Soviet Union deploys a nationwide ballistic missile defense system by the time French and British modernization plans are completed. In short, France and Britain may well increase the number of their warheads by a factor ranging from three to seven in the 1990s; but even such assets will not catapult them out of the danger zone, where their second-strike capability is kept at risk by a vast and sophisticated Soviet arsenal. As long as they remain in that zone, France and Great Britain cannot even think of extending a nuclear umbrella over their European allies.

Indeed, the French and the British umbrellas cannot substitute for U.S. guarantees because they depend for their effectiveness on the larger American umbrella. The weak can deter the strong because the strong deter each other. General Jeannou Lacaze, Chief of Staff of the French Armed Forces, underlines that point. After the standard invocation of French independence, he noted that a nuclear aggressor must fear the risk of *two* responses:

one by the Alliance and one by France. Even in assuming that he has to risk no more than our strategic strike, the aggressor would still have to consider the situation in which he would find himself after suffering the destruction of a non-negligible part of his cities [and his economic and administrative infrastructure] while *the other great nuclear powers would still have their intact economic and military potential.* This argument seems fundamental to me, and it indicates how advisable it is to view our strategy of the weak deterring the strong within the global geopolitical context.[37]

The Factor of the Hostage Relationship between the United States and Western Europe

The previous argument has focused on quantity and quality to show why French or British nuclear forces could not replace American weapons in the defense of Western Europe. Yet to reason in the same breath that superpower nuclear guarantees remain credible in spite of peril parity would surely require an excruciating scholastic effort, if not a leap of faith. Why would the West Europeans continue to believe in the solidity of a guarantee that, if executed, might trigger the swift and complete demise of its author?

The problem common to *all* alliances, before and after Hiroshima, is the fear of abandonment. Nuclear weapons have exacerbated the issue exponentially because they place the very existence of guarantors in jeopardy. Yet we must ask why NATO has nonetheless endured. The answer lies in the Atlantic Alliance's development of some potent antidotes for this deadliest bane of coalitions. The antidote for the poison of abandonment is what we now call *coupling,* and NATO has produced it in profuse variation. The technique is as old as alliances themselves. In *The Guns of August,* Barbara Tuchmann recounts a paradigmatic exchange in 1910 between French Marshall Foch and his British counterpart, Sir Henry Wilson. How many British soldiers on French soil would it take to assure the French that Great Britain would indeed fight on their side in a war against Germany? "A single British soldier," the French officer replied," and we will see to it that he is killed."[38]

In 1910 a single hostage may have been enough. In the nuclear age, the price of credibility has risen as precipitously as the level of potential damage to a guarantor if deterrence failed. Hence, great powers have been forced to add a hefty measure of redundance to their nuclear commitments. In Western Europe the supplementary guarantee consists of 330,000 American troops plus thousands of American battlefield and intermediate-range nuclear weapons. Their function is, first and foremost, to compress the gap of geography and sovereignty that separates American from Allied territory, and their message to friends as well as foes is twofold.

First, large numbers of soldiers-qua-hostages signal that an attack on Western Europe threatens values almost as precious as maintaining American core security. Hostage armies make for partial congruence between otherwise distinct national territories, thus muting the harshly divisive logic of nuclear weapons. To say that nations will not commit suicide for one another implies that each can credibly threaten suicide on its own behalf or, more to the point, on behalf of hundreds of thousands of its own citizens, even though they happen to be stationed on alien soil. The United States might not put American cities at risk in order to shelter European ones, but the deterrent threat does gain solidity when exercised on behalf of allies harboring city-sized American contingents.

Secondly, large numbers of nuclear weapons in a forward position signal that there may be no sanctuaries; that war may expand to engulf principals as well as junior partners; that an attack on America's ultima ratio in Europe is an attack on the United States itself. As long as they are in place, nuclear weapons may be used, and once even the smallest weapon explodes, there may be no firebreaks and pauses short of Moscow and Washington. Precisely because nuclear weapons might protect only their possessors, the Europeans have perennially pressed for strategies that chain patron and clients to a common nuclear fate. Pershing II and cruise missiles were merely the latest act in NATO's ongoing coupling drama.

In attacking Western Europe, the Soviet Union would have to attack a part of the American arsenal that is strategic by Moscow's own definition because it can devastate Soviet territory. Would the Soviets go for a minuscule portion of American strategic systems and spare the rest? This is not how the Soviets view the problem. For them, "a first strike in Western Europe would have no sense [sic], . . . for it would only expose our country to riposte by an absolutely intact U.S. strategic arsenal."[39] By that reckoning, there is no profit in a "small" war, and the Soviets would have to go for U.S. "central forces" if they wanted to take on Western Europe. With the United States and Western Europe so coupled, extended deterrence prevails, because an aggressor would have to face the costs of an all-out war if he contemplates an attack on Western Europe. In short, while Messrs. Herter and McNamara may well be right in terms of pure deterrence theory, their heresy is not likely to tempt the Russians to act like brazen infidels when confronting the tangible nuclear risks of the real world.[40]

Of such cloth are strategies tailored to soften the cruel verdict of Gaullist nuclear logic (according to which all nuclear alliances are impossible). Perhaps, then, such a web might also be fashioned between France and its continental neighbors—the Federal Republic in particular—so as to relieve Western Europe of its dependence on the United States. Some threads do already exist. On the French side, there have been recurrent tantalizing offers to make common military cause with West Germany, a shady tradition started by none other than de Gaulle when he tried to woo Chancellor Adenauer away from the American embrace in the early 1960s.[41] The most recent offer was the dazzling promise held out by President Mitterrand at the height of the Euromissile crisis. To provide an additional anchor to the Federal Republic, which seemed to be adrift between NATO and neutralist nationalism, the dormant military clauses of the Franco-German Treaty of Friendship and Cooperation (1963) were restored from oblivion in 1982.[42] An institutional framework was fashioned for the meeting of the foreign and defense ministers of both countries twice a year. And there is now a "security commission," consisting of a dozen high-level officials, that meets about thrice a year to discuss joint arms procurement, staff coordination, and political and strategic affairs.[43]

There are also recurrent allusions to a *sanctuaire élargi*, which might encompass France's neighbor across the Rhine, as well as to the much celebrated FAR—the French "Rapid Action Force" that might be rushed to the inter-German border to aid in the "forward battle."[44] Prime Minister Mauroy has opined that France's vital interests extend beyond the borders of the 'Hexagon' [to] their approaches. Aggression against France does not begin when an enemy invades the nation's territory."[45] And Defense Minister Hernu has praised the FAR as a boon to the security of the Federal Republic because, once the Force is dispatched, "our closest neighbors and allies would profit from a valuable reinforcement."[46] Finally, the 1990s will witness the entry of the Hadès missile into the French tactical nuclear arsenal, replacing the Pluton. The key difference between these two tactical missiles is range (120 versus 350 kilometers), and that difference translates into a significant political message. At this point, Pluton missiles can only deliver their "final warning," as French doctrine has it, by targeting enemy troops on Allied soil—meaning, at a juncture when Soviet forces have already overrun most of West Germany. The Hadès, however, can reach into Warsaw Pact territory. This fact spells out a doubly heartening message to *les voisins d'outre-Rhin:* the French might join the battle while it is still raging up front, and they will not necessarily devastate West Germany in the process.

On the other hand, there is the First Principle of French defense policy, as laid down by Prime Minister Mauroy in language echoing the iciest of Gaullist dogmas: "France does not intend to suffer the consequences of conflicts that are not its own."[47] Thus the new dispositions set in motion by the Mitterrand government in the first half of the 1980s merely increase French options; they do not limit those options, as all anti-abandonment strategies must do, in order to forge a community of risks that would truly assure the West Germans. Whereas American troops are deployed in a "hostage" position close to the inter-German border, French forces in Germany (apart from a symbolic contingent in West Berlin) are grouped in the southwest, that is, close to the *French* frontier where they do not endanger France's nonbelligerency option. While American tactical nuclear weapons are stationed near the potential locus of battle— thus dramatizing the link between regional and global war—French forces are based at home. The FAR may join the forward battle, but then it may not. Indeed, if the establishment of FAR was meant to underline the possibility of France's commitment, the simultaneous effect of separating its tactical weapons from its conventional force structure was clearly designed to make sure that such a commitment does not compromise France's ability to stay out of a nuclear war.[48]

Nor are such decoupling strategies destined to disappear with the passage of time. The French are right in claiming that small nuclear forces protect only their possessors, and therefore that a West European deterrent could not consist solely of a French force "on loan." Or as Mitterrand said in a 1984 speech in The Hague: "The Atlantic Alliance is not about to be replaced by a European Alliance. The reason is that no [European] military power can substitute for the American arsenal. France, at any rate, will use its nuclear strike force for its own deterrence strategy only." While France may have intensified military cooperation with West Germany and Britain, it had "never hidden from its allies that, apart from protecting its national sanctuary and related vital interests, it cannot take charge of Europe's security."[49] A former associate of Defense Minister Hernu, François Heisbourg, put it even more brutally. "A middle-power cannot deliver an explicit nuclear guarantee to others without, at best, appearing ridiculous. Paris could not do what is already less than credible when coming from Washington. Deterrence of the strong by the weak has its rules."[50]

Nor did his superior mince any words when asked whether France could extend a nuclear umbrella to the Federal Republic. "By nature and definition," said Charles Hernu, "nuclear deterrence exists to protect the inviolable national territory. We would lie if we said that the French are ready to shield Germany with their nuclear deterrent." There are good reasons why France could not extend, and West Germany could not accept, such an umbrella in lieu of America's: it is the Atlantic security system that allows the weak to deter the strong. Demolish it, and the weak will not even be able to take care of themselves, let alone others. Hence, concluded the French defense minister, "We do not intend to replace the Americans. . . . I will even go this far: For the sake of Europe's future and indispensable unity, that would be very dangerous. France will play no part in this."[51]

France's independence flourishes because, for the first time in modern history, it is no longer on the front line but rather is sheltered by a glacis to the East manned by American and German troops and buttressed by American nuclear weapons. Such "collective good"—never enjoyed by France from the Hundred Years' War onward, as it fought Britain, Habsburg Spain, the anti-Napoleon coalition, and Prussia-Germany—is not foregone for the pleasure of extending nuclear umbrellas to friends who are also rivals.[52] Without the American "force multiplier," as even the French have come to admit implicitly, the French deterrent would be impoverished to the point of sheer pretense.[53] There is a reason why Prime Minister Chirac deplored "sterile debates on the eventual extension of our nuclear guarantee."[54] France cannot extend such a guarantee.

The "maturation of its nuclear effort" in the 1990s is designed to multiply options, not obligations—to allow France to "explore in *complete independence* ways and means of reinforcing deterrence in Europe."[55] Power and security that depend on imported leverage cannot replace the weight supplied by the American provider. Nor can more and better French weapons unhinge the dominant power relationships in the contemporary international system. At best, a French force "on loan" would merely replicate on a smaller scale the age-old conundrums of extended deterrence, and it would certainly be less credible than even the fraying American umbrella. Why then would a country like West Germany place greater faith in the puny nuclear force of its middle power ally across the Rhine (or across the Channel) than in the massive arsenal of its American protector?

One Europe, Many Bombs

If nuclear weapons protect only their possessors, then the ultimate implication of a Western Europe minus the United States is a nuclear-armed Federal Republic, with other West European states following suit. Accepting such a scenario requires first of all several leaps of faith: that four decades after World War II, history no longer matters; that Europe's "separate pasts" have vanished; and that the historical memories flowing from them have also disappeared. Yet with France in the vanguard, the nations of Western Europe accepted West Germany's integration into their common defense and economic communities only because the Federal Republic accepted some extraordinary constraints on its power— among them, the contractually sanctified renunciation of nuclear weapons. If cooperation depended on constraints in the past, have those constraints loosened their hold over leaders and nations enough to permit cooperation without them?

Every once in a while, even the French talk as if history has at last been transcended. Yet for all their attempts at proffering a continental anchor to an apparently more restless Federal Republic, the French can offer to their German allies neither community nor equality in matters nuclear. Nuclear weapons and residual Four Power rights over Germany as a whole are the only badges of distinction that France can display in answer to the superior economic, demographic, and conventional potential of its ancient rival. In a Baden-Baden press conference, President Mitterrand put it more politely when he said, "Since World War II, our two countries . . . do not share the same international status."[56] Since nuclear weapons are the supreme "positional good" that, by definition, cannot be shared, the French will always beckon but never deliver. Making common nuclear cause with the Federal Republic founders regularly on the immovable rock of French *raison d'état*. When two Gaullist deputies floated such a nuclear trial balloon in 1979, President Giscard d'Estaing swiftly set aside his vaunted friendship with Chancellor Schmidt and declared, "I categorically exclude any proposal for France to create nuclear weapons in the Federal Republic of Germany. . . . It does not fit the interests of France, of the Federal Republic, of Europe or of détente."[57]

But assume that history does indeed no longer matter. If so, the rationale for West German and other West European nuclear weapons also requires a leap of faith: namely, the belief that defense self-sufficiency, as symbolized by national deterrents, will make for unity among many small nuclear powers rather than for disintegration. But the logic of nuclear weapons points in the opposite direction. Far from dissolving borders, they in fact harden the shell of national sovereignty. They make alliances more difficult; indeed, they may make alliances unnecessary. Classic alliances depend on the aggregation of strength. Yet national deterrents cannot be summed like yesterday's conventional armies because they have severed what was once a fairly tight link between numbers and strength. In prenuclear times, a state's security ultimately depended on the men and materiel it could array against an enemy. In a nuclear world, safety rests not so much in sheer numbers as in the certainty of the vast damage a few dozens of weapons can achieve; if, that is, certain qualitative criteria are met.

In the prenuclear era, armies and fleets carried the silent message, "Do not attack us because we will repel you." To pose a credible threat against the would-be aggressor, the forces of the intended victim had to be at least roughly matched; otherwise, they could neither impress nor repel the enemy. In the post-Hiroshima age, however, the message is, "Do not attack us because we will destroy you." Numbers still count where tanks and troops can form a physical shield against aggression. Yet the nuclear sword is the decisive threat—spelling instantaneous and horrible devastation across boundaries and continents. To render that threat credible, it is quality rather than quantity that matters.

Quality, however, does not grow from aggregates. To deter, nuclear forces must be able to withstand surprise attack, cover vast distances, elude defenses, and hit with precision. "The technology of warheads, of delivery vehicles, of detection and surveillance devices, of command and control systems, count more than the size of forces."[58] Linking national deterrents in alliance will add to numbers but not to sophistication. A state either has the requisite (qualitative) assets, or it does not. If a state has them, it does not need the help of others. If it does not have them, it will not get them from nations that are self-sufficient already, because there are no profits in such sharing. To share would merely add to costs—such as the loss of status, and perhaps even the transformation of today's ally into tomorrow's rival.

The logic of nuclear egotism, then, does not bode well for cooperation among states. If nations cannot—and need not—rely on others for nuclear security, why should they engage in alliance? (The French quest for nuclear independence was designed precisely to produce options *beyond* alliance.) If national deterrents buttress national sovereignty, why would the West Europeans yield theirs for the sake of a more perfect union? Whatever else a Europe of nuclearized nation-states might be, it will not be the security community of decades past. With their national security policies once more nationalized, the states of Western Europe would return to the not so halcyon setting of yesterday—in which they would again conduct their affairs in a self-help system. Too strong to need one another, they would still be too weak to hold their own against the Soviet Union, the nation that is both a European and a superpower.

America without Europe

Western Europe left to its own devices is not likely to achieve what the critics of the Alliance expect it to do. Looking at the consequences rather than at the cause of European stability, NATO's detractors ignore the central role played by America in pacifying a state system that almost consumed itself in two world wars. As noted by Georg Leber, then the West German defense minister, "There is neither a political nor a military nor a psychological substitute for the American commitment [in Western Europe]. No European state could provide it, whether acting alone or with others."[59] Significantly, American policy makers have usually understood and accepted this momentous responsibility, even though it was acquired by default rather than by design. "The presence of our forces in Europe under NATO," said Secretary of State Dean Rusk in 1967, "has also contributed to the development of intra-European cooperation. . . . But without the visible assurance of a sizeable American contingent, old frictions may revive, and Europe could become unstable once more."[60]

   In the 1950s and 1960s, the main argument against the American role as a power-in-Europe was the financial burden; in today's age of peril parity, the weighty factor of existential risk has been added to the cost side of the ledger. That point was driven home in the language of popular fantasy by the television film, "The Day After," shown in late 1983. The nuclear war that engulfed America had not started out as a battle between the two nuclear giants; it was triggered by an escalating crisis in Europe. The moral hardly needs belaboring. It is America's commitments that endanger America's existence. It is Europe, the Middle East, or the Persian Gulf—contested areas that bear the stamp of American commitment without being fully controlled by American might—where confrontation with the Soviet Union might degenerate into murderous collision. That risk prompts American critics of the Alliance to invoke the specter of "mutual nuclear annihilation"[61] and to advocate a strategy of retraction.

In addition to dispatching the frustrations of dealing with allies who are usually less than cooperative and rarely grateful, such a strategy would surely reduce the risk of entrapment in conflicts which are not of America's choosing. If the United States abandoned its commitment to Western Europe, if the country retreated into a refurbished "Fortress America," nuclear insecurity would surely diminish. Without obligations to allies and clients in Western Europe, the risks of mutual nuclear annihilation would vanish along with numerous points of friction where Soviet and American interests inevitably collide. Pleading "no contest" in Europe, the United States could dispatch in one fell swoop a host of motives that prompt the Soviet Union to challenge America's position. Nor would sea-lanes have to be kept open as today when the two superpowers vie for control of the Atlantic Ocean.

The neo-isolationist message can be put more forcefully still. Its underlying logic would have us conclude that alliances in fact diminish the security of great powers. Alliances did so in prenuclear times as well, but then the risk of entrapment in other nations' conflicts was balanced by the presumptive gains of power by aggregation. Not so today. For a full-fledged nuclear power like the United States, such gains are *sensu strictu* nil as to its core security, that is, the protection of borders and populations. By defintion, a superpower is capable of deterring any conceivable combination of challengers, and for that task, the United States does not need the help of allies. The United States underwrites the security of Western Europe; the armed forces of Western Europe do not protect the integrity of American territory. Indeed, for the first time since the British Navy ruled the Atlantic, nuclear weapons and intercontinental missiles have brought the will-o'-the-wisp of isolationism within theoretical grasp.

Robert W. Tucker has adumbrated the logic of a nuclear Fortress America.

Having withdrawn once again from the world beyond this hemisphere, though now possessed of a surfeit of deterrent power in the form of nuclear missile weapons, we would have little reason to fear attack, for an attacker would know with virtual certainty that he had far more to lose than to gain from so acting. To this extent, nuclear missile weapons give substance to the long-discredited isolationist dream. So long as it is clear that they will be employed only in the direct defense of the homeland, they confer a physical security that is virtually complete, and that the loss of allies cannot alter.[62]

In other words, the absolute weapon promises absolute security only if employed for an absolute cause: the nation's survival. Why, then, does the impeccable logic of nuclear neo-isolationism ring so hollow? To begin with, there are two critical assumptions behind the neo-isolationist plea, one sanguine, the other unstated. The sanguine assumption is the educational power of withdrawal: disengagement will have an entirely salutary influence, reminding the "free riders" of Western Europe of their responsibility for their own security and forcing them to assume the heavy burden the United States has carried so long at no charge. The unstated assumption of neo-isolationism is that Europe no longer matters.[63]

The former, optimistic assumption cannot be taken for granted; it is more likely that if left to its own devices, Western Europe may fall short of managing either its internal order or the military balance on the Eurasian continent. Arguments for change, of course, can be proven true or false only by trial and error. Yet such a method poses two nasty problems. First, the optimists may gamble on Western Europe's hidden strengths only to find out that they have lost the wager to the manifest might of the Soviets. Secondly, the next experiment with a policy of abandonment may also be the last. Twice in this century, the United States entered the European state system with a mission that history has not yet proven obsolete: to prevent Europe's unification under a hostile hegemony. In both cases, America's entry came late, but not too late to break the hold of German power. The rationale for staying in Europe to deter a third try by the Soviets was outlined succinctly by Harry S. Truman when he asked, "Which is better for the country—to spend twenty or thirty billion dollars [over the next four years] to keep the peace or to do as we did in 1920 and then have to spend 100 billion dollars for four years to fight a war?"[64]

Deterring a war is surely cheaper than having to fight one, but today there is an additional problem that eludes monetary calculations. Were the United States to withdraw from Europe today, the consequences of a wrong bet might no longer be so quickly undone as they were after 1917 and 1941, if at all. A third rescue effort would have to be undertaken in the shadow of nuclear weapons—and against an entrenched opponent who would have the great psychological advantage of forcing the United States to take the first step into the nuclear unknown. Assuming that the United States had left Europe in order to unshoulder the abstract nuclear risks of alliance, it is inconceivable that the United States would court the *real* risks of nuclear war that a forcible reentry would impose.

To abandon Europe under conditions in which a wrong bet could no longer be reversed by another return attempt, requires faith in the second, unstated assumption: that Europe no longer matters; indeed, that allies no longer matter. True, the United States would gain a margin of freedom and physical security once it forced its troublesome allies to fend for themselves. But it would gain little else. In fact, the United States would lose everything that great powers cherish above and beyond their core security. Great powers define themselves not only by their great strength but also by their great interests. Their character as great powers cannot be divorced from *les vastes entreprises,* as Charles de Gaulle always reminded his compatriots. Nor do such visions spring merely from misbegotten imperial ambitions. Nations are not just security-maximizing entities; they are also political communities beholden to moral norms and aspirations. As such, they seek legitimacy—*le juste milieu* where their own values will flourish. To preserve a compatible setting, they seek influence beyond their borders; and to preserve their values, they seek not only security but friends. In short, it is not just sentiment or hubris but the sober calculation of self-interest that motivates the acceptance of obligations to other nations. To argue that Western Europe does not matter, or does not matter enough to eschew the wager of abandonment, is also to argue that totalitarian domination of the largest bastion of democracy outside the United States will not grievously affect American national interests.

It is not even clear whether security would thrive behind a palisade of intercontinental missiles. Nations must fend off threats to other values besides territorial integrity; yet against threats that are less than existential, nuclear weapons are impotent. Assume a radical neo-isolationist stance whereby the United States would renounce the quest for balance in all arenas save the nuclear one (a "semi-isolationist," Pacific-based policy is assessed below). In such a world, the United States would expose itself to all manner of threats ranging from limited conventional attacks to the psychological nightmare of being alone in opposition. Or take threats to the nation's economic well-being. It is true that trade does not necessarily depend on political control, let alone ideological sympathy. (Otherwise, the Soviet Union and South Africa would hardly dominate the global diamond market.) Yet only a latter-day "Angellian" would assert that markets are immune to power.[65] Politico-military power is regularly used to deny access, expropriate assets, withhold resources, and skew the terms of trade to favor the strong. While the United States would undoubtedly survive under conditions of autarky, it would not survive very well.

Pure deterrence theory, then, captures only part of international reality—and not necessarily the most important part. In the real world, nations have interests above and beyond their core security. These interests invariably extend beyond each nation's territorial base, therefore requiring order beyond borders. To achieve order, power must be balanced across the full spectrum, not just in the nuclear band. Rivals must be contained, and their moves must be blunted. Strategic assets that affect the balance must be secured or, at a minimum, be denied to adversaries. How to do so without allies—and commitments to them—defies even the postnuclear imagination. And so there is no exit. Even a surfeit of deterrent power does not eliminate the necessity of extending it to others—and of shouldering the risks that such sharing entails.

"Pure" isolationism, however, is not what motivates contemporary, neo-conservative critics of the Alliance. Theirs is a vision of unilateralist activism that would oppose the Soviet Union across the board. Though they see the global balance as endangered, they regard the West Europeans as allies defending only their own parochial interests, and hence as a drain on American resources that would be better invested elsewhere. They want to shift the focus of America's postwar policy away from its Eurocentric base—to the Pacific, perhaps, where China and Japan loom as tomorrow's giants in a partnership of containment against the Soviet Union. In 1987, however, Japan's defense spending breached the one-percent barrier for the first time (the major Western European powers allocate between three and five percent); in addition, Japan is even more thoroughly cocooned by American might than is Western Europe. How such a country, the quintessential "free rider," could serve as the maritime sword of the United States in the Pacific, defies the most optimistic imagination. Nor is China a card that can be played by anyone but China; it will oppose the Soviet Union where its interests so dictate, but not as the handmaiden of American policy.

The key issue, however, is not the future role of Southeast Asia in the global balance, but the present weight of Europe in that balance. The United States could only count on a net gain in disposable resources if the West Europeans proved willing and able to defend themselves, thus neutralizing a considerable portion of Soviet power on their own. And if they did not? "In that event," argues the lapsed isolationist, Robert W. Tucker, with incontrovertible logic,

Moscow would have much less to worry about in the theater of greatest importance to it. Freed from this concern, while progressively strengthened by the resource base Western Europe would then afford it, Moscow might be able to turn its attention elsewhere and with greater effect. . . . Having abandoned what had heretofore been the center of our interest for the periphery, we would find the periphery increasingly difficult to secure against the improved power position of the Soviet Union.[66]

Unlike the contemporary critics of America's Eurocentric policy, the Soviet Union has never underestimated Western Europe's true weight in the global balance. The Soviet Union has probed American positions in the Middle East and in Southeast Asia, in Africa and in the Caribbean. Not once, though, did it ever lose sight of Europe, the grandest prize of them all. The 1950s' Cold War was about the containment of the Soviet advance into Europe and, in particular, into the pivotal country of Germany. The 1980s' cold war was not about Angola or Afghanistan but about Europe again, and the sway of Soviet influence beyond the Elbe River. Nor should this recurrent contest come as a surprise. Soviet Russia is not an island power, but a superpower in Europe. To either balance or best the United States, Moscow must try to dominate the approaches beyond its borders. Not only is Western Europe the landmass to the west whence Russia has been invaded thrice in the nineteenth and twentieth centuries; it also happens to represent the largest combination of economic, demographic, technological, *and* military power outside the United States and the Soviet Union. To yield such an asset, or even to merely shift toward a policy that would knowingly accept the risk of Soviet primacy on the Continent, can only amount to a prescription for American self-defeat.

If these are the costs of disengagement, what are the costs of commitment and the great nuclear risks purportedly entailed by America's continued entanglement? Unlike in other areas around the world—the Middle East or Cuba, for instance—where the United States and the Soviet Union have intermittently come to the brink of confrontation, stability in Europe has an astounding record. Nor is so much tranquility merely a fluke of history. In the nuclear arena, where no contestant would wittingly start a war that might be the last, it is not too much but too little commitment that bears the seeds of confrontation. The United States is vulnerable where it extends deterrence without bridging the gap of geography and sovereignty that separates core from periphery – separating, say, Boston from Beirut. Obligations that go beyond the writ of a nation's sovereignty are always blurred, and such interests are always less than "vital," no matter now solemn the incantations. The single most important threat to the nuclear peace arises from this uncertainty: the miscalculation of interests and will, of stakes and obligations. Ambitious adversaries may underestimate the value of the stake at hand, as did Hitler vis-à-vis Poland in 1939. But unruly allies may overestimate the extent of their patron's tolerance, as may have been the case when Israel expanded the war in Lebanon in 1982, ultimately embroiling U.S. Marines.

The clarity of commitment and the certainty of control compress the dangers of entangling alliances, and this is why Europe, with only two exceptions in the distant past, has not served as a locus of confrontation.[67] The presence of large numbers of American troops and nuclear weapons demonstrates a clarity of commitment to Western Europe that reduces the chance of miscalculation to almost zero. That presence and the rigorous integration of the North Atlantic coalition under an American supreme commander make for enough control over allies to militate against entrapment in conflicts that could escalate into a confrontation of the two principals. Conversely, the lack of clarity and control has been at the bottom of all the great power crises of the postwar period – most notably, in the Middle East, where the two superpowers lined up on opposite sides of the conflict, but then did not fully clarify the extent of their commitments or gain full control over their clients. Not all bonds, then, breed existential risks – only loose ones. And thus to cut, or merely lengthen, the tie that binds the United States to Europe is likely to bring about precisely the calamity that disengagement is said to forestall.

Costly as it may be, America's investment in Europe has yielded enormous profit to both sides – the most important benefit being decades of tranquility on a continent whose strategic importance in this century has only been dwarfed by its inability to maintain order and stability when left alone. As Western Europe and the United States face the future of their relationship, the foggy mirror of the past reflects endless crisis, but also a glaring absence of trumps and options. Interdependence is painful when there is neither the unifying bond of a true community nor the relief afforded by an exit. Neither Western Europe nor the United States would suffer the misfortunes of allliance if either was free to abandon alliance. Yet the contemporary setting, unlike the more fluid European state system of centuries past, is short on alternatives. By virtue of its propinquity, power, and ideology, the Soviet Union is Western Europe's natural adversary. And the United States—clumsy rather than overbearing, oblivious rather than oppressive—is Western Europe's natural ally. Theoretically, the West Europeans are free to part with the United States, but at the price of exchanging one dependence for another. The freedom to change allegiance pales when it may only lead into the embrace of another patron who would not permit another change of heart.

Nor is the United States free to reconsider. While amply equipped to assure its own security, the United States can abandon Western Europe only at the risk of yielding the world's foremost strategic asset to its one and only global adversary. To do so would invite a strategic defeat of the first order. When shackles are strong and tight, they chafe—but they continue to hold.

Notes

1. In the course of the missile contest, that logic—and the threat to the European balance—was enunciated most clearly by the French. Dispensing with France's earlier aspersions against the American guarantee, Prime Minister Pierre Mauroy declared, "Certain European countries, which doubt this, ought to become convinced that [the U.S.] medium-range nuclear weapons . . . will not be deployed in order to wage a war limited to Europe but, quite to the contrary, to make a potential adversary understand that such a limited war is impossible." Pierre Mauroy, "Vers un nouveau modèle d'armée" (Address before the Institut des Hautes Etudes de Défense Nationale, September 20, 1982), reprinted in *Défense Nationale* (November 1982): 18.
2. Irving Kristol, "Foreign Policy in an Age of Ideology," *The National Interest*, no. 1 (Fall 1985): 14.
3. Erhard Eppler, as quoted in Wolf Perdelwitz, "Deutschstunde: Der neue Patriotismus," *Stern*, 22 Oct. 1981, p. 28.
4. Heinrich Albertz (formerly the SPD mayor of West Berlin), "Von der Nation— und von Wichtigerem," in Walter Jens, ed., *In letzter Stunde* (Munich: Kindler, 1982), p. 139.
5. George F. Kennan, *Memoirs 1925–1950* (Boston: Little, Brown, 1967), p. 464.
6. This functional definition of an international order is not as parsimonious as it could be. One could well imagine an international order that preserves the security and independence of its members, but at the same time is both labile and violent. Strictly speaking, system preservation requires only one condition: that each member act to oppose the ambitions of all others. Indeed, shifting coalitions and the resort to violence may well be proof of the system's vitality, because these features show that members take their "systemic obligations" seriously enough to oppose the hegemonic designs of other members with countervailing coalitions and/or the use of force. Normatively, however, a system that is both stable (i.e., bereft of hegemonic ambitions) and

violence-free is preferable to a "Hobbesian equilibrium" that is preserved only through an endless battle of each against all.

7. The exceptions were perpetual civil strife in Northern Ireland and, farther afield, the clashes between Greece and Turkey over Cyprus. In Soviet-dominated Eastern Europe, force was used regularly in the service of imperial recentralization but not *between* Eastern European states, most of which have unresolved territorial claims against each other.

8. Karl W. Deutsch, *Political Community at the International Level* (n.p.: Archon Books, 1970), p. 33.

9. The protector/pacifier distinction was borrowed from Uwe Nerlich, "Western Europe's Relations with the United States," *Daedalus* (Winter 1979): 88.

10. See John H. Herz, *International Politics in the Nuclear Age* (New York: Columbia University Press, 1959); and Herbert Butterfield, *History and Human Relations* (London: William Collins & Sons, 1961), and *Christianity, Diplomacy and War* (London: Epworth, 1953).

11. In October of 1950, almost half of all French respondents opined that German rearmament would diminish France's security. *Sondages*, no. 1 (1951), as cited in Frank R. Willis, *France, Germany and the New Europe* (Stanford, Cal.: Stanford University Press, 1965), p. 140.

12. See C.L. Sulzberger, "Dulles Cautions Europe to Ratify Arms Treaty Soon," *New York Times*, 15 Dec. 1953. Dulles' warning was reinforced by the Richards Amendment of the appropriations bill under the Mutual Security Assistance Program, according to which one-half of the aid given to Western Europe in FY 1954 was to be tied to the ratification of the EDC Treaty.

13. Anthony Eden, *Full Circle* (London: Cassell, 1960), pp. 151, 149–150.

14. Statement by Anthony Eden at the London Conference, 28 September–3 October 1954, "The London Conference: Final Act, United States, United Kingdom and Canadian Assurances," in Council on Foreign Relations, ed., *Documents on American Foreign Relations, 1954* (New York: Harper Brothers, 1955), p. 113.

15. Ibid., p. 117.

16. Ibid., p. 113.

17. Kenneth N. Waltz, *Theory of International Politics* (Reading, Mass.: Addison-Wesley, 1979), p. 105.

18. As recounted by Louis Halle, *The Cold War as History* (London: Chatto & Windus, 1962), p. 82. Roosevelt also did not want the United States to assume the burden of "reconstituting France, Italy and the Balkans" because that "was definitely a British task." Franklin D. Roosevelt, as quoted in Herbert Feis, *Churchill, Roosevelt, Stalin* (Princeton, N.J.: Princeton University Press, 1957), p. 340.

19. It may be no coincidence that Europe proved most successful in these areas. The issue was not to merge sovereignties but to protect shrinking sectors in each economy—coal, steel, agriculture—against the ravages of global competition from subsidy and cartel arrangements. The EEC's agricultural cartel, also known as the Common Agricultural Policy, has turned into an impenetrable bulwark of unification because it is based on the lasting confluence of *national* policies, which reflect the disproportionate political power of each member state's agrarian sector.

20. Charles de Gaulle, *Lettres, notes et carnets, juin 1958-décembre 1960* (Paris: Plon, 1985), pp. 398–399.
21. Dean Acheson, "Europe: Decision or Drift?" *Foreign Affairs* (January 1966): 200.
22. Stanley Hoffman, "Fragments Floating in the Here and Now," *Daedalus* (Winter 1979): 2, 5.
23. From the mid-1960s to the early 1970s, Senator Mike Mansfield led a congressional campaign for the reduction of U.S. troops in Europe.
24. Willy Brandt, *Begegnungen und Einsichten: Die Jahre 1960–1975* (Hamburg: Hoffman und Campe, 1976), p. 348. He added that "those gentlemen in the Senate" who were pushing for reductions could "not be bought off" with larger European offset payments. Nor could the West Germans make up for U.S. troops; increasing the weight of the German defense contribution would pose a political problem "not only vis-à-vis the East but also within the Western alliance." Brandt also did not think (in 1973) that the Vienna troop reduction talks (MBFR), which were mainly conceived to hold off unilateral U.S. withdrawals, "would achieve great things" (p. 365).
25. Edouard Herriot, as quoted in Richard J. Barnett, *The Alliance* (New York: Simon & Schuster, 1983), p. 162.
26. Valéry Giscard-d'Estaing, Address before the National Assembly, as quoted in "L'interview du chef de l'Etat à TF1," *Le Monde*, 7 May 1976.
27. Ministère de la Défense, *Livre blance sur la défense nationale, 1972*, vol. 1, p. 8.
28. With regard to the "employment of pre-strategic weapons," France might be willing to consult with the Federal Republic, said President Mitterrand at a press conference in Baden-Baden on January 16, 1986. "But I repeat, the very nature of this type of combat means that the decision cannot be shared." François Mitterrand, as quoted in Ministère des Rélations Extérieures, *La Politique Etrangère de la France: Textes et Documents*, January–February 1986, p. 26. For a virtually identical statement by Prime Minister Jacques Chirac, see "La politique de défense de la France" (Address before the Institut des Hautes Etudes de Défense Nationale, September 12, 1986), reprinted in *Défense Nationale* (November 1986): 12.
29. Mauroy, "Vers un nouveau . . .," p. 26.
30. Christian A. Herter, as quoted in U.S. Senate, Committee on Foreign Relations, *Hearings on the Nomination of Christian A. Herter*, 86th Cong., 1st sess., April 21, 1959, p. 10.
31. Robert S. McNamara, "The Military Role of Nuclear Weapons," *Foreign Affairs* (Fall 1983): 79.
32. Mauroy, "Vers un nouveau . . .," pp. 12–13.
33. Charles Hernu, as quoted in "Wir können Amerika nicht ersetzen" (Interview with Charles Hernu) *Der Spiegel*, no. 26 (June 26, 1983): 110.
34. See President de Gaulle's press conference of July 23, 1964, reprinted in Charles de Gaulle, *Discours et Messages, 1962–1965* (Paris: Plon, 1970), pp. 232–233.
35. The Redoutable, with sixteen single-warhead M-20 missiles; four submarines of the same class with sixteen M-4 missiles per boat and six warheads per missile; one Inflexible-class submarine with a 16 times 6 warhead complement (put to sea in 1985); and another boat of this type (with ninety-six

warheads) that is supposed to enter service in 1994. On the other hand, there is an uncertainty factor. The Redoutable is scheduled for demobilization in the mid-1990s, to be followed by the Terrible at the end of the decade, by which time France's SLBM force would be reduced to five, unless additional ones are ordered in the next few years. For the best recent analysis of French doctrine, and of present as well as scheduled capabilities, see David S. Yost, *France's Deterrent Posture and Security in Europe*, Adelphi papers nos. 194 and 195 (London: International Institute for Strategic Studies, 1984). For a critical assessment of French ambitions, see Jolyon Howorth, "Begrenzte Mittel und strategische Optionen: Frankreichs Verteidigungspolitik am Scheideweg?" *Europa-Archiv*, no. 9 (1986). For a comparison of the French and the British nuclear programs for the 1990s, see John Prados, Joel S. Wit, and Michael J. Zagurek, Jr., "The Strategic Nuclear Forces of Britain and France," *Scientific American* (August 1986).

36. According to Defense Minister Quilès, there are plans for "ordering two more in coming years." Paul Quilès, "L'Avenir de notre concept de défense face aux progrès technologiques" (Address before the Institut des Hautes Etudes de Défense Nationale, November 12, 1985), reprinted in Défense Nationale (January 1986): 22.

37. Jeannou Lacaze, "Concept de défense et sécurité en Europe" (Address before the Institut des Hautes Etudes de Défense Nationale, May 19, 1984), reprinted in *Défense Nationale* (July 1984): 13 (emphasis added).

38. Barbara Tuchman, *The Guns of August* (New York: Macmillan, 1962), p. 49.

39. *The Threat to Europe* (Moscow: Progress, 1981), p. 20.

40. See notes 30 and 31 above.

41. See, for instance, de Gaulle's address before the Academy of the Bundeswehr on September 7, 1962, when he pleaded for the "solidarity of our arms." For the text of the address (in German), see Presse- und Informationsamt der Bundesregierung, *Bulletin*, no. 168, 11 Sept. 1962.

42. "Pacifism is in the West, and the Euromissiles are in the East," said Mitterrand during a dinner speech in the Royal Palace in Brussels on October 12, 1983. François Mitterrand, as quoted in Ministère des Rélations Extérieures, *Textes et Documents*, September–October 1983, p. 85.

43. For the details, see François Heisbourg (formerly a high official in the French defense department), "Coopération en matière d'armements: rien n'est jamais acquis," in Institut Français des Rélations Internationales, ed., *Le couple franco-allemand et la défense de l'Europe* (Paris: IFRI, 1986), p. 119.

44. The "Force d'Action Rapide" comprises 47,000 men and more than 200 helicopters, the bulk of which will be configured in an antitank mode. It is theoretically capable of fighting as far as 200 kilometers from the initial zone of deployment. The new strike force has a dual mission: to allow for intervention in the third world, and to serve as an expeditionary corps that would aid NATO forces "in any zone where it would be needed." Defense Minister Charles Hernu, as quoted in "Le débat dur la loi programmation militaire," *Le Monde*, 7 Dec. 1982, p. 14.

45. Pierre Mauroy, Address before the Institut des Hautes Etudes de Défense Nationale, 14 September 1981, reprinted in Ministère des Rélations Extérieures, *Textes et Documents*, September–October 1981, p. 17.

46. Charles Hernu, "Equilibre, dissuasion, volonté: la voie étroite de la paix et de la liberté" (Address before the Institut des Hautes Etudes de Défense Nationale, November 15, 1983), reprinted in *Défense Nationale* (December 1983): 16.
47. See note 29 above.
48. The Pluton regiments have been regrouped in a special command distinct from France's main conventional force, the First Army. The army's Hadès, to become operational in 1992, will be under the direct control of the Armed Forces Chief of Staff. Given the ASMP (the medium-range air-to-ground standoff missile) and the Hadès, said Chief of Staff Lacaze, the "use of tactical nuclear weapons will no longer . . . be necessarily linked to the maneuver of our ground forces" (Lacaze, "Concept de defense . . .," p. 21). In fact, these weapons will be "dissociated from the deployment of our classical forces in the theater." While the new dispositions are designed to "concretize . . . France's solidarity with its allies" (Jeannou Lacaze, "L'Avenir de la défense française," *Défense Nationale* (July 1985): 25, 20), none of these reforms, especially the establishment of the FAR, "signifies the beginning of a return to the integrated structure (of NATO) or the 'manning of the battlements' in the forward-defense according to Allied planning" (Lacaze, "Concept de defense . . .," p. 20). For more details, see Yost, *France's Deterrent Posture*, no. 194, pp. 60–64, and no. 195, pp. 26–32.
49. François Mitterrand, as quoted in Ministère des Rélations Extérieures, *Visite officielle aux Pays-Bas de Monsieur François Mitterrand*, 6–7 February 1984, p. 18.
50. François Heisbourg, "Défense et sécurité extérieure," *Politique Etrangère* (Summer 1985): 392.
51. Charles Hernu, as quoted in "Wir können Amerika nicht ersetzen," *Der Spiegel*, no. 26 (June 26, 1983): 110. In this interview, Hernu also added a few ironical asides that shed an instructive light on the difficulties of cooperating on less than vital matters. As to a joint helicopter project: "There were protracted discussions between French and German military commands whether the pilots should be placed side-by-side or one-behind-the-other." (The project is still under discussion.) With regard to a Franco-German tank, a project that was swiftly aborted, Hernu said caustically, "Now we are building a Franco-French tank" (p. 109).
52. This is the basic reason why a recent (nonofficial) French proposal for moving French forces into a hostage position, i.e., "on the Elbe and not on the Rhine" (Pierre Lelouche, *L'Avenir de la guerre* (Paris: Mazarine, 1985), p. 281), has about as great a chance of realization as Helmut Schmidt's idea of a Franco-German force of thirty divisions as the nucleus of a European deterrent. Schmidt outlined that idea in the Bundestag two years after his ouster from the chancellorship. Two key advantages of a Franco-German force, as he saw it, were the almost complete denuclearization of West German forces and the possibility of "substantially reducing" the American presence in Europe. See Helmut Schmidt's address to the Bundestag on 28 June 1984, as reprinted in *Verhandlungen des Deutschen Bundestages*, 28 June 1984, p. 5601 ff; he repeated the point in Helmut Schmidt, "Europa muss sich selbst behaupten," *Die Zeit*, 21 Nov. 1986. In response to the Schmidt proposal, Defense Minister Hernu said, "Schmidt knows very well that France's deterrent protects only France, and it cannot deliver a guarantee to Europe" (As quoted in

"Schmidt's Vorschlag stösst in Paris auf Interesse und Skepsis," *Die Welt,* 6 July 1984, p. 5). Foreign Minister Claude Cheysson added the biting rejoinder that it would have been more interesting if Schmidt had launched his proposal while still chancellor (Ibid., p. 5).

53. See Lacaze, "Concept de défense . . .," p. 13.
54. Chirac, "La politique de défense . . .," p. 13.
55. Ibid., p. 11 (emphasis added).
56. François Mitterrand, at a press conference in Baden-Baden, Jaunary 16, 1986, as quoted in Ministère des Relations Extérieures, *Textes et Documents,* January–February 1986, p. 24.
57. Valéry Giscard d'Estaing, in a televised interview on September 17, 1979, as quoted in "Précision et commentaire," *Le Monde,* 19 Sept. 1979, p. 8.
58. Kenneth N. Waltz, *The Spread of Nuclear Weapons: More May Be Better,* Adelphi papers no. 171 (London: International Institute for Strategic Studies, 1981), p. 3.
59. Georg Leber, "Goodwill allein reicht nicht," *Süddeutsche Zeitung,* 24 Feb. 1973, p. 9.
60. Dean Rusk, as quoted in U.S. Senate, Combined Subcommittee on Foreign Relations and Armed Services, *Hearings on United States Troops in Europe,* 90th Cong., 1st sess., p. 100.
61. For instance, see Kristol, "Age of Ideology."
62. Robert W. Tucker, "Containment and the Search for Alternatives: A Critique," in Aaron Wildavsky, ed., *Beyond Containment* (San Francisco: Institute for Contemporary Studies Press, 1983), p. 81. Tucker states the case only to refute it.
63. For a cautious argument according to which Europe no longer matters *as much* as it did in the 1950s, while having also turned into a "strategic liability," see Eliot A. Cohen, "Do We Still Need Europe?" *Commentary* (January 1986). He observes, however, that "we can . . . recognize that new strategic realities exist without concluding that we must discard old instruments of security" (p. 35).
64. Harry S. Truman, as quoted in John L. Gaddis, *Strategies of Containment* (New York: Oxford University Press, 1982), p. 62.
65. In his famous book, *The Great Illusion* (New York: Putnam, 1913), Norman Angell argued that war, which he saw as caused by the quest for resources, was a costly atavism. If nations let themselves be guided by the principle of mutual economic gain, they could satisfy their economic needs more cheaply and completely through free trade than through war.
66. Robert W. Tucker, "Isolation and Intervention," *The National Interest* (Fall 1985): 24.
67. The exceptions are the Berlin Blockade in 1948 and the erection of the Berlin Wall in 1961. In both cases, there was a remote chance of military clashes— significantly, however, because American commitments were not clear. In 1948 Stalin underestimated America's stake in the freedom of the West Berlin enclave within the Soviet Occupation Zone; in 1961 Khrushchev thought he could count on Kennedy's connivance because Kennedy himself had publicly speculated about Soviet–East German measures that would stop the mounting tide of refugees from the GDR.

Index

Pershing II missiles *(cont.)*
  détente and, 35
  Mitterrand and, 36
  peace movement and, 93, 102, 103, 112, 121, 134
  political issues and, 48, 51, 83–84
  psychological process of deterrence and, 82–83
  public opinion on use of, 97–98, 99
  Schmidt and, 74
  survivability and penetrability of, 81
Pleven Plan, 181
Pluton missiles, 197
Poland
  deep strike capacity and, 162
  détente and, 19, 20, 21, 37–38
  1980 crisis in, 5, 37
  Solidarity movement in, 28, 37
Polaris missiles, 47, 58, 76, 193
Political factors
  alliance and, 183–184
  coupling and decoupling policies and, 50–52, 83
  détente and, 28–29
  deterrence and, 83–84
  Multilateral Force (MLF) and, 56–57
  nuclear weapons and, 52, 54–55
  Pershing II and cruise missiles and, 48, 51, 83–84
  politics of transcendence and, 184–189
Political parties
  peace movement and, 110–119
  see also Democratic left; Social democratic parties; *and specific parties*
Poniatowski, Michel, 4
Populist movements
  elections and, 96
  political institutions in Europe and, 95–96
  see also Peace movement
Poseidon missiles, 68
Precision-guided munitions (PGMs), 151
Protestantism, and peace movement, 100, 107–108
Psychological factors, and deterrence, 82–83
Public opinion
  concerns about nuclear weapons in, 99
  détente and, 10, 28–29
  electoral choices and, 96–97, 99–100
  peace movement and public policy and, 95–100

  religious factors in, 108
  resist or surrender options in, 100–101, 103, 108
  threat perception and, 97, 98, 108
  U.S. participation in Europe's defenses in, 97
  West German views of détente in, 5

Quilès, Paul, 146–147

Raimond, Jean-Bernard, 85
Rand Corporation, 157
Rapid Action Force (FAR), 197–198
Reagan administration, 105
  arms control and, xiv, 41
  cruise missile deployment and, 84–85, 121
  détente and, 28, 41
  Euromissiles and, 40–41
  Reykjavík summit (1986) and, xiv, 84
  Strategic Defense Initiative (SDI) of, 146–147
Religious factors, and peace movement, 100, 107–108
Reykjavík summit (1986), xiv, 84, 85–86
Rogers, Bernard, 156
Rogers Plan, 156
Romania, 21
Rusk, Dean, 202
Russia, *see* Soviet Union

Sadat, Anwar, 140–141
SALT I, 69
  détente and, 7
  Intermediate-range nuclear forces (INF) and, 63, 64, 65
  nuclear balance and, 23
  parity under, 48–49
SALT II, 122
  nuclear balance and, xiv
  protocol of, 65, 66
  West Germany and, 54
Schlesinger, Arthur, 57
Schlesinger, James, 62
Schlesinger doctrine, 61–62, 63
Schmidt, Helmut, 152
  Afghanistan invasion by Soviet Union and, 3, 4, 5
  arms control and, 86
  cruise missile deployment decision and, 72–73, 74
  détente and, 16, 22, 23–24, 34–35, 38

About the Author

Born in Europe, **Josef Joffe** has spent much of his adult life alternating between the two shores of the Atlantic. For his higher education, he attended Swarthmore College, Johns Hopkins University, and Harvard University, where he received his Ph.D. in government. He has taught international relations at the University of Munich, the Salzburg Seminar, and the School of Advanced International Studies in Washington, D.C. He has held research positions at the Woodrow Wilson International Center for Scholars and at the Carnegie Endowment for International Peace in Washington, D.C.

Joffe's journalistic career spans senior editorial positions at the weekly, *Die Zeit,* in Hamburg and at West Germany's largest circulation quality daily, *Süddeutsche Zeitung,* in Munich. He is currently foreign editor and columnist at the *Süddeutsche Zeitung.* His columns and opinion pieces have appeared in the *Wall Street Journal,* the *New York Times,* the *Washington Post,* the *Los Angeles Times, Encounter,* and the *New Republic.* His contributions on Alliance affairs, arms control, and international relations have been published in *Foreign Affairs, Foreign Policy, International Security,* the *Washington Quarterly,* and in many scholarly collections on either side of the Atlantic.